KEY IDEAS in CRIMINOLOGY and CRIMINAL JUSTICE

KEY IDEAS in CRIMINOLOGY and CRIMINAL JUSTICE

Travis C. Pratt
Arizona State University

Jacinta M. Gau
California State University, San Bernardino

Travis W. Franklin
Sam Houston State University

Los Angeles | London | New Delhi
Singapore | Washington DC

Copyright © 2011 by SAGE Publications, Inc.

All rights reserved. No part of this book may be reproduced or utilized in any form or by any means, electronic or mechanical, including photocopying, recording, or by any information storage and retrieval system, without permission in writing from the publisher.

For information:

SAGE Publications, Inc.
2455 Teller Road
Thousand Oaks,
California 91320
E-mail: order@sagepub.com

SAGE Publications India Pvt. Ltd.
B 1/I 1 Mohan Cooperative
Industrial Area
Mathura Road, New Delhi 110 044
India

SAGE Publications Ltd.
1 Oliver's Yard
55 City Road
London EC1Y 1SP
United Kingdom

SAGE Publications Asia-Pacific Pte. Ltd.
33 Pekin Street #02-01
Far East Square
Singapore 048763

Printed in the United States of America.

Library of Congress Cataloging-in-Publication Data

Pratt, Travis C.
Key ideas in criminology and criminal justice / Travis C. Pratt, Jacinta M. Gau, Travis W. Franklin.
p. cm.
Includes bibliographical references and index.
ISBN 978-1-4129-7013-6 (cloth : alk. paper)
ISBN 978-1-4129-7014-3 (pbk. : alk. paper)
1. Criminology. 2. Criminal justice, Administration of. I. Gau, Jacinta M., 1982- II. Franklin, Travis W. III. Title.

HV6025.P66 2011
364—dc22 2010032177

This book is printed on acid-free paper.

10 11 12 13 14 10 9 8 7 6 5 4 3 2 1

Acquisitions Editor: Jerry Westby
Associate Editor: Aja Baker
Editorial Assistant: Nichole O'Grady
Production Editor: Karen Wiley
Copy Editor: Teresa Herlinger
Typesetter: C&M Digitals (P) Ltd.
Proofreader: Laura Webb
Indexer: Holly Day
Cover Designer: Glenn Vogel
Marketing Manager: Erica DeLuca

BRIEF CONTENTS

DETAILED CONTENTS

PREFACE

Scattered throughout the history of criminology and criminal justice are a variety of scholarly works that have left enduring marks within their respective fields. For example, it would be impossible to discuss the nature of punishment in the United States (and much of Europe) without acknowledging the profoundly influential work of Cesare Beccaria in his short treatise, *On Crimes and Punishments*. Likewise, an understanding of crime causation would be decidedly inadequate without recognition of Shaw and McKay's work on social disorganization or Gottfredson and Hirschi's more recent work on low self-control. One would, furthermore, be hard-pressed to explain the recent shift away from offender rehabilitation without affording Martinson's assessment of correctional treatment its due attention. These contributions, along with several others discussed in this text, have carved out unique positions in criminology and criminal justice—they have, in a sense, risen to the top and have become *key ideas* within their disciplines.

For the dedicated student, it does not take long to realize that certain scholarly contributions stand out among others. To be sure, it is these works that are usually first introduced to the student of criminology or criminal justice, and over the years various texts have been written to do just that. Identifying and explaining key works is certainly important in its own right, but vital questions still remain. For example, what are the circumstances that cause one work to rise to the top when other similar works seem to have gone unnoticed? After all, many key contributions, however compelling and articulate they may have been, were not necessarily the first (or at times, the most well-developed) pieces of work to address a particular idea, yet they rose up as dominant contributions to the field. Is there something about the work itself that caused it to stand out and to gain an unusual amount of attention? Does social context have anything to do with the apparent success or failure of certain ideas?

To more fully understand the rich history of criminology and criminal justice, the answers to these questions are particularly important. This book argues that the most influential research in the fields of criminology and criminal justice have earned their status as *key ideas* for reasons that extend beyond the theoretical developments and general findings of the research itself. Accordingly, this book is organized around a single unifying theme: explaining how two factors—(1) the broader sociopolitical context or climate of the time and (2) the unique style and manner in which the research was marketed to its intended audience—are central to understanding the emergence of key ideas in criminology and criminal justice.

In doing so, each chapter in this text is dedicated to a key idea, or contemporaneous set of ideas, and adopts an organizational strategy that takes a four-part approach. First the key idea is introduced and explained to provide an essential understanding of its central components. Second, the sociopolitical climate during which the work was written is highlighted to bring attention to the importance of external conditions for understanding the widespread acceptance of the idea. Here it is demonstrated how social context is responsible for propelling some ideas to the forefront of criminology and criminal justice while repressing others from gaining much, if any, attention at all. Third, to more fully explain why the key work, as opposed to similar works, "rose to the top" and became a primary contribution to its field, the specific manner in which the idea was marketed or packaged to its audience is discussed. Ultimately, this provides clarity as to exactly how the key work was successfully disseminated for maximal influence in the field. Finally, the fourth part of each chapter explains the far-reaching effects of the key idea, demonstrating specifically how it has impacted or changed the discipline. This strategy provides the reader with not only a clear understanding of the key works themselves, but also with a complete picture of precisely how and why certain research efforts have come to yield such powerful influences while similar works have gone relatively unnoticed.

Chapter 1 introduces the book. Theories in criminal justice and criminology, this chapter explains, cannot be viewed as independent of or divorced from the social and political milieu from which they sprang, nor can their content be understood as distinct from their discourse. Criminological ideas catch on because they are consistent with prevailing sociopolitical attitudes at the time, and because the authors of those ideas offered something unique and compelling that other authors working in the same time periods and promulgating similar ideas failed to provide.

The remaining chapters are organized chronologically, rather than thematically, to illustrate the sequential development of criminology and criminal justice over the centuries and to demonstrate to students how social, political, and theoretical trajectories ebb, flow, and sometimes even come full circle. "New" ideas are rarely entirely novel or unique; rather, they rely on prior theories and either affirm, challenge, or modify those existing ideas. Chapter 2 describes Cesare Beccaria's *On Crimes and Punishments* and the inception of the Classical School of criminology. The Enlightenment and the American Revolution provide the historical backdrop, and Beccaria's succinct, pragmatic writing style and ability to synthesize various philosophical viewpoints combined to make this treatise one of the key ideas in criminology.

Chapter 3 describes the downfall of the Classical School in the 1800s as the Positivist School gained popularity. Cesare Lombroso is the star of this chapter. Lombroso, combining existing biological theories such as phrenology with what at that time was the new Darwinian theory of evolution, proposed a theory of the born criminal whose innate atavism propelled him into crime. His vivid writing, massive data collection efforts, and status as the first criminologist to devote specific attention to female criminals as a separate class from male criminals earned him a permanent place in history.

Chapter 4 outlines the demise of the individual-level studies of crime and the rise of macro-level criminological research. Robert Merton's anomie/strain theory and Clifford Shaw and Henry McKay's social disorganization theory are the focus of this chapter. The American Industrial Revolution provides the sociopolitical backdrop. Merton's theory that crime is spawned by the lower classes' adherence to materialistic standards is contrasted against Shaw and McKay's conjecture that it is the rejection of mainstream values that results in deviant behavior. Both theories have a distinguished legacy in criminology.

Chapter 5 is devoted to Travis Hirschi's social bond/social control theory and the way in which Hirschi revamped the traditional question of "why do people commit crime?" and instead asked "why don't they?" Hirschi's theory fit well in the post–World War II context of the United States where the booming war economy had created a large middle class, and where rising social discontent and crime rates led this "new bourgeoisie" to claim that the traditional institutions of social order (e.g., families, schools, churches) were crumbling and that the younger generation was out of control. Hirschi also tantalized academic criminologists with a new method of research: empirical-based theory testing.

In Chapter 6, Robert Martinson's (in)famous "nothing works" assessment of correctional rehabilitation is reviewed. Martinson released his report in the mid-1970s, at a time when conservative politicians and right-wing commentators called for harsher criminal penalties and liberals called for reduced discretion and greater uniformity in sentencing. Rehabilitation appeared to be at the heart of the problem and, as it turns out, Martinson's research provided a rather large segment of society with just the "scientific" evidence they had been waiting for. He was not the first scholar to criticize rehabilitation as implemented in the United States, but favorable timing helped him to become the first to expand his message beyond the confines of academic journals, drawing considerable media attention to his findings.

Chapter 7 works in tandem with Chapter 6 and covers James Q. Wilson's *Thinking About Crime*. The disintegration of the rehabilitation monolith left American corrections without a guiding theoretical paradigm, and Wilson quickly interjected a proposed replacement: selective incapacitation of high-risk offenders. Soaring (and, it would turn out, greatly exaggerated) estimates of the crime-reduction potential of selective incapacitation captured public and academic attention and helped usher in the mass incarceration movement.

Chapter 8 shifts the discussion from corrections to policing with James Q. Wilson's and George L. Kelling's broken windows thesis. People in the United States in the 1980s increasingly complained about the dilapidated, squalid conditions of cities and the seemingly uncontrollable behavior of wayward vagrants and idle youth. Wilson and Kelling spoke to people's fears and legitimized them by arguing that unchecked disorder caused serious street crime. Their theory also put police in charge of disorder reduction, which breathed new life into the policing institution and offered both police and the public the hope of a "quick fix" to the crime problem. Broken windows theory was, and continues to be, enormously popular in policing and the focus of much contentious debate among academics.

Along the same line of quick fixes, Chapter 9 describes Nancy Reagan's "Just Say No" campaign targeting drug use. The Reagan administration's "war on drugs" launched a series of offensives against the supply side of the drug trade. Nancy Reagan's popularity sprang from her prominence as the First Lady, from her attention to the demand side of drug use, and from her reliance on the politically conservative language of rational choice to depict drug use as a simple "yes or no" decision that would be easy for youth to make and would result in a fast and sure victory for society in its battle against the drug scourge.

Chapter 10 covers the reemergence of correctional rehabilitation with Andrews, Zinger, Hoge, Bonta, Gendreau, and Cullen's delineation of risk, need, and responsivity as the three components to effective rehabilitation. This group of mostly Canadian scholars was distressed at the Martinsonian wholesale rejection of rehabilitation and collaborated with American criminologists to refute the notion that offenders could not be treated. Hope for rehabilitation was revitalized with the argument that treatment can work if it follows evidence-based procedures and adheres to the three core tenets. Andrews et al. used quantitative meta-analysis to demonstrate what types of programs show positive outcomes and which do not, in an attempt to provide guidance to practitioners and, most importantly, they offered explanations for *why* some programs succeeded and some failed.

Chapter 11 reviews the life course theories articulated by Terrie Moffitt and by Robert Sampson and John Laub. Researchers in the years leading up to the introduction of life course theories had specified an enduring relationship between individuals' personal traits and their criminal behavior that allegedly persisted uniformly throughout the life span. This contradicted everything known in criminology about the age-crime curve and the fact that criminality in youth usually does not persist into adulthood. Moffitt offered a theory of why some delinquent youth persist in deviance (stability), while most do not (change), and Sampson and Laub proposed an alternative version that focused on intra-individual dynamic change over time. Sampson and Laub's life course perspective also incorporated elements of Hirschi's social bond theory, thus linking these two key ideas in important ways. Both life course theories were presented in systematic, well-articulated manners that lent themselves to empirical testing, and they therefore became popular quickly in the academic arena.

Chapter 12 concludes the volume with a brief justification for why certain key ideas covered in this book were chosen to the exclusion of other important works that also, it could also be argued, put forth key ideas. Some of the major theories that were excluded (e.g., social learning theory) are summarized. This chapter also offers a "Looking Forward" section that discusses some promising but as-yet-underdeveloped theories in criminology and criminal justice, any of which may be the next "key idea" on the horizon.

ACKNOWLEDGMENTS

The authors wish to extend gratitude to Jerry Westby and the rest of the Sage team for their invaluable patience and assistance with this book. We also thank the following reviewers who offered comments on earlier versions of some chapters: Gad J. Bensinger, Loyola University Chicago; Ellen G. Cohn, Florida International University; AnnMarie Cordner, Kutztown University; C. Nana Derby, Virginia State University; Phil Harris, Temple University; George E. Higgins, University of Louisville; Dennis Longmire, Sam Houston State University; Mary Maguire, California State University, Sacramento; Nancy E. Marion, The University of Akron; Jerome McKean, Ball State University; J. Mitchell Miller, University of Texas at San Antonio; Xin Ren, California State University, Sacramento; Tara Kay Shaw, University of Oklahoma; and Scott Vollum, James Madison University.

We also appreciate Teresa Herlinger for her editorial assistance. Her efforts and those of the reviewers have ensured that any and all errors, misinterpretations, or limitations contained within this book are ours and ours alone . . . but we really wish we could blame them anyway.

ONE

INTRODUCTION

We have a tendency to assume that things wouldn't be the same in the arts—regardless of the medium—had it not been for the influence of certain select individuals. For example, the impressionist tradition would not have been the same without Monet; literature wouldn't be the same without Shakespeare, Jane Austen, John Steinbeck, or Toni Morrison; and music certainly wouldn't be the same without Bob Dylan or Jimi Hendrix—without them, we may not have been blessed with Bruce Springsteen or Stevie Ray Vaughn. Each of these figures explored new directions that fundamentally altered the way we look at those particular slices of the world, and the influence of each is heralded as his or her own. Indeed, we see these works (or bodies of work) as the result of individual creativity that broke new ground that, were it not for them, may never have been broken (even if it's questionable in some cases whether such a reputation is deserved).

We tend to think about science much differently, where major scientific breakthroughs—whether empirical or theoretical—have often been viewed through the lens of "scientific inevitability." To be sure, science doesn't operate in a social vacuum. Even Charles Darwin and Albert Einstein were working within the larger disciplinary traditions of biology and physics, with numerous scholars treading over similar territory at the time (Gould, 1998). Others, like James Watson and Francis Crick, whose work is synonymous with the "discovery" of the DNA molecule, actually got the visual for the double helix from Rosalind Franklin—a female scientist who was never allowed to be part of the winning team's roster for the Nobel Prize that followed and was snubbed in the subsequent historical record (Strathern, 1999).

These examples aren't provided in an effort to downplay the contributions of a few notably influential scholars. They are merely meant to illustrate that new ideas emerge within particular social contexts where certain ideas would "makes sense" when formerly they may not have (Kuhn, 1962). In short, the notion of scientific inevitability holds that great scientific breakthroughs, even if not made by the particular scientists known for them, probably would have been made by someone else anyway. This sentiment is echoed by Isaac Newton's 17th-century statement regarding the cumulative—as opposed to individualistic—nature of scientific discovery (one that even he wasn't the first to use, though he's often credited for it), that, "If I have seen further it is by standing on the shoulders of giants" (Hawking, 2003, p. ix). Gould (1998) even took it a step further in his discussion of science's "myth of inexorability in discovery," in which he argued that scholars have been depicted as "interchangeable cogs in the wheel of [scientific] progress—as people whose idiosyncrasy and individual genius must be viewed as irrelevant to an inevitable sequence of advances" (p. 54).

The result is that it tends to be the idea—not the idea producer—that is viewed with critical importance within various scientific fields. The point here is not to dispute the existence of a few "rock star" scientists that operate within particular disciplines. Such popularity is, however, exceptionally rare within scientific ranks. What is far more likely is that even though we might not recall the names of Joseph Fourier or Svante Arrhenius, we still have an intuitive idea of what the "greenhouse effect" is; we may never have heard of Walter Fiers, J. Craig Venter, or Pieter J. de Jong, but most of us are familiar with the Human Genome Project; and even if we don't know who Tim Berners-Lee or Luis Furlan are, we certainly know what the Internet is.

These are but a few examples (and others certainly abound), but what they highlight is clear: We're familiar with the outcomes of scientific advances even if we're ignorant of the scientists responsible for them. By extension, this also indicates that ideas lurk in competition with each other, and for a host of reasons, certain ones rise above the others and take prominence. Accordingly, many "revolutionary" scientific ideas—independent of who was touting them—either gained credence or were killed (or at least delayed) by the sociopolitical context in which they were advanced.

The field of criminology/criminal justice is no different. To be sure, certain ideas about the causes of crime and the appropriate response to crime have emerged and gained popularity for reasons that have little or nothing to do with their scientific merit (see the discussion in Pratt & Cullen, 2000). Instead, scholars have noted that certain theories have become popular because they may be "interesting" and contrary to common sense (Hagan, 1973), because they provide "puzzles" that can be easily researched by scholars seeking publications (Cole, 1975), or because the policy implications of a particular theory may be either pleasing or controversial (Gould, 1996). The dominant explanation within the sociology of science, however, specifies a much more straightforward explanation for why certain ideas do, or do not, "catch on": that changes in the social and political context of the time shift the way people think about issues of crime and justice. Accordingly, particular ways of thinking about crime/criminal justice will inevitably seem more plausible in certain periods of history than in others (Lilly, Cullen, & Ball, 2007).

Criminologists themselves have certainly reinforced this concept. For example, scholars have noted how spiritual explanations of crime in the 19th century were consistent with more general societal notions of the "evil" nature of criminal behavior (Vold & Bernard, 1986); how early positivist theories about genetic and physiological sources of criminal behavior fit well within the general shift in scientific assumptions of the early 1900s (Lilly et al., 2007); how social disorganization and strain theories made sense in the early part of the 20th century amid growing concerns over the consequences of urbanization, poverty, and geographic mobility (Pratt & Cullen, 2005); how control theories of crime and delinquency in the late 1960s fit within the emerging perception of the WWII generation that the permissive American society is allowing crime to happen (Hirschi, 1969); and how the wide spectrum of contemporary explanations of crime—from rational choice, to biosocial perspectives, to life-course frameworks—reflects a more pluralistic nature of contemporary American society and the increasingly interdisciplinary nature of criminology as an academic discipline (Pratt, Maahs, & Stehr, 1998).

This social-contextual view isn't necessarily wrong. There is truth to the observation that all of the works noted above (and those to be discussed in this book) were, in fundamentally important ways, consistent with the prevailing social context of the time. Such an explanation is nevertheless incomplete. In particular, we contend in this book that such a viewpoint fails to specify why *certain* works distinguished themselves from the pack of other pieces of scholarship produced within the same intellectual tradition at the same time and, in turn, went on to enjoy lasting influence while their contemporaries—many of which contained a nearly identical message—remain mired in obscurity.

To address this issue, in this book we contend that the way in which the idea was delivered is just as important as the idea itself for determining why a particular concept became a "key idea" in criminology and criminal justice. Put simply, there are reasons why, for example, Travis Hirschi has become the Bruce Springsteen of criminology, and the purpose of this book is to illustrate those reasons. To that end, the book follows the flow of influence in contemporary ideas about crime and criminal justice chronologically—rather than thematically—so that the sequence of ideas from time period to time period will be most clear. We also devote chapters to key ideas that address both the causes (criminology) and the consequences (criminal justice) of crime. Although contemporary higher education (and the academy itself) tends to view criminology and criminal justice as somehow separate and distinct, we see the two as fundamentally intertwined. Specifically, ideas concerning what to do about the crime problem will inevitably draw upon a set of assumptions concerning what causes the crime problem in the first place. Conversely, ideas about crime causation have consequences—they will inevitably shape in important ways our thoughts about how to best combat crime.

With these goals in mind, each of the remaining chapters will address one or two primary works in the field of criminal justice or criminology.

(In two cases where key contributions are highly related, they will be addressed within the same chapter.) Furthermore, each of the chapters will follow a similar format, organized into four main sections. The first section will address the social and political climate during which the work was written, highlighting the external conditions that led to such wide acceptance of the idea. The second section will introduce and discuss the general content of the key contribution being addressed, highlighting its most significant aspects. Once the reader has become familiar with the work and its relative importance, the remaining sections will clarify *how* and *why* it, as opposed to other similar works, "rose to the top" and became a key contribution to its field. Specifically, the third section will discuss how the particular piece of work was marketed or "packaged" in a way that aided its subsequent impact on the field. Finally, the fourth section will demonstrate its far-reaching influence, showing specifically how it has impacted or changed the discipline. The broader point of this book, then, is not only to give readers an appreciation for these ideas themselves, but also to provide an understanding of why a certain scholar's take on a particular concept can come to define the nature of that idea for future generations of criminologists.

REFERENCES

Cole, S. (1975). The growth of scientific knowledge: Theories of deviance as a case study. In L. A. Coser (Ed.), *The idea of social structure: Papers in honor of Robert K. Merton* (pp. 175–200). New York: Harcourt Brace Jovanovich.

Gould, S. J. (1996). *The mismeasure of man* (Rev. ed.). New York: Norton.

Gould, S. J. (1998). *Leonardo's mountain of clams and the diet of worms: Essays on natural history.* New York: Three Rivers Press.

Hagan, J. (1973). Labeling and deviance: A case study in the "sociology of the interesting." *Social Problems, 20,* 447–458.

Hawking, S. (2003). *On the shoulders of giants: The great works of physics and astronomy.* Philadelphia: Running Press.

Hirschi, T. (1969). *Causes of delinquency.* Berkeley: University of California Press.

Kuhn, T. S. (1962). *The structure of scientific revolutions* (3rd ed.). Chicago: University of Chicago Press.

Lilly, J. R., Cullen, F. T., & Ball, R. A. (2007). *Criminological theory: Context and consequences* (4th ed.). Thousand Oaks, CA: Sage.

Pratt, T. C. & Cullen, F. T. (2000). The empirical status of Gottfredson and Hirschi's general theory of crime: A meta-analysis. *Criminology, 38,* 961–964.

Pratt, T. C., & Cullen, F. T. (2005). Assessing macro-level predictors and theories of crime: A meta-analysis. *Crime and Justice: A Review of Research, 32,* 373–450.

Pratt, T. C., Maahs, J. R., & Stehr, S. D. (1998). The symbolic ownership of the corrections "problem": A framework for understanding the development of corrections policy in the United States. *Prison Journal, 78,* 451–464.

Strathern, P. (1999). *Crick, Watson and DNA: The big idea.* Norwell, MA: Anchor.

Vold, G. B., & Bernard, T. J. (1986). *Theoretical criminology* (3rd ed.). New York: Oxford University Press.

TWO

KEY IDEA: RATIONAL OFFENDING AND RATIONAL PUNISHMENT

KEY WORK

Beccaria, C. (1986). *On crimes and punishments* (D. Young, Trans.). Indianapolis, IN: Hackett Publishing. (Original work published 1764).[1]

The Western history of criminology began with Cesare Beccaria (1738–1794), who experienced sudden fame with the publication of *On Crimes and Punishments* in 1764. Beccaria was the first person to construct a philosophy concerning crime's cause and solution. He designed a utilitarian framework of law and punishment that was grounded in his fundamental belief that people are rational, that they exercise free will, and that deterrence is the only ethical foundation for criminal punishment. His philosophical arguments and policy proposals were simple but elegant, and they resounded well among a populace eager to embrace a new system of justice. Beccaria's ideas inspired later figures like Jeremy Bentham and formed the basis for the Classical School of criminology, which reigned for a century and is to this day an integral aspect of criminal justice in the United States. This chapter is devoted to Cesare Beccaria's master work and the impact it has had on criminal law and sanctions.

THE SOCIAL CONTEXT OF CRIMINAL PUNISHMENT

The criminal justice system in Europe during the 18th century was a scene of caprice, torture, and death (Maestro, 1973). Even a minor offense could form the basis for an execution order. Executions were generally carried out in public so that citizens could bear witness to the bloody spectacle. Many death-eligible offenses were, moreover, petty property crimes for which capital punishment was an extraordinarily severe response (Maestro, 1973; Rustigan, 1981). Criminal codes and their judicial applications were largely provincial (e.g., Foucault, 1977); that is, criminal matters were typically adjudicated at the local level with little or no oversight by centralized national governments. This decentralization resulted in tremendous judicial discretion over convictions and sentences. Magistrates used criminal codes as they saw fit and designed punishments on an offender-specific basis (Foucault, 1977; Maestro, 1973). There was no requirement that offenders be treated in an equitable or uniform fashion—punishments were tailored to the individual characteristics of an offender and his or her crime. Vicious penalties could be exacted upon petty thieves, while cold-blooded killers could be pardoned at judges' whims (Tibbetts & Hemmens, 2010).

The status of the criminal justice system (or lack of system, as it were) in Europe during the 1700s was the product of a long tradition of aristocracy. An aristocratic government is one in which land is owned by particular families and is bequeathed through the generations of a family line. The monarch of the region grants titles and powers to the landed gentry, who in return keep order within their land and swear loyalty to the monarch. Property and power in an aristocracy are privileges of birth alone; merit is irrelevant. Aristocrats' lives center around maintaining—and even hopefully expanding—their wealth and clout; as a class, aristocrats historically have cared little for the poor and have been inclined to appoint assistants, such as magistrates and police, to whom they can delegate the responsibility of keeping order among the lower classes. This frees aristocrats to concentrate on other matters of consequence.

Ancient Europe was ruled by aristocracies and the economy was driven by agriculture, but the 18th century saw the beginning of the Industrial Revolution and the concomitant rise of enterprises like mining and textile manufacturing that rivaled agrarianism for economic dominance. The rise of big industry created something that Europe had never seen before: a middle class. This class consisted of economic entrepreneurs who built fortunes using savvy business strategies, hard work, and capital investment. They became the first group in European history to move up through the socioeconomic ranks and actually *earn* wealth rather than stumble upon it by the haphazard fortune of birthright. In the 1700s, birthright-based aristocracies still controlled governments across Europe, but that power was weakening as the middle class gained ground.

Two different but mutually-dependent movements in the 18th century marked an inevitable and fundamental change in the way European governments operated. The first was the Enlightenment, a philosophical movement that began in the early 1700s[2] and pulsed through Western Europe for a century. At the heart of the Enlightenment was the use of reason and logic to improve political systems, enhance social justice, and generally better the lot of humanity. Some Enlightenment devotees were wealthy aristocrats and others were paupers. Some desired only minor alterations in the system and others spent their lives attempting to foment revolution. All, though, sought to bolster justice in social and political institutions; the criminal justice system was therefore a primary target of reformers' writings and commentaries.

A select few sovereigns throughout Europe also embraced Enlightenment ideas. These "enlightened monarchs" were princes, empresses, and other royals who displayed enthusiasm for political and social changes that would improve life for all citizens (Maestro, 1973). One hallmark of the Enlightenment was the belief that religion and politics should be separated. The Church, at that time in history, was a powerful and insular monolith of political leverage. Church leaders were not just religious figures, but political figures as well. Law was a mixture of secular legislation and allegedly-divine doctrine. Enlightenment supporters—many of whom were Christians—espoused the conviction that the Church as an institution had become too politically-potent and that the marriage between law and religion threatened freedom, reason, and prosperity. Monarchs liked the thought of secularization, too, as they stood to absorb the power and clout formerly possessed by the ousted clergy.

The second series of events revolves specifically around the criminal justice system. Criminal punishments became a primary target of middle-class reform efforts. As described above, sanctions were harsh during this time period and even trivial crimes carried harrowing physical penalties, including execution. What irritated the middle class was that in some countries, juries began refusing to convict defendants accused of petty offenses because the punishments were so grossly disproportionate to the crimes. The existence of unduly harsh penalties meant that, in practice, property and other crimes of moderate severity often carried no penalties at all. This spate of jury nullification ignited fears among the ruling echelons that the legitimacy of the criminal justice system was crumbling. The middle class favored making penalties milder so that juries would willingly impose them and punishment would thus become more certain and predictable (Humphries & Greenberg, 1981; Rothman, 1983; Rustigan, 1981).

To make matters worse for the ruling classes, the famous Enlightenment thinker Voltaire started a crusade to expose miscarriages of justice. In 1762, he personally investigated the case of a Protestant

Frenchman named Jean Calas who had been convicted of murdering his own son when the latter allegedly professed a desire to convert to Catholicism. Calas, as per his court-imposed sentence, was executed by being broken upon the wheel. His widow appealed to Voltaire who, when he discovered that Calas' son had in fact committed suicide, flooded France with pamphlets trumpeting the awful truth that the state had tortured an innocent man to death. He succeeded in getting the verdict overturned and Calas' name cleared in 1765. The French populace was outraged and became even more so as Voltaire's campaign of post-conviction exonerations continued (Maestro, 1973). In France and beyond, Europeans' faith in their governments plummeted and in some countries, the specter of rebellion began surfacing. The ruling classes knew they had to do something, be it out of genuine sympathy for those terrorized by the bloodthirsty criminal justice system or out of a desire to preserve their own power.

Cesare Beccaria, an Italian lawyer and legal philosopher, entered the political scene at the height of this controversy. Beccaria joined a group of educated men enmeshed in the Milanese Enlightenment in the Italian province of Lombardy. Milan was the largest city in Lombardy and the hub of the Italian Enlightenment there. Aristocrats in many Italian provinces—Lombardy in particular—were eager participants in the Enlightenment. Beccaria was an aristocrat, albeit one of modest means, and was enamored with Enlightenment thought (Young, 1986). He studied, lectured, and wrote on topics ranging from crime to economics to religion to law. He toiled in almost total obscurity until being propelled to the pinnacle of fame virtually overnight with the 1764 publication of *On Crimes and Punishments* (Maestro, 1973). This treatise earned him a place in history as the first criminologist (Tibbetts & Hemmens, 2010), though he hardly would have self-applied the label (see Rafter, 2009). Beccaria's arguments were firmly grounded in philosophical, moral, and ethical tenets, yet the treatise is heavily pragmatic and can be seen, for all intents and purposes, as an administrative text designed to inform the bureaucracy of criminal justice. Even Beccaria himself did not anticipate the wild popularity his essay would earn or the fact that posterity would place *On Crimes and Punishments* on a pedestal as the first treatise on the nature of crime, the criminal law, and the philosophical basis for punishment.

BECCARIA'S PROPOSAL

Cesare Beccaria (1764/1986) saw the then-extant criminal law as a hodgepodge of laws, customs, and traditions deriving primarily from ancient Roman and Germanic cultures (see also Maestro, 1973). He sought to rationalize this antiquated, tangled mess into a uniform system that embodied the spirit of modernity and would be consistent, principled, and predictable.

True to Enlightenment ideals, Beccaria—a self-professed Christian—aimed much criticism at the role of institutional religion in what he considered to be an unquestionably secular sphere of society. The Church had conflated "crime" and "sin" in a manner that allowed it to assume authority over both. The Roman Inquisition had shaped criminal procedure across continental Europe and had made the use of secret witnesses and torture-compelled confessions standard practice in criminal cases (Maestro, 1973). Beccaria rejected the Church as a political institution and argued with particular vehemence that religious leaders and doctrines had no place in the criminal justice system.

Beccaria drew heavily on the ideas and written works of other philosophers; in fact, there was really nothing unique or novel in the actual substance of his treatise. The text is full of references to, for instance, Rousseau's contractualism and Helvetius' utilitarianism. Beccaria also relied extensively upon Montesquieu, who in 1748 published a book detailing many of the same principles that Beccaria would echo in his 1764 treatise (Maestro, 1973). Beccaria made no attempt to conceal that he was in the debt of several intellectual predecessors.

The starting point of Beccaria's argument was the philosophical theory of *contractualism.* He conceptualized law as a contract between individuals and society: Each person in society relinquishes a small portion of his or her liberty to the sovereign and in exchange, the sovereign provides the people with the security they require in order to live free and happy lives (see also Rousseau, 1762/1973). Under a contractualist viewpoint, violating the law is tantamount to breaking the social contract and, therefore, the sovereign has the right—indeed, the obligation—to punish the person who overstepped his or her bounds and threatened the security and happiness of society.

To determine the permissible scope of punishment for those who violated the social contract, Beccaria (1764/1986) turned to utilitarian principles. He operated under the precept that the fundamental purpose of law is to ensure "the greatest happiness shared among the greatest number" (p. 5) and to this end, he sought ways to exact criminal penalties in a manner that ultimately benefitted society. One of the most important contributions Beccaria made to criminology and criminal justice was his insistence that criminal penalties be devised and administered on the basis of the crime that has been committed and not upon the character or social standing of the person who committed that crime. He was resolved that "the only true measurement of crimes is the harm done to the nation" (p. 16). This proposition seems self-evident today because offense type is the foremost factor in criminal sentencing, but it has not always been that way. Contemporary society has Beccaria to thank for institutionalizing this notion (Lilly, Cullen, & Ball, 2007).

The utilitarian underpinnings of Beccaria's (1764/1986) thinking gave rise to *deterrence* as the guiding force behind criminal law and punishment.

He declared that, "The purpose of punishment is nothing other than to dissuade the criminal from doing fresh harm to his compatriots and to keep other people from doing the same" (p. 23). Deterrence theory presumes that people are rational actors with free will (e.g., Caulkins & MacCoun, 2003; Rafter, 2009) who conscientiously compare the costs and benefits of a contemplated act before executing that act. Beccaria believed that people's behavior is guided by self-interest and that people generally avoid doing anything that carries more pain than reward. It seemed obvious to him, then, that penal sanctions would curb crime via their role as consequence enhancers. Awareness of the ramifications, Beccaria theorized, would cause would-be criminals to rethink their planned law-breaking and would lead them to ultimately decide against it in most cases. Deterrence, then, was meant to reduce crime through prevention (see Beccaria, 1764/1986, pp. 74–75).

Three elements dominated Beccaria's (1764/1986) analysis of penal sanctions: certainty, severity, and promptness. Certainty, he said, was the single most important characteristic of effective deterrence. He reasoned that the effectiveness of deterrence hinges upon citizens being absolutely sure that they will be caught and punished if they misbehave. There must be no possibility that punishment will be evaded because so long as a glimmer of hope for impunity exists, deterrence is compromised. He considered certainty superior to severity; to wit, he wrote, "One of the greatest checks on crime is not the cruelty of punishments but their inevitability" (p. 46). Beccaria saw certainty and severity as inversely related: Mild penalties enjoyed enhanced certainty because conscientious judges and juries might balk at forcing convicted persons to suffer atrocities of the body or mind but would, conversely, be far more consistent in their application of temperate, humane penalties.

Regarding severity, he held that penalties should be as mild as they could possibly be while still effecting deterrence. Anything more severe than what is absolutely necessary to deter, he said, is by definition excessive, abusive, and unjustifiable. It would, as aforementioned, also undermine certainty. The determination of appropriate severity was to be made based on the amount of harm done to society by the crime. Beccaria delineated a sentencing tariff (see also von Hirsch, 1983) whereby greater levels of harm to society warranted stiffer penalties and, likewise, lesser crimes merited milder sanctions. Proportionality was vital to Beccaria because he believed that tariffs helped ensure that when people did commit crimes, they would avoid those that carried onerous sanctions and would opt instead for less serious offenses. As Beccaria (1764/1986) put it, "If an equal punishment is meted out to two crimes that offend society unequally, then men find no stronger obstacle standing in the way of committing the more serious crime if it holds a greater advantage for them" (p. 16).

The final element of Beccaria's (1764/1986) formulation of deterrence was the promptness of punishment. He argued,

> [T]he less time that passes between the misdeed and its chastisement, the stronger and more permanent is the human mind's association of the two ideas of *crime* and *punishment,* so that imperceptibly the one will come to be considered as the cause and the other as the necessary and inevitable result. (p. 36, emphasis in original)

The deterrent value of a penalty, he theorized, is maximized when very little time elapses between the crime and the penalty so that the relationship between the two will be permanently imprinted upon offenders' minds.

The primary reason for the lasting influence of Beccaria's treatise in criminology and criminal justice[3] was that it offered both a theory of crime causation and a policy proposal for crime's reduction/prevention (see Rafter, 2009). Beccaria conceived of human beings as rational, self-interested, possessing of free will, and capable of making decisions based on cost-benefit analyses. It followed logically from this premise that crime results when the perceived benefit of a criminal act outweighs the perceived consequences—this was the first cogent theory of crime ever produced in the modern Western world (Rafter, 2009).

The theories of free will and rational choice offer the distinct benefit of making human behavior amenable to control by social institutions. Up to and even during Beccaria's time (and obviously owing to the Church's influence), noncompliance with the law was considered by many to be the product of demonic possession or predetermined, immutable wickedness (Tibbetts & Hemmens, 2010). Clearly, exorcism is a bit beyond the purview of the criminal justice system and if Calvinistic predetermination were the operative force behind human activity, then the system would certainly have its hands tied. If crime is seen as a free choice, though, then controlling this behavior suddenly becomes much easier. The theory of free will legitimizes the use of punishment as a way to shape behavior. It is in this way that Beccaria simultaneously offered a theory of why people commit crime (i.e., because they choose to do so, using their innate rationality and freedom of thought) and a proposed method of curbing it (i.e., certain, proportionate, and prompt penalties).

WHY IT CAUGHT ON

On Crimes and Punishments fascinated the public and earned its respect. The treatise was translated immediately into languages such as French, German, and English, which aided its dissemination throughout Europe and into the American colonies. Beccaria offered a captivating theory of crime that fit tidily with Enlightenment ideas about human nature. The principles of free will and rational choice affirmed the dignity and value of all people, hail as they might from majestic castles or lowly hovels. It also, as described above, made the solution to crime rather convenient because if crime is a choice made by rational people, then punishment—or, better yet, the mere *threat* of punishment—can quash this antisocial behavior.

Although the substance of *On Crimes and Punishments* was of course critical to its success, Beccaria's communication method was profoundly instrumental in the work's rise to fame. The treatise was simple and tidy. The document itself is quite short—a fraction of the length of most books—and his writing is concise and his reasoning succinct. *On Crimes and Punishments* was a pragmatic, administrative document more so than a philosophical or theoretical one. It was cobbled together using fragments of numerous philosophies, yet was streamlined, to-the-point, and free from tangents and other sources of distraction and obfuscation. Beccaria (1764/1986) wove complex philosophies into a straightforward text that offered guidance, direction, and recommendations and was accessible to a wide audience (see also Jenkins, 1984; Morris, 1973).

The absence of a strong ideological bent also made the text appealing to people from a variety of schools of thought. It is easier to get people to reach a consensus about "what" than about "why." During the Enlightenment, all of the major thinkers and enlightened monarchs agreed that torture and other forms of brutality were wrong, but they proposed different and sometimes incompatible explanations for *why* barbaric methods should be abandoned. Beccaria deftly sidestepped the whole issue of "why" by refraining from a dogmatic propounding of philosophical ideas and instead devoting attention to the actions that must be taken to improve the system and bring justice to penology. This practical take on crime policy appealed greatly to reformers from a variety of schools of thought because there was no need to sacrifice one's own beliefs to see the merit in Beccaria's proposals.

Another reason for Beccaria's popularity is one that has earned him both praise and criticism. Beccaria, as aforementioned, was a member of the Italian aristocracy. He favored monarchies and believed that only land owners, business owners, and others with a tangible stake in politics should be permitted to participate in government. He was not a radical reformist like some of his contemporaries, such as Rousseau (Cole, 1955/1973) and Voltaire (Maestro, 1973). He was, quite simply, conservative (Jenkins, 1984; Klang, 1984). Nowhere in *On Crimes and Punishments* or in any of his other writings did he so much as hint at major political reform or governmental upheaval—he wanted a change in function, not in structure. He saw the monarchy as having the potential for enormous social good, and his arguments were all framed so as to preserve the aristocracy while advancing humanistic ideals. He repackaged and mainstreamed the ideologies upon which his thinking was based and thereby cleverly made palatable to power-holders the very same ideas they rejected outright when proposed by rebels of the establishment (Jenkins, 1984). He gave monarchs and the landed gentry the best of both worlds by offering them a way to preserve their own power while simultaneously gaining popularity with the people by embracing the Enlightenment.

A final reason for the success of Beccaria's ideas actually postdates his death by nearly 200 years. Beccaria held center stage in criminology and criminal justice for a century before his ideas were eclipsed by the Positivist School of criminology (see Chapter 3 of this book), macro-level criminology (Chapter 4), and the rehabilitation ideal (Chapter 6), each of which rose to prominence and then faded through the course of criminological history. In the 1970s and ensuing decades, however, the nation's attention shifted away from criminogenic structural conditions and offender rehabilitation and took on a conservative, punitive orientation that advocated tough sentences (Lilly et al., 2007; see Chapters 7 and 9). Deterrence reemerged as a major focus of penology and correctional policy (von Hirsch, 1983) because of its punishment-based approach to crime control. This point will be elaborated upon in the next section.

INFLUENCE: THE RISE OF THE CLASSICAL SCHOOL OF CRIMINOLOGY

Beccaria's influence in the United States, just like in Europe, was a combination of good ideas and good timing. The late 1700s saw increasing unrest in the American colonies, which in 1775 exploded into the Revolutionary War. It is noteworthy that the first American printing of *On Crimes and Punishments* appeared in 1778 (Rafter, 2009), which plunked the text right into the height of the war. After Britain surrendered and withdrew, the brand-new United States of America faced the daunting task of establishing a federal government and was in need of guidance on the matter. Many people who were instrumental in the years both before and after the war, including notable persons such as Thomas Jefferson and John Adams (Maestro, 1973; Morris, 1973), were Enlightenment followers and held Beccaria in high esteem. Principles Beccaria expounded upon in his treatise—such as due process of law and trial by jury—had become established and necessary features of modern, civilized, rational governments. It is not surprising, then, that the U.S. Constitution and Bill of Rights codified into law many of Beccaria's proposals and permanently absorbed *On Crimes and Punishments* into the country's criminal justice system.

Beccaria's lasting influence on criminology and criminal justice is attributable partially to his own work and partially to the impression that *On Crimes and Punishments* made on a British utilitarian philosopher named Jeremy Bentham. Bentham wrote extensively on the ways in which utilitarianism could be used to improve law and government.

Bentham's (1789/1988) ideas about criminal sanctioning echoed and expanded upon Beccaria's thoughts (see also Young, 1986). The cumulative body of work produced by Beccaria, Bentham, and other utilitarians concerned with crime came to be known as the Classical School of criminology (Bankston & Cramer, 1974). This was the first school of criminological thought in the Western world. The Classical School held that deterrence was the only morally-defensible rationale for criminal punishment and that although it is distasteful to ever purposefully inflict harm, crime is sufficiently deleterious to society so as to legitimize punishment. Neither Beccaria nor Bentham had much of a stomach for penal harm; Beccaria (1764/1986), for instance, advocated abolition of the death penalty, and Bentham (1789/1988) asserted that "all punishment is mischief; all punishment in itself is evil" (p. 170). Bentham conceded that the principles of utility do permit criminal penalties, though he maintained that punishment is permissible only when it "promises to exclude some greater evil" (p. 170). The Classical School adopted Beccaria's three tenets of efficacious punishment (certainty, severity, and swiftness) and his assumption that humans are rational, self-interested actors who possess and exercise free will in decision making and are therefore deterrable by the threat of punishment.

The Classical School facilitated the rise of the prison as a primary method of punishment.[4] Bentham was a vocal prison advocate (Foucault, 1977; Semple, 1993) and he was not alone in his thinking. During the 1700s and 1800s, people across Europe and in the United States reached a general consensus that the era of corporal punishment was over and that it was time for a new strategy. The question was what, exactly, the substitute would be. Jails had been in existence since the early 1600s, but they were used only for holding offenders who were awaiting trial or exile and were not viewed as methods of punishment in and of themselves (Takagi, 1981). Reformers gave jails a second look and decided they had potential (Rothman, 1983). Prisons seemed to promise both a more humane mode of punishment and an opportunity to reform criminals during their stints as wards of the state (see Clear, 1994; Pratt, 2009). The idea of punishing offenders by confining them became a staple of penology across the Western world.

The Classical School of criminology was shattered in the latter portion of the 1800s when the Positivist School rose to take its place (see Chapter 3 of this book), but Classicism experienced a resurgence in the mid-1900s (Maestro, 1973; Morris, 1973; von Hirsch, 1983) when the United States' attention was drawn toward domestic crime problems and politicians revived the language of deterrence in their efforts to convince the public that harsh penalties were necessary to bring skyrocketing crime rates under control (e.g., Blumstein & Nagin, 1978). The systemic entrenchment of deterrence in the United States can be seen most vividly in the get-tough, pro-prison movement that began in the early 1970s, picked up speed in the 1980s, and today helps account for the country's reliance on mass incarceration as a preferred crime control strategy (Clear, 1994; Currie, 1998; Pratt, 2009). Capital punishment, too, owes its continued existence in the United States—despite having been abandoned by other Western democracies years ago (Zimring, 2003)—in part to the claims of its proponents that it serves a deterrent purpose (Cochran & Chamlin, 2000; Cochran, Chamlin, & Seth, 1994). Today, although the espoused rationale for penal sanctions is no longer a single doctrine and is instead somewhat of a philosophical mishmash of deterrence, retribution, and incapacitation (see Rothman, 1983), one is hard-pressed to find a conversation about the purposes of sanctioning that does not contain some reference to the prevention of crime through the threat of punishment.

EMPIRICAL ANALYSES AND CRITIQUES OF FREE WILL, RATIONALITY, AND DETERRENCE

Beccaria lived before the rise of the scientific method. In his time, philosophy still reigned as the method for determining the nature of man, the purpose of law, and the efficacy of social policies. Positivism—the emphasis on theory-driven hypothesis testing using established scientific methods—began in the late 1700s (Rafter, 2009), well after the publication of *On Crimes and Punishments,* and did not become a standard feature of criminology until the late 1800s and early 1900s (Pratt, 2009). The question of whether there existed any empirical support for Beccaria's theory about rationality and deterrence was simply never asked in the 18th and 19th centuries; his philosophy was logical and it fit with the general sentiment of the time, so it was incorporated into popular "wisdom" and public policy (see Tullock, 1974). By the time Positivism had taken hold and empirical testing became standard practice in all sciences, the Classical School's epoch had ended. The resurrection of deterrence, beginning in the early 1970s, sparked a rash of criminological research devoted to the topic (Paternoster, 1987).

Does deterrence work? Well, yes and no. "Yes" because sanctions probably do tend to discourage people from committing prohibited acts; all else being equal, people are more likely to engage in a behavior that carries no penalty than one that does. In the sense of the simple *existence* of sanctions, then, deterrence might have crime-prevention value (Klepper & Nagin, 1989; Nagin, 1978; Tittle, 1969; von Hirsch, 1983; Zimring & Hawkins, 1973) at least to some extent (Bankston & Cramer, 1974; Pratt et al., 2006; but see Paternoster, 1987; Worrall, 2004).

The "no" answer arises from the fact that researchers have not found a clear relationship between enhanced sanctions and lower crime rates.

To borrow a metaphor, it is easier to assess people's reactions to the thought of putting their hand on a hot burner than it is to figure out how much more frightened they are of a burner that is 300 degrees relative to one that is 200 degrees (see von Hirsch, 1983). The threat of being sent to prison may suffice to deter the majority of the public from stealing cars, robbing gas stations, and doing violence to their neighbors, but how much more deterrence does society reap when it increases a prison sentence from 5 years to 10? From 20 years to 30? It is in this question that deterrence theory gets murky (Spelman, 2000b).

Whether and to what extent greater deterrence can be achieved by increasing the severity of criminal penalties has been the subject of many empirical analyses. Some researchers have claimed that harsher prison sentences do reduce crime (e.g., Levitt, 1996; Tittle, 1969; Tittle & Rowe, 1974), but studies of the relationship between imprisonment and crime tend to suffer from three problems. First, they typically conflate deterrence and incapacitation so that it becomes unclear whether the crime-reduction effect of longer prison sentences is the result of people deciding not to commit crime at all (i.e., deterrence) or whether it is due to the fact that people in prison cannot commit crimes outside of prison (i.e., incapacitation; Levitt, 1996; Piquero & Blumstein, 2007; see also Blumstein & Nagin, 1978; Worrall, 2004).

Second, most studies fail to control for bidirectionality in the prison–crime relationship (for exceptions, see Fisher & Nagin, 1978; Levitt, 1996). An inverse relationship between sanction severity and crime rates could mean that harsher sanctions cause crime reductions, but it is just as readily interpreted as indicating that higher crime rates result in less severe sanctions because there are simply too many criminals for the system to handle (Blumstein, 1983; Pratt & Cullen, 2005; Spelman, 2000a, 2000b). Third, sanction severity may be confounded with the informal, norm-based proscriptions on certain types of behavior. Proportionality in punishment means that greater sanctions are attached to more serious crimes, but more serious crimes are also associated with greater social disapproval. People may shy away from these crimes for reasons unrelated to formal punishment, such as out of fear of being embarrassed or of being rejected by loved ones (Grasmick & Bursik, 1990; Nagin & Paternoster, 1994; Nagin & Pogarsky, 2001).

An additional issue is that there is disagreement among scholars as to whether deterrence is a sociological theory wherein certainty, severity, and celerity exist as a factual, objective reality or whether it is, conversely, a psychological theory in which the individual and/or combined effect of these three aspects hinges upon people's perceptions of these conditions (see Bankston & Cramer, 1974; Caulkins & MacCoun, 2003; Paternoster, 1987; Williams & Gibbs, 1981; Zimring & Hawkins, 1973). These unresolved questions have cast doubt upon the efficacy of deterrence as a crime-control strategy.

Capital punishment is frequently justified on grounds of deterrence, which is ironic because Cesare Beccaria considered the death penalty heinous and he advocated its abolition. The deterrence-based argument offered in favor of the death penalty today is that the existence of capital punishment will make would-be murderers decide not to viciously strip another human being of life. The potential deterrent effects of the death penalty on murder have been investigated and the results are equivocal—the death penalty may be a slight deterrent for some types of murder, but it can increase other types, resulting in an overall null effect (Cochran & Chamlin, 2000; Cochran et al., 1994).

The rationality assumption underlying deterrence theory is the linchpin of the Classical School and, ergo, the most damning criticism of the theory has come from empirical studies that have failed to find support for the idea that crime is a purely rational decision (e.g., Cullen, Pratt, Miceli, & Moon, 2002; Nagin, 1978, 1998; Paternoster, 1987; Pratt & Cullen, 2005). This is not to say that choice itself is a trivial concept in criminology; to the contrary, the search for the genesis of crime is, at its most basic, a search for the reasons why people choose to engage in criminal acts (Lilly et al., 2007). The hang-up is not necessarily in the assumption that crime is a choice but, rather, in the presumption that it is a *rational* choice made by actors who accurately and objectively evaluate costs and benefits without being influenced by emotion and self-serving biases (Nagin, 2007; Nagin & Pogarsky, 2003; see also Tullock, 1974). Rational choice theory ignores the fact that cognitive ability is implicated in criminal behavior (e.g., Moffitt & Silva, 1988; White et al., 1994; see Chapters 3 and 11 of this book) and it overlooks the ways in which social factors like poverty, income inequality, racism, and other injustices may alter the cost-benefit calculus of crime[5] (see Pratt & Cullen, 2005). Finally, it neglects the ways that rationality can be bounded by differential incentive structures (Caulkins & MacCoun, 2003; Cherbonneau & Copes, 2006; Copes & Vieraitis, 2009). The omission of these key considerations in deterrence theory helps explain why the theory has met with shaky empirical support. Their absence also, as will be seen in the next chapter on the Positivist School, contributed to the Classical School's demise because positivists attacked the Classical School for painting an unrealistic picture of the mind of offenders (Jenkins, 1983).

CONCLUSION

The influence of Cesare Beccaria's *On Crimes and Punishments* (1764/1986) was vast and enduring; the core elements of the Classical School, based on his work, are firmly embedded in the modern criminal justice system. His contribution, though, is somewhat bittersweet. On one hand, his work formed the foundation for greater humanity and justice in penology. He admirably sought to rationalize penalties and introduce fairness and equity into the system. On the other hand, his failure to acknowledge the existence and power of individual traits and of macro-level criminogenic conditions is a serious flaw in deterrence theory. The rationality and free will assumptions evince a narrow, reductionistic simulacrum of the tremendously complex human psyche. *On Crimes and Punishments,* then, deserves accolades as the first attempt to modernize and humanize the criminal justice system, but it also lives in infamy as "the first great effort to cure crime without curing the society which produced it" (Jenkins, 1984, p. 128).

DISCUSSION QUESTIONS

1. What characteristics of the social context made the timing of *On Crimes and Punishments* optimal?
2. Why did Beccaria's treatise have such a profound impact on criminology and criminal justice?
3. Explain the reasons for the resurgence of the Classical School in the 1970s.
4. Have empirical studies found support for deterrence theory? Explain your answer.

REFERENCES

Bankston, W. B., & Cramer, J. A. (1974). Toward a macro-sociological interpretation of general deterrence. *Criminology, 12*(3), 251–280.

Beccaria, C. (1986). *On crimes and punishments* (D. Young, Trans.). Indianapolis, IN: Hackett Publishing. (Original work published 1764)

Bentham, J. (1988). *Introduction to the principles of morals and legislation.* Amherst, NY: Prometheus Books. (Original work published 1789)

Blumstein, A. (1983). Prisons: Population, capacity, and alternatives. In J. Q. Wilson (Ed.), *Crime and public policy* (pp. 229–250). San Francisco, CA: ICS Press.

Blumstein, A., & Nagin, D. (1978). On the optimum use of incarceration for crime control. *Operations Research, 26*(3), 381–405.

Caulkins, J. P., & MacCoun, R. (2003). Limited rationality and the limits of supply reduction. *Journal of Drug Issues, 33*(2), 433–464.

Cherbonneau, M., & Copes, H. (2006). "Drive it like you stole it": Auto theft and the illusion of normalcy. *British Journal of Criminology, 46,* 193–211.

Clear, T. R. (1994). *Harm in American penology.* New York: State University of New York Press.

Cochran, J. K. & Chamlin, M. B. (2000). Deterrence and brutalization: The dual effects of executions. *Justice Quarterly, 17*(4), 685–706.

Cochran, J. K., Chamlin, M. B., & Seth, M. (1994). Deterrence or brutalization? An impact assessment of Oklahoma's return to capital punishment. *Criminology, 32*(1), 107–134.

Cole, G. D. H. (1955/1973). Introduction. In J. H. Brumfitt & J. C. Hall (Eds.), *Jean-Jacques Rousseau: The social contract and discourses* (pp. viii–xvi). London: Everyman's Library.

Copes, H., & Vieraitis, L. M. (2009). Bounded rationality of identity thieves: Using offender-based research to inform policy. *Criminology & Public Policy, 8*(2), 101–126.

Cullen, F. T., Pratt, T. C., Miceli, S. L., & Moon, M. M. (2002). Dangerous liaison? Rational choice theory as the basis for correctional intervention. In A. R. Piquero & S. G. Tibbetts (Eds.), *Rational choice and criminal behavior: Recent research and future challenges* (pp. 279–296). New York: Routledge.

Currie, E. (1998). *Crime and punishment in America*. New York: Owl Books.

Fisher, F. M., & Nagin, D. (1978). On the feasibility of identifying the crime function in a simultaneous equation model of crime rates and sanction levels. In A. Blumstein, J. Cohen, & D. Nagin (Eds.), *Deterrence and incapacitation: Estimating the effects of criminal sanctions on crime rates* (pp. 361–399). Washington, DC: National Academy of Sciences.

Foucault, M. (1977). *Discipline and punish* (A. Sheridan, Trans.). New York: Vintage Books.

Garland, D. (2001). *The culture of control.* Chicago: University of Chicago Press.

Grasmick, H. G., & Bursik, R. J., Jr. (1990). Conscience, significant others, and rational choice: Extending the deterrence model. *Law & Society Review, 24*(3), 837–861.

Humphries, D., & Greenberg, D. F. (1981). The dialects of crime control. In D. F. Greenberg (Ed.), *Crime and capitalism* (pp. 209–254). Palo Alto, CA: Mayfield Publishing.

Jenkins, P. (1983). Erewhon: A manifesto of the rehabilitative ideal. *Journal of Criminal Justice, 11*(1), 35–46.

Jenkins, P. (1984). Varieties of Enlightenment criminology. *British Journal of Criminology, 24*(2), 112–130.

Klang, D. M. (1984). Reform and Enlightenment in eighteenth-century Lombardy. *Canadian Journal of History, 19,* 39–70.

Klepper, S., & Nagin, D. (1989). The deterrent effect of perceived certainty and severity of punishment revisited. *Criminology, 27*(4), 721–746.

Levitt, S. D. (1996). The effect of prison population size on crime rates: Evidence from prison overcrowding litigation. *Quarterly Journal of Economics, 111*(2), 319–351.

Lilly, J. R., Cullen, F. T., & Ball, R. A. (2007). *Criminological theory: Context and consequences* (4th ed.). Thousand Oaks, CA: Sage.

Maestro, M. (1973). *Cesare Beccaria and the origins of penal reform.* Philadelphia: Temple University Press.

Moffitt, T. E., & Silva, P. A. (1988). IQ and delinquency: A direct test of the differential direction hypothesis. *Journal of Abnormal Psychology, 97*(3), 330–333.

Morris, N. (1973). *Forward: Cesare Beccaria and the origins of penal reform.* Philadelphia: Temple University Press.

Nagin, D. (1978). *General deterrence: A review of the empirical evidence.* Washington, DC: National Academy of Sciences.

Nagin, D. (1998). Criminal deterrence research at the outset of the twenty-first century. In M. Tonry (Ed.), *Crime and justice: A review of research* (pp. 1–42). Chicago: University of Chicago Press.

Nagin, D. (2007). Moving choice to center stage in criminological research and theory: The American Society of Criminology 2006 Sutherland Address. *Criminology, 45*(2), 259–272.

Nagin, D., & Paternoster, R. (1994). Personal capital and social control: The deterrence implications of a theory of individual differences in criminal offending. *Criminology, 32*(4), 581–606.

Nagin, D., & Pogarsky, G. (2001). Integrating celerity, impulsivity, and extralegal sanction threats into a model of general deterrence: Theory and evidence. *Criminology, 39*(4), 865–892.

Nagin, D., & Pogarsky, G. (2003). An experimental investigation of deterrence: Cheating, self-serving bias, and impulsivity. *Criminology, 41*(1), 167–194.

Paternoster, R. (1987). The deterrent effect of the perceived certainty and severity of punishment: A review of the evidence and issues. *Justice Quarterly, 4*(2), 173–217.

Piquero, A. R., & Blumstein, A. (2007). Does incapacitation reduce crime? *Journal of Quantitative Criminology, 23,* 267–285.

Pratt, T. C. (2009). *Addicted to incarceration: Corrections policy and the politics of misinformation in the United States.* Thousand Oaks, CA: Sage.

Pratt, T. C., & Cullen, F. T. (2005). Assessing macro-level predictors and theories of crime: A meta-analysis. In M. Tonry (Ed.), *Crime and justice: A review of research* (pp. 373–450). Chicago: University of Chicago Press.

Pratt, T. C., Cullen, F. T., Blevins, K. R., Daigle, L. E., & Madensen, T. D. (2006). The empirical status of deterrence theory: A meta-analysis. In F. T. Cullen, J. P. Wright, & K. R. Blevins (Eds.), *Taking stock: The status of criminological theory—Advances in criminological theory* (Vol. 15, pp. 367–395). New Brunswick, NJ: Transaction.

Rafter, N. (2009). *The origins of criminology: A reader.* Abingdon, Oxon, UK: Routledge.

Rothman, D. J. (1983). Sentencing reforms in historical perspective. *Crime & Delinquency, 29*(4), 631–647.

Rousseau, J. (1973). *The social contract* (G. D. H. Cole, Trans.). London: Everyman's Library. (Original work published 1762)

Rustigan, M. (1981). A reinterpretation of criminal law reform in nineteenth-century England. In D. F. Greenberg (Ed.), *Crime and capitalism* (pp. 255–278). Palo Alto, CA: Mayfield Publishing.

Semple, J. (1993). *Bentham's prison: A study of the Panopticon penitentiary.* Oxford, UK: Clarendon Press.

Spelman, W. (2000a). The limited importance of prison expansion. In A. Blumstein & J. Wallman (Eds.), *The crime drop in America* (pp. 97–129). Cambridge, UK: Cambridge University Press.

Spelman, W. (2000b). What recent studies do (and don't) tell us about imprisonment and crime. In M. Tonry (Ed.), *Crime and justice* (Vol. 27, pp. 419–494). Chicago: University of Chicago Press.

Takagi, P. (1981). The Walnut Street Jail: A penal reform to centralize the powers of the state. In D. F. Greenberg (Ed.), *Crime and capitalism* (pp. 279–291). Palo Alto, CA: Mayfield Publishing.

Tibbetts, S. G., & Hemmens, C. (2010). *Criminological theory: A text/reader.* Thousand Oaks, CA: Sage.

Tittle, C. R. (1969). Crime rates and legal sanctions. *Social Problems, 16*(4), 409–423.

Tittle, C. R., & Rowe, A. R. (1974). Certainty of arrest and crime rates: A further test of the deterrence hypothesis. *Social Forces, 52*(4), 455–462.

Tullock, G. (1974). Does punishment deter crime? *The Public Interest, 36,* 103–111.

von Hirsch, A. (1983). "Neoclassicism," proportionality, and the rationale for punishment: Thoughts on the Scandinavian debate. *Crime & Delinquency, 29*(1), 52–70.

White, J. L., Moffitt, T. E., Caspi, A., Bartusch, D. J., Needles, D. J., & Stouthamer-Loeber, M. (1994). Measuring impulsivity and examining its relationship to delinquency. *Journal of Abnormal Psychology, 103*(2), 192–205.

Williams, K. R., & Gibbs, J. P. (1981). Deterrence and knowledge of statutory penalties. *Sociological Quarterly, 22,* 591–606.

Worrall, J. L. (2004). The effect of three-strikes legislation on serious crime in California. *Journal of Criminal Justice, 32,* 283–296.

Young, D. (1986). *On crimes and punishments.* Indianapolis, IN: Hackett Publishing.

Zimring, F. E. (2003). *The contradictions of American capital punishment.* Oxford, UK: Oxford University Press.

Zimring, F. E., & Hawkins, G. J. (1973). *Deterrence: The legal threat in crime control.* Chicago: University of Chicago Press.

NOTES

1. This is but one of many translations of this work.

2. Estimates concerning the starting date of the Enlightenment vary. Some sources place the start of the Enlightenment as early as the mid-1600s.

3. Beccaria's theory of crime and his proposed system of criminal punishment was but one element of his treatise. He also offered a detailed and influential treatment of criminal procedure, such as the presumption of innocence, the right to confront one's accusers, the right to a trial by a jury of one's peers, and the right to be free from compelled self-incrimination (see Beccaria, 1764/1986). For reasons of space and topical relevance, these other aspects of Beccaria's treatise cannot be covered in this chapter. The reader should be aware, though, that the present coverage of *On Crimes and Punishments* does not do justice to the full range of Beccaria's influence on criminal law and procedure.

4. The argument has been raised that the impact of philosophers—especially Bentham—in doing away with corporal penalties and transforming prisons into the

major punishment modality is misplaced and that the shift is actually attributable to the middle class's demands that penalties become more humane so that laws would actually be enforced and offenders punished (an issue that was detailed earlier in this chapter). To some extent, then, the influence of Bentham and Beccaria has been confounded with other pro-prison social forces (Rustigan, 1981). A detailed account of this counterpoint is beyond the scope of this chapter, but readers should be aware that even though Beccaria and Bentham typically get the "credit" for the shift to a prison-based sanctioning system, the Classical School was not the only impetus behind this change. See also Garland (2001) for a detailed treatment of the topic.

5. Oddly enough, Beccaria did make a link between crime and resource deprivation. He claimed that one way to reduce crime is to improve the quality of life and condition of living for all citizens. He did not interpret macro-level conditions, however, as a set of structural constraints that affect choice and thereby constrain rationality. In essence, then, Beccaria assumed the existence of a relationship between crime and environment, yet he simultaneously failed to consider that there might be a direct relationship between a person's environment and his or her behavior.

THREE

KEY IDEA: THE SCIENCE OF CRIMINAL BEHAVIOR

KEY WORKS

Lombroso, C. (2006). *Criminal man* (M. Gibson & N. H. Rafter, Trans.). Durham, NC: Duke University Press. (Original work published 1876)

Lombroso, C., & Ferrero, G. (2004). *The criminal woman, the prostitute, and the normal woman* (N. H. Rafter & M. Gibson, Trans.). Durham, NC: Duke University Press. (Original work published 1893)

Cesare Lombroso (1835–1909) is widely regarded as the father of criminal anthropology and the Positive School of criminology, sometimes called the Italian School. He is famous for his research on the physical attributes of criminals. He coined the term "born criminal" and classified this type of offender as a holdover from an earlier evolutionary period. Lombroso's fame lies in the fact that he pioneered the use of science in the study of criminal behavior. He was displeased by the domination of philosophy over law and he believed that penology should be the province of those who actually study the human mind rather than those who merely theorize about it. He brought the study of the criminal's mind and body to the forefront of scientific and public awareness, thereby paving the way for the modern field of criminology and, in particular, for the study of the influence of biological characteristics on offenders' behavior. His theories have been discredited, but Lombroso still occupies a space in criminological texts for his groundbreaking work that fundamentally restructured the study of crime and criminals. This chapter is devoted to the father of scientific criminology.

THE SOCIAL CONTEXT: A TIME WITHOUT CRIMINOLOGY

In the 19th century, there was no "criminology" as it is conceptualized today. The original brand of criminology belonged to the philosophers, not to the scientists. Criminal law and penology operated under the Classical School—ruled by the ideas of Cesare Beccaria and Jeremy Bentham—and the emphasis was on rationality, free will, and deterrence (see Chapter 2 of this book). The process of developing theories and hypotheses, gathering data, and conducting empirical tests was not part of criminology; quite the opposite, ideas about crime were embedded in philosophers' abstractions about human nature and the capacity of the mind to reason. It was taken as a given in the United States and countries across Western Europe that human beings are inherently rational and self-interested and that because lawbreaking is a choice made on the basis of a cost-benefit calculus, crime can be deterred via penal sanctions.

But are humans truly and purely rational? Does reason always triumph over emotion, impulse, and desire? Those who subscribed to the Classical School in the 1800s believed the answer to these questions was "Yes"; however, their assertions were grounded not in science but in detached musings of the sort that conjure images of middle-class white men lounging in armchairs, swilling cognac, puffing cigars, and waxing philosophical about the nature of man. The presumptions of rationality, free will, and informed choice pose a significant problem for deterrence theory because it is not at all clear that offenders' minds operate in this fashion (Williams & Gibbs, 1981; see also Chapter 2). It is to this unfounded assumption of the Classical School that Lombroso's work spoke.

THE ROAD TO LOMBROSO

Around 1830, the French philosopher Auguste Comte spearheaded a new idea called *positivism*. The characteristic that distinguished this branch of philosophy from its predecessors was that positivism rejected abstract notions about the nature of man and the world in favor of concrete, empirically demonstrable phenomena. He criticized philosophers and psychologists for failing to offer testable premises or tangible demonstrations of the truth of their propositions. Appeals to "reason" and other amorphous, intangible concepts were pointless because they were merely the form of words, devoid of substance and true meaning (Comte, 1893). Comte advocated a full-scale overhaul of the procedures by which people acquire knowledge; specifically, he argued for the use of scientific inquiry to advance the state of humans' understanding about their world and about themselves. Comte's was an empirical approach. He contended that "no function can be studied but with relation to the organ that fulfills it" (p. 382), meaning that to understand human intellect, reason, and emotion, one must study the human body itself.

In the same general time period in which Comte's positivism was gaining ground, scientists from diverse backgrounds were seeking greater knowledge about the human physique and the relationship between physical characteristics, intelligence, and criminality. Students of phrenology attempted to link criminality and other human behavior to the shape of the skull. Later, physiognomists expanded the inquiry from the skull alone to the entire body (Tibbetts & Hemmens, 2010). These early investigators into the biology–crime link got a major boost in the mid-1800s when Charles Darwin (1859) published his theory of evolution based on the observations he made during his voyages around the world. Darwin detailed his theory that modern species descended from primitive ancestors and that their contemporary physical and mental form was the product of millions of years of genetic trial-and-error wherein organisms that were better adapted to their environment survived and procreated while those less suited to their surroundings died off. It was the confluence of positivism, theories about the relationship between biological traits and crime, and the theory of evolution that created the propelling force that would drive Cesare Lombroso's work.

LOMBROSO AND THE BODY OF THE CRIMINAL

Cesare Lombroso was born in Italy in 1835. From childhood, he had an insatiable appetite for knowledge. He read books of all types, attended lectures, and ultimately pursued a career in academic medicine. Deviant behavior was a topic of particular interest to him, and he wanted to know why some people obey the law and others do not. He shared the positivists' disillusionment with traditional philosophy and he espoused a belief in the need for scientific, not philosophical, inquiries to guide knowledge acquisition and policy development. Lombroso argued forcefully against the rational choice assumption of the deterrence-based framework under which the criminal law operated as a result of Beccaria and the Classical School (Chapter 2). He took issue with the presumption that all people have equal, innate capacities for reason and that all criminal behavior is the product of free will. He believed, instead, that behavior was *deterministic* (Glaser, 1969; Martin, Mutchnick, & Austin, 1990); that is, that certain biological traits embedded in people's anatomies determine how those people behave. He sought to demonstrate to the world that some people are disadvantaged by organic defects in intellectual ability and reasoning capacity and that decisions about guilt and punishment should, therefore, take into account the nature of the criminal himself. He found the dry, detached, utilitarian analysis of crime fundamentally at odds with the thought processes of criminals and, therefore, with the way the criminal law should behave. He believed the analysis should be of the criminal, not of the crime.

He found empirical support for his anti-utilitarian position in the fact that crime in Italy had been escalating for years and was becoming a very serious problem. He also noted extremely high recidivism rates—up to 80 percent—among offenders who had been caught and punished, and he argued that this was proof of the failure of deterrence theory (Lombroso, 1876/2006, p. 44). Punishment, he concluded, was misapplied via its narrow focus on legal definitions rather than on humans' personal traits and, therefore, it lacked any crime-reduction value. At the heart of Lombroso's quest, then, was the desire for a criminological approach capable of informing penal policy to deal effectively with offenders and to protect public safety.

Before discussing Lombroso's research, it should be acknowledged that his assumptions and conclusions were patently racist, classist, and sexist. He is criticized today for advancing theories pertaining to the inferiority of non-white racial groups, the poor, and women, but it must be kept in mind that he was a product of his time. Europe had been male-dominated and imperialistic for centuries. White male Europeans built ships and weapons and sailed around the world in search of precious gems, spices, and fertile land. When native populations were encountered, they were ignored, killed, or taken as slaves. Women, too, occupied a low status in society. They were generally prohibited from owning land or obtaining an education. They were forcibly relegated to the domestic sphere based on the assumption that their biological characteristics made them ill-suited for anything other than attending to the needs of their husbands and children. Had Europe and the United States been more progressive and enlightened during the 1800s, Lombroso could be justly condemned for his biases; however, since prejudice was ingrained in the mainstream culture, it understandably provided the social backdrop for his work (see Rafter & Gibson, 2004).

Lombroso took as his subject the physical body of the criminal. This was no simple task: Lombroso's major work, *L'uomo Delinquente* (*Criminal Man*), went through a total of five editions as he continually expanded and revised his theories. Fundamental to Lombroso's theories, analyses, and conclusions was the idea that criminals were anatomically different from "normal" individuals (i.e., those who do not commit crime). In keeping with the theory of evolution, Lombroso believed that the physical differences were manifestations of evolutionary disruptions. His theory of "atavism" embodied the notion that criminals were, in essence, evolutionary throwbacks: Successive generational transference over eons of time had failed to purge their blood of its primal ancestry. These physical differences were linked to mental abnormalities (Morrison, 1898); specifically, Lombroso believed that physical markers could be used to identify those whose mental faculties were deficient and who were, as a result, prone to criminality.

Lombroso's data collection methods were diverse, to say the least. He meticulously measured and recorded head sizes and body types of live persons; he gathered the skulls of dead criminals donated to him by prisons and museums; he visited prisons to observe criminals and speak with them; he kept written and pictorial records of the types of tattoos criminals had and the location of those tattoos upon their body; and he analyzed literature and artwork crafted by prisoners. He squirreled away scads of records, measurements, artifacts, drawings, poems, and photographs.[1] It was upon all this that Lombroso based his theories and conclusions about atavism and born criminality.

"Born criminal" is an inherently ambiguous term; it has never been defined clearly, and it has been used by multiple people to explain various types of offenders (Rafter, 1997). To Lombroso, the born criminal was the man or woman with the misfortune to enter the world bereft of a civilized mind capable of higher-order thought. Lombroso offered many artifacts of evidence. One exhibit consisted of the measurements and characteristics of 66 skulls of men known to have been criminals. He reported abnormally small cranial capacities among the majority of the skulls, as well as a high incidence of unusual protrusions, fissures, and other anomalies. Upon his examination of 832 live criminal subjects, Lombroso concluded that criminals' facial features were noticeably different from those of noncriminals. He stated that, "there is nearly always something strange about their [criminals'] appearance. It can even be said that each type of crime is committed by men with particular physiognomic characteristics" (Lombroso, 1876/2006, p. 51). He examined and categorized criminals' noses, eyes, ears, foreheads, and jaws. Was the nose atypically large or small, did the eyes have a strange sparkle or film, were the forehead and jaw heavy? He also paid attention to criminals' hair, noting texture, thickness, and length. He measured their height and compared it to that of the "normal" population. Lombroso exhaustively analyzed and classified the facial and bodily features that he believed were the marks of the born criminal—stigmata, so to speak. He concluded the following:

> Prognathism, thick and crisp hair, thin beards, dark skin, pointed skulls, oblique eyes, small craniums, overdeveloped jaws, receding foreheads, large ears, similarity between the sexes, muscular weakness—all these characteristics . . . demonstrate that European criminals bear a strong racial resemblance to Australian aborigines and Mongols. (p. 57)

He also analyzed the practice of tattooing and surmised that the practice "occurs only among the lower classes" (Lombroso, 1876/2006, p. 58) and was especially prevalent among criminals. Criminals, moreover, were likely to have tattoos depicting violence and to have tattoos on their genitals, the latter of which prompted Lombroso to infer that criminals harbored an unusual insensitivity to pain. He reasoned that tattoos must be a manifestation of latent atavistic tendencies. He pointed to the use of tattooing in tribal cultures and remarked, "It is only natural that a custom widespread among savages and prehistoric peoples would reappear among certain lower-class groups" (p. 62). Tattoos, according to him, could be used as a sort of "criminal record" marker to identify recidivistic criminals. At that time, of course, there were no electronic databases or centralized record-keeping facilities to track criminals and identify repeat offenders. Lombroso believed that the presence, number, type, and location of tattoos could be a clue to law enforcement officials that they were dealing with a born criminal.

Lombroso was the first criminologist to give attention to female offenders; in fact, he was the only one to study female offenders and offending until the torch was passed to the feminist criminologists in the 1970s (see also Rafter & Gibson, 2004). He believed criminality varied markedly between male and female offenders and, therefore, he kept the two lines of research distinct from one another. In *La Donna Delinquente, la Prostituta, e la Donna Normale* (*The Criminal Woman, the Prostitute, and the Normal Woman,* coauthored with Guglielmo Ferrero, 1893/2004; hereinafter referred to as *Criminal Woman*), Lombroso detailed his theory of female criminality.

Lombroso started with the premise that all women are atavistic to some extent and are thus born lacking the skills necessary to reason effectively. He summarized women's presumed lack of moral and intellectual sense succinctly: "Woman, therefore, feels less, just as she thinks less" (Lombroso & Ferrero, 1893/2004, p. 64). He concluded that women are childlike in that they are irrational, they cry often and sometimes at will as a means of getting what they want, and they are vengeful and cruel when angered. He believed them untrustworthy, too: "Women have something close to what might be called an instinct for lying" (p. 77). The only thing standing between ordinary women and criminality, according to Lombroso, was their piety, physical weakness, lack of interest in sex, and low intelligence. It was when these buffering conditions were absent and/or when women were born especially atavistic that the female became criminal. Lombroso searched for the physical stigmata on female offenders that signified the absence of the buffers. As the title of his book suggests, he divided women into normals, criminals, and prostitutes. He found more anomalies in the skulls of female criminals and prostitutes than in those of normal women, though the substantial variability in cranial circumferences and capacities among *all* women—criminal, prostitute, or normal—led him to temper his conclusion in this regard. He observed that female offenders had uncannily masculine appearances. (He also observed in *Criminal Man* a strange prominence of feminine features among some types of criminals.) Prostitutes and criminal women, he explained, each had distinct facial stigmata.

Lombroso was undoubtedly a misogynist by today's standards, but there is evidence that he was disconcerted by his own biases. He offered the somewhat backhanded compliment that "women's intensity of feeling and maternal sentiment more than makes up for women's deficiency of intellect" (Lombroso & Ferrero, 1893/2004, p. 37). Tellingly, he prefaced *Criminal Woman* with the admonition to readers that, "Not one line of this work justifies the great tyranny that continues to victimize women . . . that which impedes them from studying, and worse, from practicing a profession once they are educated. These [are] ridiculous and cruel constraints" (p. 37). Lombroso's conscience wrestled with itself over this issue, and the struggle was due primarily to the fact that he had daughters, Gina and Paola, and it is obviously more difficult to make hateful statements about a certain group when one's own children happen to be members of it. Through his daughters, too, Lombroso was exposed to and very impressed by the feminist movement that was growing as a result of the spreading of socialism (Rafter & Gibson, 2004). Lombroso seemed to want to let go of his prejudices, but he just could not quite bring himself to do it.

THE DISSEMINATION OF LOMBROSO'S THEORIES

Lombroso's influence was initially confined to Europe because scholars were slow to translate his writings into languages readable by a wider audience. His ideas spread quickly in Europe for two primary reasons: (1) The controversial nature of his theories made them attractive to other researchers in the field; and (2) the discourse he used to communicate these theories drew much attention. Regarding the first, it can be said simply that talk of Lombroso's research spread quickly because it was rather shocking. The Classical School still dominated legal thinking, so Lombroso's research stood in stark contrast to the conventional wisdom of the time. His theories bringing positivism together with physiognomy and Darwinian evolution, his shotgun approach to research, and the breadth and strength of his convictions about the nature of criminals were too tempting a target for supporters and critics alike to pass up. Lombroso posited new, intriguing ideas, and he provided scads of empirical "proof" of their validity—how could anyone resist the challenge? In addition, Lombroso was the chair of anthropology at the University of Turin (Gibson & Rafter, 2006), which made it easy for his ideas to be transferred to countless students during his lifetime and beyond. Lombroso's work, in short, bucked the status quo and became the subject of much attention.

The second primary reason for Lombroso's influence across Europe concerned not so much the substance of his ideas but, rather, the way he communicated them (see Walker & Boyeskie, 2001). *Discourse* refers to the way ideas are transformed into words and passed on to others. Discourse is as important as ideas themselves because all scientific theories depend on effective formation, delineation, and communication of central precepts (Walker & Boyeskie, 2001). Language is a medium for disseminating ideas, and certain communication techniques can either enhance or hinder the conveyance of ideas. Lombroso used flamboyant, vivid language. He crafted chilly images of bloodthirsty, cannibalistic murderers; "fallen" women; and cunning, sparkly eyed thieves. He used tables of numbers to classify his subjects and present information in a visually appealing manner. He also used many pictures, including illustrations of naked, tattoo-speckled bodies; creepily malformed faces; and, in *The Criminal Woman,* a page devoted to sketches of differently shaped vaginas. The reader really cannot help but stare. Lombroso's descriptions of atavistic individuals (the so-called "throwbacks") cause one's mind to drift to modern caricatures of cavemen: low foreheads; bulging brows; heavy jaws; and large, protruding ears. Lombroso's use of language, tables, and pictures made his ideas readily accessible to his fellow scientists and to the public, and it helped capture their attention more effectively than if he had confined his descriptions to more formal, clinical reports.

CRITICISMS OF LOMBROSO'S THEORIES

Not surprisingly, Lombroso's work was the subject of rancorous debate, and he amassed no shortage of critics bent on discrediting his theories. The criticisms centered primarily on two separate but related issues: The ambiguity in his definitions and classifications; and his nonscientific data collection and analysis (see, e.g., Martin et al., 1990). Lombroso delineated multiple types and subtypes when classifying his subjects. First, there was the designation of criminals as one of four types: born criminals, criminals by passion, insane criminals, and occasional criminals. The occasional criminal category was further divided into pseudocriminals, criminaloids, habitual criminals, and epileptics (Martin et al., 1990). Given the variety of classifications Lombroso proposed, it is not surprising that other scientists had some trouble keeping up. The definition issue was exacerbated by the fact that Lombroso's categories sometimes overlapped, that his typology changed over time as the multiple editions of *Criminal Man* were published, and that he failed to define how many stigmata offenders must have to be classified as "born criminals" versus other types of offenders, such as occasional criminals or epileptics. The imprecision with which offenders were typed and labeled remains, to this day, a serious problem (Glaser, 1969).

Ambiguous definitions, however, might have actually served Lombroso and others who studied the (supposed) relationship between physical traits and criminality quite well. The phrase "born criminal" so eludes precise definition that it can pretty much be interpreted to mean anything. Being vague is tantamount to being unfalsifiable because it is impossible to disprove a theory that is not clearly defined (Rafter, 1997). Strangely enough, even those who scoffed at Lombroso did not reject his basic thesis that lawbreakers are set apart from law abiders by a distinct set of physical traits. Charles Buckman Goring (1913), one of Lombroso's most vocal adversaries, espoused the belief that biology and crime were related even as he went about attempting to discredit Lombroso (see also Lilly, Cullen, & Ball, 2007). In the 1940s and 1950s—long after Lombroso's theory of atavism had been relegated to the trash bin—work by William H. Sheldon and by Sheldon and Eleanor Glueck continued to search for biological explanations for offending behavior to the neglect of sociological/environmental influences (Lilly et al., 2007). A century after Lombroso, crime theorists Wilson and Herrnstein (1985) claimed that "there is no such thing as a 'born criminal'" (p. 69), yet went on to consider what sorts of biological, genetic, and general constitutional factors might set offenders apart from non-offenders. Lombroso's work inspired others to keep looking for biological etiologies even after Lombroso himself fell out of favor. The perpetuation of the "born criminal" idea is due in part to the absence of a single, consistent definition and the resultant malleability of the concept.

The second major problem with Lombroso's work was the absence of systematic procedures for gathering and analyzing data. The plethora of evidence he gathered from a multitude of sources and the way he sifted through it and culled from it the bits and pieces that he thought were relevant rendered his studies unreplicable. One hallmark of scientific methodology is that anyone wishing to confirm the results of a given study should be able to reproduce the original analytic method. This was not the case with Lombroso—the steps he took on his subjective, atheoretical, exploratory path through data analysis were impossible to retrace.

Lombroso also failed to use control groups in most of his research. Goring (1913) made much of this shortfall. Lombroso did attempt some rough use of control groups, such as comparing criminals to deviant soldiers, and both groups to non-deviant soldiers. He also used non-deviant women as the controls in *The Criminal Woman.* Overall, however, control groups were either missing altogether or were rough accounts of aggregate demographic data pulled from various sources. Because of this, the comparisons Lombroso made between criminals and "normals" were severely suspect because it is impossible to claim that something is "abnormal" when one has no conception of what "normal" looks like.

To be fair to Lombroso, he was born before the advent of sophisticated statistical theories and methods that today facilitate data analysis and replication. Lombroso's analytic methods were not radically different from other scientists of his time and, indeed, criminologists even today face serious imperfections in the measurement and analysis of theoretical constructs. In addition, the field of criminology was in its infancy during the late 1800s; Lombroso, being the first criminologist in the positivist tradition, obviously had no prior scientific models upon which to premise his own studies. To use a Lombrosian metaphor, the fledgling field of criminology was still in the process of emerging from its own primordial ooze to evolve into what it is today. Lombroso's scientific methods were modern during his lifetime despite seeming quite primitive by contemporary standards. The field at that time was staffed by academics who hailed from several different disciplines and employed a variety of research techniques (Rafter, 1997). Even Goring's methodology had problems, and some of his conclusions were either ambiguous or actually supported some of Lombroso's propositions (Piers, 1988). Many of the criticisms of Lombroso's methods, then, are a bit harsh, as he obviously cannot be faulted for using techniques that were accepted at the time, or for failing to utilize statistical concepts that did not exist yet (Wolfgang, 1960).

Lombroso's theory of atavism and his typologies of born criminals and other offender types were doomed from the start because, to put it plainly, they were wrong. In many ways, Lombroso did science backward: He started with a conviction (i.e., atavism) and he interpreted his data in the way that best supported his preconceived notions. At times, his writing in both *Criminal Man* and *Criminal Woman* betrayed his confusion and frustration over the fact that the data he analyzed and the logical premises he constructed from his observations actually contradicted the theory of atavism (Rafter & Gibson, 2004). Given that Lombroso himself saw—but would not admit to—serious flaws in his theory, it comes as no surprise that his ideas have been thoroughly discredited, with the potential exceptions of a very limited number of his minor observations (Morris, 1951; see also Adams, 2009; Nachshon & Denno, 1987).

LOMBROSO'S INFLUENCE

It is difficult, in some respects, to pinpoint the exact influence that Lombroso's ideas had on criminology, criminal justice, and public policy because Lombroso has been and continues to be one of the most misunderstood figures in the history of criminology. This is primarily the fault of language barriers and translation impediments: *The Criminal Woman* and the five editions of *Criminal Man* were translated into English and other non-Italian languages slowly and in a piecemeal fashion that gave readers only snippets of his ideas (Rafter & Gibson, 2004). As Rafter and Gibson put it, "Misunderstandings of Lombroso's work are so widespread as to constitute a distinct mythology" (p. 5). Much of the early praise and criticism alike were unwarranted because nobody actually knew what portion of his work they were reading or how accurate the translation was. This problem is illustrated most poignantly by the astounding fact that the first full (i.e., all five editions in one volume) English translation of *Criminal Man* did not appear until 2006 (Gibson & Rafter, 2006), more than 100 years after Lombroso wrote them. Lombroso's legacy, then, has unfortunately been rife with misunderstandings and misinterpretations of his work.

Europe

Havelock Ellis (1890/1972), a post-Lombroso biocrime investigator, remarked of Lombroso's criminological progeny that "A continuous stream of studies . . . is constantly pouring forth. It is still impossible to gather up this mass of investigation, often necessarily discordant, into a tentative whole, but its existence is sufficient to prove the vitality of the new science" (p. 40). Lombroso's work fed what came to be called the Italian School of criminology (or the Positivist School), though it was by no means confined to Italy. French and British anthropologists, criminologists, and legal scholars took up attempts to confirm, elaborate upon, or falsify his work. Scientists long after his death continued his work on the anatomy of the criminal and on identifying the traits that separate born criminals from "normal" persons and from persons with noncriminal mental abnormalities. His studies of female offenders also led some researchers to further examine the relationship between anatomy and crime in terms of chromosomal differences between the sexes and the types of abnormal chromosomes that might be associated with crime (Frossman & Hambert, 1967).

Raffaele Garofalo and Enrico Ferri are among the most famous of the post-Lombrosian Italian criminologists (Lilly et al., 2007). First his students, later his colleagues, and eventually his successors, Garofalo and Ferri each adapted Lombroso's anthropological work to his own pursuits in law and sociology, respectively. In 1922, Ferri was commissioned by the Italian government to write a proposal for an overhaul of the criminal justice system. He submitted a design premised upon positivist criminology, but it was rejected by the government for being too radically different from the classical Beccarian system in place at the time (Lilly et al., 2007; Martin et al., 1990).

The United States

Lombroso's influence in the United States is less obvious, and decidedly more moderate, than that in Europe. Again, this was largely due to delays in translating the work into English, which impeded U.S. citizens' access to it. Fragments of *Criminal Man* were translated early and made their way across the Atlantic, but the translations were incomplete and of dubious quality (Rafter & Gibson, 2004). The first English edition was prepared by Lombroso's daughter Gina Lombroso-Ferrero in 1911 and was assumed by Americans to be a direct translation of Lombroso's work, but it was actually a distorted, oversimplified interpretation that Lombroso-Ferrero herself had created (Gibson & Rafter, 2006). As a result, readers in the United States missed the proverbial boat. Lacking the foundational texts, scholars and the public alike were denied the requisite level of understanding of Lombrosian criminology and, as a result, his theories failed to gain a foothold.

By the time translated chunks of Lombroso's work became common in the United States, his popularity in Europe was waning because his ideas had been disproved (Rafter, 1997); however, Americans paid little heed to the European experience. Lombroso's influence in the United States came less from Lombroso's work *per se,* but rather from the work of others who were inspired by his ideas. Notable among these criminologists were Earnest Albert Hooton, Henry H. Goddard, William H. Sheldon, and Sheldon and Eleanor Glueck (Lilly et al., 2007; Rafter, 2004). Sheldon, for instance, became known for his studies with delinquent youth and his classification of criminals as mesomorphs, endomorphs, and ectomorphs, based upon their different body shapes. Sheldon's work was denigrated for shoddy methodology, murky operationalizations of key variables, and questionable conclusions (Sutherland, 1951), charges reminiscent of those that had been leveled against Lombroso himself.

Those who were influenced by Lombroso applied his work to various areas of study. Lombroso's influence can be seen primarily in four areas: positivism, eugenics, feminist criminology, and the recently renewed interest in biological studies of crime. As aforementioned, Lombroso pioneered the Positivist School of criminology. Much like the way the Classical School of criminology outlasted its figurehead, Cesare Beccaria, the Positivist School continued unabated well after the sun had set on its leader, Cesare Lombroso. In the late 1800s and through the first decades of the 1900s, white, middle-class reformers in the United States sought to improve conditions for the working poor and to find ways to rehabilitate criminal offenders. Biological determinism à la Lombroso gave way to a version of positivism—called the Progressive movement—wherein offenders were viewed not as hopelessly primitive but as "sick" and in need of treatment (Lilly et al., 2007). The Progressives were the champions of the rehabilitation ideal (see Chapter 6 of this book) and the ones responsible for the decades of the 1900s during which rehabilitation was the dominant philosophy of the criminal justice system. Lombroso himself played little part in the ultimate form that positivist criminology took, though.

The eugenics movement was the most insidious and terrifying of the post-Lombroso efforts to incorporate the alleged biology–crime link into public policy. This movement was strong in the United States and Europe during the 1930s and 1940s (Lilly et al., 2007; Rafter, 2004) and played no small part in the Nazi plan to eliminate "undesirable" populations. Darwin's theory of evolution and the reports issued by the Austrian monk Gregor Johann Mendel in his study of genetic inheritance among pea plants sparked several chains of scientific inquiry into the hereditability of various physical and mental traits in humans. If certain traits were passed genetically from parents to their children, then "bad" traits—so the proponents of eugenics believed—could be "bred out" of the population. Since Lombroso had argued and offered evidence seeming to prove that criminality sprung from a constitutional abnormality, the American biocriminologists of the era wondered if perhaps crime could be reduced through the systematic prevention of reproduction among born criminals. The eugenics movement and criminology thus dovetailed. Social Darwinism was born, and its advocates sought ways to use public policy to ensure the survival of the fittest (Lilly et al., 2007).

Lombroso never advocated eugenics or selective breeding. He did acknowledge the potential for some forms of criminality to be passed on genetically; however, he made no assertions that criminal parents would have criminal offspring, and he did not insinuate that society should attempt to control the procreation of born criminals. His solutions for dealing with criminals—such as incarceration or, in extreme cases, execution—were intended to protect society and prevent reoffending by *those* individuals, not to reduce crime in future generations (Rafter, 1997; see also Rafter, 1992). Some of Lombroso's U.S. followers, though, took the biocrime concept a step further.

Ernest Hooton was perhaps the most vocal criminological proponent of eugenics. Hooton, a criminal anthropologist at Harvard, made a career of splashing academia and the public with pro-eugenics propaganda. He advocated sterilization of criminals and all other persons suffering from mental and physical diseases that were (supposedly) heritable, and he opposed governmental welfare programs that kept alive a segment of the population that he thought the nation would be better off allowing to die out. While academics such as Robert Merton and Edwin Sutherland considered Hooton's work garbage, much of the popular press and even some scientific reviews applauded his pro-eugenics arguments (Rafter, 2004; see also Lilly et al., 2007). Eugenics-based policies are also apparent in the histories of the early penitentiaries and asylums. Evidence suggests that these early institutions were meant not only to isolate from society those who might harm themselves or others, but also to prevent these individuals from having children (Rafter, 1997). Lombroso's work was undeniably—although perversely—absorbed into the American eugenics movement.

The third area of influence that Lombroso had in America was in the advent of the study of female criminals. As mentioned in the previous sections, Lombroso published a study of female criminals, prostitutes, and "normals." He made many assertions about the nature of women, in general, and that of female deviants, in particular. Lombroso was one of the few early criminologists to devote more than passing mention to the study of female delinquents and to treat them as subjects worthy of independent study (Adler & Simon, 1979; Flowers, 1995). His ideas, however, understandably upset American criminologists—and non-criminologists, undoubtedly—due to their reliance on stereotypes about women as weak and unintelligent. Much like Lombroso's work in general, his research on women found its way into the criminological study of female criminals because it was provocative and controversial and because, in the case of women, it stood out as one of the only texts that had been devoted to the subject at the time. In the 1970s, when feminism took off in the United States, Lombroso's work became a rallying cry for women's rights advocates. It was a symbol of men's subjugation of women and a tangible manifestation of the wretched biases lurking in the patriarchal arrangement (see Rafter & Gibson, 2004). As hated as it was, then, it served feminists well as a point of unification for the movement.

Lombroso's direct influence and his brand of positivist criminology began waning in the 1920s and all but disappeared after World War II. The demise can be attributed to two things: the rise of the sociological study of crime and the fall of eugenics. In the 1920s, the Chicago School sociologists (see Chapter 4 of this book) assumed control over the discipline of criminology, bringing the study of crime from the micro level (i.e., the individual) to the macro level (i.e., communities and society). The anthropologists, with their focus on individual-level causes of crime, were forced to cede control to the sociologists, who sought social and economic etiologies (see Laub, 2003; Rafter, 2004). All individual-based studies—including but not limited to Lombroso's—fell out of favor. The second reason Lombroso's research agenda died was that Lombroso's name had been attached (though arguably unfairly) to the eugenics movement, and eugenics became a dirty word after World War II when the Allies found the concentration camps and the world learned that the Nazi regime had attempted a large-scale extermination of Jews, homosexuals, criminals, and others. Eugenics became taboo after the war, which meant the end of many of the lines of research stemming from Lombroso's original studies. It is worth noting, though, that attempts to prevent criminals from procreating by sterilization and institutionalization continued into the 1970s (Lilly et al., 2007).

Lombrosian-like ideas are still around. The final line of influence that Lombroso had on American criminology can be seen in the recent resurgence of the study of biological explanations for criminality (see Chapter 12 of this book). Clearly, Lombroso's theory was one of biology; however, he focused on the outward characteristics of offenders. Today, with the development of sophisticated equipment for studying humans at the molecular—rather than phenotypic—level, biocrime researchers have advanced well beyond Lombroso's rather crude biological reductionism. Modern biocrime researchers are in no way criminological "descendents" of Lombroso; quite to the contrary, today's biocriminologist has a hefty burden to overcome the assumption that modern biocrime research is naught but a resurrection of the long-discredited theory of atavism and biological determinism. Lombroso's infamy tainted the field of biocrime research (Farrington, 1987). Nonetheless, modern researchers do owe Lombroso a debt as the pioneer of biological criminology, even though he obviously did not have the last word on the subject.

CONCLUSION

Lombroso's greatest contribution to criminology was not the substance of his ideas—we have seen that it was actually quite poor—but, rather, the very fact that he had these ideas at all. That he entertained these hypotheses and engaged in a heated enterprise to demonstrate to the world what he thought he knew about the origins of criminality marked a fundamental shift in European (and, eventually, American) thought about crime and punishment. Lombroso's rapid accumulation of a mountain of motley factoids and the stream of conclusions he produced sparked and fueled a heated controversy that would last beyond Lombroso's death and would feed a new brand of criminology and penology in Europe and the United States. Lombroso earned both supporters and critics—the former sought to continue Lombroso's line of work and further the scientific study of born criminality, while the latter disseminated scathing castigations of Lombroso's methods and conclusions. The skeptics ultimately won the debate, but that is beside the point, for Lombroso's legacy lives not in how the debate ended but in the fact that it ever began.

DISCUSSION QUESTIONS

1. What was Lombroso's primary criticism of the Classical School of criminology?
2. What role did discourse play in the dissemination of Lombroso's ideas?
3. Describe Lombroso's influences on criminology and society in the United States and in Europe. How much of this influence was due to Lombroso himself, and how much was due to those who either misinterpreted or reinterpreted his ideas?
4. Is modern biocriminology a new version of Lombrosian criminology? Explain your answer.

REFERENCES

Adams, J. (2009). Marked difference: Tattooing and its association with deviance in the United States. *Deviant Behavior, 30,* 266–292.

Adler, F., & Simon, R. J. (1979). Introduction. In F. Adler & R. J. Simons (Eds.), *The criminology of deviant women* (pp. 2–5). Boston: Houghton Mifflin.

Comte, A. (1893). *Positive philosophy* (Vol. 1; H. Martineau, Trans.). London: Kegan Paul.

Darwin, C. (1859). *The origin of species.* New York: Bantam Books.

Ellis, H. (1972). *The criminal.* New York: AMS Press. (Original work published 1890)

Farrington, D. P. (1987). Implications of biological findings for criminological research. In S. A. Mednick, T. E. Moffitt, & S. A. Stack (Eds.), *The causes of crime: New biological approaches* (pp. 42–64). Cambridge, UK: Cambridge University Press.

Flowers, R. B. (1995). *Female crime, criminals and cellmates.* Jefferson, NC: McFarland.

Frossman, H., & Hambert, G. (1967). Chromosomes and antisocial behavior. *Excerpta Criminologica, 7*(2), 113–117.

Gibson, M., & Rafter, N. H. (2006). Introduction. In C. Lombroso, *Criminal man* (M. Gibson & N. H. Rafter, Trans.). Durham, NC: Duke University Press.

Glaser, D. (1969). Criminality theories and behavioral images. In D. R. Cressey & D. A. Ward (Eds.), *Delinquency, crime, and social process* (pp. 515–530). New York: Harper & Row.

Goring, C. B. (1913). *The English convict: A statistical study.* Montclair, NJ: Patterson Smith.

Laub, J. H. (2003). The life course of criminology in the United States: The American Society of Criminology 2003 Presidential Address. *Criminology, 42*(1), 1–26.

Lilly, J. R., Cullen, F. T., & Ball, R. A. (2007). *Criminological theory: Context and consequences* (4th ed.). Thousand Oaks, CA: Sage.

Lombroso, C. (2006). *Criminal man* (M. Gibson & N. H. Rafter, Trans.). Durham, NC: Duke University Press. (Original work published 1876)

Lombroso, C., & Ferrero, G. (2004). *The criminal woman, the prostitute, and the normal woman* (M. Gibson & N. H. Rafter, Trans.). Durham, NC: Duke University Press. (Original work published 1893)

Martin, R., Mutchnick, R. J., & Austin, W. T. (1990). *Criminological thought: Pioneers past and present.* New York: Macmillan.

Morris, N. (1951). *The habitual criminal.* Westport, CT: Greenwood Press.

Morrison, W. D. (1898). Introduction. In C. Lombroso & W. Ferrero, *The female offender.* New York: D. Appleton.

Nachshon, I., & Denno, D. (1987). Violent behavior and cerebral hemisphere function. In S. A. Mednick, T. E. Moffitt, & S. A. Stack (Eds.), *The causes of crime: New biological approaches* (pp. 185–217). Cambridge, UK: Cambridge University Press.

Piers, B. (1988). Heredity versus environment: A reconsideration of Charles Goring's *The English Convict. British Journal of Criminology, 28*(3), 315–339.

Rafter, N. H. (1992). Criminal anthropology in the United States. *Criminology, 30*(4), 525–545.

Rafter, N. H. (1997). *Creating born criminals.* Urbana: University of Illinois Press.
Rafter, N. H. (2004). Earnest A. Hooton and the biological tradition in American criminology. *Criminology, 42*(3), 735–771.
Rafter, N. H., & Gibson, M. (2004). Introduction. In C. Lombroso & G. Ferrero, *The criminal woman, the prostitute, and the normal woman* (N. H. Rafter & M. Gibson, Trans.). Durham, NC: Duke University Press.
Sutherland, E. (1951). Critique of Sheldon's *Varieties of Delinquent Youth. American Sociological Review, 16*(1), 10–13.
Tibbetts, S. G., & Hemmens, C. (2010). *Criminological theory: A text/reader.* Thousand Oaks, CA: Sage.
Walker, J. T., & Boyeskie, J. A. (2001). The discourse of criminality: From Beccaria to postmodernism. *Critical Criminology, 10,* 107–122.
Williams, K. R., & Gibbs, J. P. (1981). Deterrence and knowledge of statutory penalties. *Sociological Quarterly, 22,* 591–606.
Wilson, J. Q., & Herrnstein, R. J. (1985). *Crime and human nature.* New York: The Free Press.
Wolfgang, M. E. (1960). Cesare Lombroso. In E. Glover, H. Mannheim, & E. Miller (Eds.), *Pioneers in criminology* (pp. 168–227). Chicago: Quadrangle Books.

NOTE

1. It would, ultimately, take an entire museum to house Lombroso's collection.

FOUR

KEY IDEA: UNDERSTANDING CRIME AND SOCIETY

KEY WORKS

Merton, R. K. (1938). Social structure and anomie. *American Sociological Review, 3*, 672–682.

Shaw, C. R., & McKay, H. D. (1942). *Juvenile delinquency and urban areas.* Chicago: University of Chicago Press.

Popular culture is replete with examples of how the circumstances people find themselves in—often through no fault of their own—can exert a strong influence on their behavioral choices. For instance, with regard to inner-city environments, hip-hop music by artists ranging from Kanye West to DMX to Easy-E has long been a repository for the kind of storytelling relevant to the plight of the urban underclass (Kitwana, 2003). Even television shows like HBO's *The Wire* are making their way into social science classrooms at places as prestigious as Harvard University. And artists such as Bruce Springsteen have built careers on singing about how social forces larger than individuals can breed the kind of anger and frustration that may set the stage for criminal behavior. Springsteen's message comes through most clearly when he sings "some folks are born into a good life; other folks get it any way, any how" from "Darkness on the Edge of Town"; or "you're born into this life paying for the sins of somebody else's past" from "Adam Raised a Cain"; or when he sings of the crimes committed by an out-of-work auto worker, saying, "it was more than all this, Judge, that put that gun in my hand" in his song "Johnny 99."

Of course, Springsteen wasn't the first to recognize these problems and to put them down on paper. To be sure, his message is rooted and reflected in the work of social scientists that came along a half-century before him. In particular, these sentiments reflect the work of early 20th-century criminologists like Robert Merton, Clifford Shaw, and Henry McKay. Together, the works of these theorists demonstrate how individuals' behavior is shaped by their surroundings in general, and how social conditions influence criminal behavior in particular. While Shaw and McKay's social disorganization theory and Merton's anomie/strain theory posit different—and at times, seemingly contradictory—propositions concerning what causes crime, they are wedded to the common notion that criminal behavior cannot be understood as merely an individual phenomenon. Put differently, understanding crime requires an understanding of society.

THE SOCIAL CONTEXT OF THE EARLY TWENTIETH CENTURY

Early perspectives on criminological theory and research were guided by the assumption that the explanation for crime can be found within the individual. These theories differed, however, in terms of their propositions regarding what it is about individuals that *should* cause crime. For example, some criminological theorists maintained that crime could be a function of biological determinism (Dugdale, 1877), of substandard intelligence or "feeble-mindedness" (Goddard, 1914), or of dissocial manifestations of psychic forces (Aichorn, 1925/1979). Others were even so bold as to assert that individuals' criminal propensity can be indicated by the existence of "criminal bumps" on their heads (Lombroso-Ferrero, 1911; see also Gould, 1996). Regardless of their differences, all of these early perspectives shared the underlying premise that individual variations, not social conditions, were responsible for criminal behavior (see the discussion in Pratt, Maahs, & Stehr, 1998).

Social and economic changes beginning in the early 1900s, which were largely fueled by mass industrialization, resulted in new social problems and new ways of thinking about the sources of criminal behavior (Palen, 1981). Rapid increases in urbanization, residential mobility, and the rise of racially and ethnically heterogeneous neighborhoods in American cities seemed to occur in concert with increases in crime rates. In particular, crime became visibly concentrated among the urban poor (Rothman, 1980). The recognition of these problems found its way into popular culture in many ways; most notable among them was Upton Sinclair's book *The Jungle,* which focused on the problems immigrant workers faced in finding work and merely "getting by" in early 20th-century Chicago. These problems were also reflected among the rural poor at around the same time that John Steinbeck's *The Grapes of Wrath* detailed the plight of the economically deprived Midwest dustbowl farmers migrating to California.

In the midst of the Progressive movement, however, a liberal reform movement that occurred in early 20th-century America, criminologists began to reject the notion that the poor were somehow biologically inferior and that they therefore deserved their meager lot in life as the natural outcome of their collective pathology (Cullen & Gilbert, 1982; Rothman, 1980). Instead, the Progressives "preferred a more optimistic interpretation: The poor were pushed by their environment, not born, into a life of crime" (Lilly, Cullen, & Ball, 2002, p. 39). As a consequence, a number of new formulations of criminological thought began to emerge that sought to shift the assumed "causes" of crime away from individuals themselves and instead toward society as a whole (Matza, 1969). Among these new traditions were social disorganization theory as articulated by Chicago School of criminology researchers Shaw and McKay (1942), and Robert Merton's (1938) anomie/strain theory.

SOCIAL DISORGANIZATION AND ANOMIE/STRAIN THEORIES

Social Disorganization Theory

The social disorganization tradition grew out of the research conducted in the early 1900s in Chicago by Shaw and McKay (see their 1942 work). Upon studying Chicago's juvenile court records over a period of several decades, Shaw and McKay noted that rates of crime were not evenly dispersed across time and space in the city. Rather, crime tended to be concentrated in particular areas—namely, slum neighborhoods. Further, crime rates were highest in these neighborhoods regardless of which racial or ethnic group happened to reside there at any particular time. Moreover, as the previously crime-prone groups moved to other lower-crime areas of the city, their rate of criminal activity decreased accordingly (Lilly et al., 2002). These observations led Shaw and McKay to the conclusion that crime was likely a function of neighborhood dynamics and not necessarily a function of the individuals within such neighborhoods (see also the discussions by Lowenkamp, Cullen, & Pratt, 2003; Sampson & Groves, 1989). The question that remained was, what are the characteristics of the "slum neighborhoods" that set them apart from low-crime neighborhoods, and therefore seemed to foster criminal activity?

In answering this question, Shaw and McKay focused on the urban areas experiencing rapid changes in their social and economic structure—that is, in the "zone in transition."[1] In particular, they looked to neighborhoods that were low in socioeconomic status, with high rates of residential mobility, and had higher degrees of racial heterogeneity. These neighborhoods were viewed as "socially disorganized," meaning that conventional institutions of social control (e.g., schools, churches, voluntary community organizations) were weak and unable to regulate the behavior of the neighborhood's youth (Bursik, 1988; Bursik and Grasmick, 1993). Shaw and McKay also noted that, aside from the lack of behavioral regulation, socially disorganized neighborhoods tended to produce "criminal traditions" that could be passed across successive generations of youths. This system of pro-delinquency attitudes could be easily learned by youths through their daily contact with older juveniles (see also Kornhauser, 1978). Thus, a neighborhood characterized by social disorganization would provide fertile soil for crime and delinquency in two ways: through a lack of behavioral control mechanisms, and through the cultural transmission of delinquent values from one generation to the next.[2]

It is important to note that Shaw and McKay did not specify a *direct* relationship between social disorganization and crime (see the discussion by Bursik, 1988). Rather, the socially disorganized neighborhoods observed by Shaw and McKay could indirectly influence neighborhood rates of crime in two ways. First, areas characterized by social disorganization tended to experience high levels of population turnover, which meant that they were abandoned by most people as soon as it was economically possible to do so (see also W. J. Wilson, 1987). In addition, such neighborhoods often experienced rapid changes in racial composition (i.e., racial heterogeneity) that made it difficult to resist the influx of new racial or ethnic groups. Taken together, these characteristics hindered the ability of socially disorganized neighborhoods to effectively engage in "self-regulation" (Bursik, 1986; see also Bursik & Grasmick, 1993; Sampson, Raudenbush, & Earls, 1997). In short, as Bursik (1988) stated, "the dynamics of social disorganization lead to variations across neighborhoods in the strength of the commitment of the residents to groups standards" and, as a result, to variations in community crime rates (p. 521).

Merton's Anomie/Strain Theory

Robert Merton published his "Social Structure and Anomie" in 1938. In this brief article, Merton set forth a theoretical framework for explaining crime rates that differed in important ways from that of the Chicago School criminologists. For example, theorists such as Shaw and McKay held that urban slum areas foster criminal behavior through the generational transmission of deviant cultural values. Thus, social disorganization theory assumes that the *rejection* of conventional middle-class values results in high rates of crime in urban slum communities. Merton, on the other hand, argued that it was the rigid *adherence* to conventional American values that caused high rates of crime and deviance. In essence, he believed that the widespread conformity to American culture in general—and the American obsession with economic success in particular—produced high levels of serious crime.[3] Of course, understanding why Merton made such a claim requires an understanding of how he viewed American society.

Merton noted that, in contrast to other Western industrialized nations, the United States places an unusual emphasis on economic success. Even more unique is how this emphasis seems to be universal, that all members of American society, from the well-to-do to the impoverished, ascribe to the "American dream"—the idea that if one were simply willing to work hard enough, he or she would inevitably reap the economic rewards of such labors. The problem, according to Merton, is that despite the widespread belief in the possibility of upward social mobility, the American social structure limits individuals' access to the goal of economic success through legitimate means. For example, while the probability of attaining economic success would be enhanced by getting a college education or by taking advantage of some strategic nepotism, not all members of American society are able to do so. Those lower on the socioeconomic ladder are particularly vulnerable due to their relatively disadvantaged starting point in the race toward affluence.

In essence, Merton's work contained separate (but related) discussions of how "culture" and "social structure" could cause high crime rates (Messner, 1988). Merton noted that the American culture, as stated above, places economic success at the pinnacle of social desirability. The emphasis on attaining economic success, however, is not matched by a concurrent normative emphasis on what "means" are legitimate for reaching the desired "goal." This problem is then exacerbated by the social structural component discussed by Merton, which highlights the structural barriers that limit individuals' access to the legitimate means for attaining the goal of economic success. The disjunction between a strong cultural emphasis on a particular ascribed goal (i.e., economic success) and the comparatively weak cultural emphasis on employing legitimate means to attain such goals (i.e., social structural limits) in turn puts pressure on the norms that guide what means should be used to achieve the culturally prescribed goal.[4]

Merton (1938) referred to this weakening of cultural norms as *anomie.* His adoption of the term is based on Durkheim's (1897/1951) reference to the weakening of the normative order in society, or, put differently, how institutionalized social norms may lose their ability to regulate individuals' behavior. In particular, Merton noted that institutionalized norms will weaken, and anomie will set in, in societies that place an intense value on economic success. When this occurs, the pursuit of success is no longer guided by normative standards of right and wrong. Rather, Merton (1968) asserted, "the sole significant question becomes: Which of the available procedures is most efficient in netting the culturally approved value?" (p. 189).

Thus, the exceptionally high crime rates experienced by the United States are seen through the lens of anomie theory as being a natural consequence of American culture (see also Currie, 1997). By dangling the carrot of a universally shared goal in the faces of many who cannot reach that goal through legitimate means, the anomic quality of American society "produces intense pressure for deviation" (Merton, 1968, p. 199). Indeed, the theme of the limits associated with "working hard" and "playing fair" can be seen quite clearly in a passage from John Steinbeck's (1947) *The Wayward Bus,* where a character, in describing his father, states that,

> My old man had two faiths. One was that honesty got rewarded some way or other. He thought that if a man was honest he somehow got along, and he thought if a man worked hard and saved he could pile up a little money and feel safe. Teapot Dome and a lot of stuff like that fixed him on the first, and nineteen-thirty fixed him on the other.[5] He found out that the most admired people weren't honest at all. And he died wondering, a kind of an awful wondering, because the two things he believed in didn't work out—honesty and thrift. It kind of struck me that nobody has put anything in place of those two. (p. 277)

REJECTING INDIVIDUALISM

While it is true that social disorganization and anomie/strain theories differed in the way they conceived the effects of middle-class values on criminal behavior, they agreed on one fundamental thing: that understanding crime requires a shift in focus away from individual pathology. Indeed, both of these perspectives raised a clear challenge to social scientists and policy makers alike to stop looking for the sources of crime inside of individuals and instead to start looking at the social contexts in which individuals find themselves.

For example, with regard to social disorganization theory, Shaw and McKay (1942) were clear in their argument that understanding juvenile delinquency required an equal understanding of the social contexts in which those very youth lived (see also Bursik, 1988). They even gathered detailed data from Chicago neighborhoods to bring to bear on this notion. Their work showed that regardless of race or ethnicity, any given group's rates of delinquent behavior went up when its members went to reside in socially disorganized communities, yet the rates went down once they had moved out of the socially disorganized environment.

Merton's work was also clear in its macro-level focus. Indeed, while his theory is often misunderstood to be an explanation for why individuals engage in crime and deviance, and many a criminologist has misinterpreted the theory in that way (see the excellent discussion by Baumer & Gustafson, 2007; see also Cullen, 1984), he was much more concerned with the unique conditions of the broader American society that could be criminogenic. Specifically, Merton (1968) noted that the "cardinal American virtue, 'ambition,'" is what ultimately "promotes the cardinal American vice, 'deviant behavior'" (p. 200).

Of course, prior to the work of Shaw and McKay and Merton, the major players in the business of criminology shared the assumption that "little insight on crime's origins could be gained by studying the social environment or context external to individuals" (Lilly et al., 2002, p. 31). To be sure, these early perspectives collectively pinned the cause of crime—in one form or another—on individual offenders themselves. It is also important to note that these perspectives never fully "went away"; indeed, they lingered, and they still enjoy a certain level of influence over a nontrivial portion of contemporary criminological thought (see, e.g., Herrnstein & Murray, 1994; J. Q. Wilson & Herrnstein, 1985). Yet it was the ideas of Shaw and McKay and Robert Merton that, according to Matza (1969), did the most to "relocate pathology . . . from the personal to the social plane" (p. 47).

THE LEGACY OF ANOMIE/STRAIN AND SOCIAL DISORGANIZATION THEORIES

While both social disorganization and anomie/strain theories were popular during the time in which they were written—sparking a rush of theoretical and empirical work that also focused on how structural characteristics influence the behavioral choices available to individuals (Cloward & Ohlin, 1960; Cohen, 1955)—both perspectives have endured decades after their publication as well. For example, after falling out of favor with criminologists for a time, social disorganization theory was "rediscovered" in the 1980s. Research by scholars such as Bursik (1986, 1988), Sampson and Groves (1989), and Wilson (W. J. 1987, 1996) helped to revitalize, and partially reformulate and extend, the social disorganization tradition. In doing so, a number of charges leveled against the theory have been addressed effectively (see Bursik, 1988). For example, research has been conducted to test for the "reciprocal effects"[6] of social disorganization (Bursik, 1986), and to test for the potential impact the levels of social disorganization of "surrounding communities" may have on neighboring communities (Heitgerd & Bursik, 1987).[7]

In addition, the scope of the theory was adjusted and expanded to include constructs beyond the macro-level components originally specified by Shaw and McKay (1942) (e.g., low socioeconomic status, residential mobility, racial heterogeneity). New concepts have been added that have enhanced its theoretical clarity. In particular, as stated above, recent research has explicitly tested for "intervening mechanisms" between the traditional social disorganization variables and crime rates. The intervening mechanisms noted by researchers include the effect of social disorganization on rates of family disruption and "collective efficacy" (see Sampson and Groves, 1989; Sampson et al., 1997), which, in turn, directly influence crime rates.

More recently, scholars have begun integrating concepts drawn from social disorganization theory into other individual-level theories of criminal behavior. Most notably, criminologists have linked social disorganization variables to the kinds of family processes that are related to the development of self-control in children (Pratt, Turner, & Piquero, 2004). This link is critical given the consistent empirical support for the relationship between self-control and criminal behavior (Pratt & Cullen, 2000). In particular, this research indicates that elements of parental efficacy (e.g., monitoring and supervision of children) are determined to a large extent by neighborhood context (i.e., effective parenting is made more difficult in socially disorganized communities). Such parenting problems, in turn, result in lower levels of self-control in children—an effect that also explains the apparent "race gap" in offending (see Pratt et al., 2004). In short, not only does social disorganization theory offer an explanation for community variations in crime rates, but it also provides the context for certain well-supported individual theories of criminal behavior.

As for anomie/strain theory, it remained influential throughout the 1950s and 1960s. Guided by Merton's emphasis on social stratification, the theory was even extended to notions of "status discontent" and delinquency (see, e.g., Cohen, 1955; Cloward & Ohlin, 1960). Despite its popularity, however, it was the subject of considerable criticism in the 1970s and 1980s. At this time, theorists began to take issue with some of the core theoretical assumptions of the theory—namely, that the discrepancy between individuals' life aspirations and achievements causes delinquency (Kornhauser, 1978; see also Burton & Cullen, 1992). Even more important was the changing social context of this era. Rosenfeld (1989) notes that during this time, the liberal consensus that characterized the post—WWII era began to weaken, the welfare and antipoverty programs of the "Great Society" came under attack, and crime rates continued to rise. As such, "the necessary supports for a theory universally regarded as advocating liberal social reform as a way to reduce crime withered away" (Messner & Rosenfeld, 1997, p. 14).

Criminologists' interests in the anomie/strain tradition were again piqued, however, when Messner and Rosenfeld published their *Crime and the American Dream* in 1994 (see Messner & Rosenfeld, 2001). In this important work, Merton's anomie/strain theory was extended and partially reformulated. Although Messner and Rosenfeld agreed with Merton's view of American culture, they found his analysis of social structure incomplete (see also Messner, 1988). In particular, Merton (1938) held that the American system of *stratification* was responsible for restricting individuals' access to legitimate opportunities for upward socioeconomic mobility, which, in turn, resulted in high levels of criminogenic anomie in society. What was missing from the anomie tradition, argued Messner and Rosenfeld (1997), was an understanding of how "[t]he American Dream promotes and sustains an institutional structure in which one institution—the economy—assumes dominance over all others" (p. xi). This apparent "imbalance" in the institutional structure limits the ability of other social institutions, such as the family, education, or the political system, to insulate members of society from the criminogenic pressures of the American Dream or to impose controls over their behavior. Thus, what Messner and Rosenfeld have created is a version of anomie/strain theory that sees crime rates as a function of the American Dream's cultural emphasis on economic success in *combination* with an institutional structure dominated by the economy.

Merton's work has also influenced the most recent incarnation of the strain perspective—Agnew's (1992) general strain theory (see also Agnew, 1985). In this perspective, crime is viewed primarily as the outcome of certain emotional states—most notably, frustration-induced anger (or what he refers to as "negative affect") when individuals are presented with negative stimuli (e.g., abusive relationships, financial hardship) or are faced with the possible removal of positive stimuli (e.g., the loss of a job or romantic partner). In either case, strained individuals may see engaging in various forms of criminal behavior—from violence to theft to substance abuse—as a way to cope with the strains they are feeling (similar to Merton's formulation of "adaptations to strain"). Thus, what Agnew has done is extend more fully the conversation that Merton began by discussing more explicitly the conditions under which individuals will feel a sense of strain and will react to those feelings in deviant ways.

Yet also in the tradition of Merton, Agnew has applied this theory to the social ecology of crime. In particular, his version of macro-level general strain holds that variations in crime across macro-social units can be explained in terms of "differences in strain and in those factors that condition the effect of strain on crime" (Agnew, 1999, p. 126). This perspective draws heavily upon the relative deprivation tradition (see Blau & Blau, 1982) in that "high levels of income or socioeconomic inequality lead some individuals to experience stress or frustration" (Agnew, 1999, p. 127). Such feelings of relative deprivation, Agnew argued, can lead to high levels of negative affect among social collectives and to increased frequencies of interaction between angry and frustrated individuals, which, in turn, lead to higher rates of crime (see also Pratt & Godsey, 2003). As such, social aggregates characterized by high rates of crime "are more likely to select and retain strained individuals, produce strain, and foster criminal responses to strain" (Agnew, 1999, p. 126). In short, Merton's legacy is strong enough that even a social psychologist like Agnew has recognized the need to apply his model to the broader social level if he is to truly develop a "general" theory of offending.

CONCLUSION

A "macro-level" or "ecological" analysis in criminology examines how characteristics of delimited geographic areas—such as neighborhoods, census tracts, cities, counties, states, or nations—are related to rates of crime. Macro-level theories seek to explain why certain characteristics of ecological areas, but not others, account for the distribution of crime. Empirical research attempts to establish which of these characteristics are predictors of—that is, explain statistical variation in—crime rates. In conducting this research, independent and dependent variables are typically constructed by aggregating characteristics of individuals, such as calculating what proportion of residents in a community are under the poverty level, live in single-parent families, or commit crime.

In the first half of the 20th century, Shaw and McKay's (1942) study of social disorganization and Merton's (1938) study of anomie emerged as two vibrant, macro-level criminological paradigms. Rejecting the competing thesis that crime was due merely to individual pathology (Lilly et al., 2002), these formulations illuminated how macro-level processes explained why crime was endemic to inner-city neighborhoods and to the United States. Accordingly, much of the tradition of macro-level criminology owes its existence to Merton and to Shaw and McKay (Pratt & Cullen, 2005).

Yet since its first articulation by Shaw and McKay in the early 1900s, social disorganization theory has fallen both in and out of favor with criminologists. Despite being somewhat marginalized during the 1960s and 1970s, recent research has revived the theory (see Bursik & Grasmick, 1993; Sampson & Groves, 1989; Sampson & Wilson, 1995), and it continues to make an important contribution to criminological thought. In its current iteration, researchers have specified the links through which traditional social disorganization theory variables (e.g., low socioeconomic status, residential mobility, racial heterogeneity) may influence community crime rates. In particular, levels of social disorganization may affect informal control and criminal opportunity mechanisms (e.g., unsupervised peer groups, collective efficacy), which, in turn, directly influence neighborhood crime rates. Thus, in its contemporary form, social disorganization theory continues to be a parsimonious, yet dynamic, explanation of crime at the macro level that has received considerable empirical support.

Merton's anomie/strain theory has also enjoyed considerable influence since its first introduction. Despite falling somewhat out of favor beginning in the 1960s, the theory's rather bold contention that American society itself is criminogenic has remained provocative to this day "for it suggests, in a sense, that society gets the crime it deserves" (Lilly et al., 2002, p. 73). Now in its current iterations of institutional anomie and general strain, the theory has the potential to become even more influential with its emerging body of empirical support. Nevertheless, empirical tests of anomie theory (either in its original or extended form) are still few in number. On one hand, this may diminish our confidence in the overall explanatory power of the theory, especially at this stage in the game of theoretical validation. On the other hand, however, this also hints toward a fruitful research agenda for interested and motivated criminologists to pursue. Either way, Shaw, McKay, and Merton would all likely agree with Bruce Springsteen's assessment of what seems to be the arbitrary distribution of legitimate opportunities that are beyond any one individual's control when he sings in "Atlantic City" that "I been lookin' for a job, but it's hard to find. . . . Down here it's just winners and losers and don't get caught on the wrong side of that line."

DISCUSSION QUESTIONS

1. Explain the difference between individual-level and societal-level theories about crime causation. Are anomie/strain and social disorganization theories individual or social in nature? How can you tell?
2. Explain the problems with the original formulations of social disorganization theory and what scholars did in the 1980s to rectify these problems and revitalize the theory.
3. What weakness did Messner and Rosenfeld see in Merton's version of anomie/strain theory, and what did they add to the theory as a result?
4. Discuss the ways in which macro-level criminogenic forces like strain and social disorganization can interact with individual-level processes to produce crime; specifically, how might the environment in which a person is raised affect his or her development of self-control, and how might societal-level strain influence individuals' behavior as they attempt to cope with and adapt to that pressure?

REFERENCES

Agnew, R. (1985). A revised strain theory of delinquency. *Social Forces, 64,* 151–167.

Agnew, R. (1992). Foundation for a general strain theory of crime and delinquency. *Criminology, 30,* 47–87.

Agnew, R. (1999). A general strain theory of community differences in crime rates. *Journal of Research in Crime and Delinquency, 36,* 123–155.

Aichorn, A. (1979). Wayward youth. In J. E. Jacoby (Ed.), *Classics of criminology* (2nd ed., pp. 167–171). Prospect Heights, IL: Waveland. (Original work published 1925)

Bates, J. L. (1963). *The origins of Teapot Dome.* Urbana: University of Illinois Press.

Baumer, E. P., & Gustafson, R. (2007). Social organization and instrumental crime: Assessing the empirical validity of classic and contemporary anomie theories. *Criminology, 45,* 617–664.

Blau, P. M., & Blau, J. R. (1982). The cost of inequality: Metropolitan structure and violent crime. *American Sociological Review, 47,* 114–129.

Burgess, E. W. (1967). The growth of the city: An introduction to a research project. In R. E. Park, E. W. Burgess, & R. D. McKenzie (Eds.), *The city* (pp. 47–62). Chicago: University of Chicago Press.

Bursik, R. J. (1986). Ecological stability and the dynamics of delinquency. In A. J. Reiss & M. Tonry (Eds.), *Communities and crime* (pp. 35–66). Chicago: University of Chicago Press.

Bursik, R. J. (1988). Social disorganization and theories of crime and delinquency: Problems and prospects. *Criminology, 26,* 519–551.

Bursik, R. J., & Grasmick, H. G. (1993). *Neighborhoods and crime: The dimensions of effective community control.* New York: Macmillan.

Bursik, R. J., & Webb, J. (1982). Community change and patterns of delinquency. *American Journal of Sociology, 88,* 24–42.

Burton, V. S., & Cullen, F. T. (1992). The empirical status of strain theory. *Journal of Crime and Justice, 15,* 1–30.

Cloward, R. A., & Ohlin, L. E. (1960). *Delinquency and opportunity: A theory of delinquent gangs.* New York: The Free Press.

Cohen, A. K. (1955). *Delinquent boys: The culture of the gang.* New York: The Free Press.

Cullen, F. T. (1984). *Rethinking crime and deviance theory.* Totowa, NJ: Rowman & Allenheld.

Cullen, F. T., & Gilbert, K. E. (1982). *Reaffirming rehabilitation.* Cincinnati, OH: Anderson.

Currie, E. (1997). Market, crime and community: Toward a mid-range theory of post-industrial violence. *Theoretical Criminology, 1,* 147–172.

Dugdale, R. (1877). *The Jukes: A study in crime, pauperism, and heredity.* New York: Putman.

Durkheim, E. (1951). *Suicide: A study in sociology.* New York: The Free Press. (Original work published 1897)

Goddard, H. H. (1914). *Feeble-mindedness.* New York: Macmillan.

Gould, S. J. (1996). *The mismeasure of man* (Rev. ed.). New York: Norton.

Heitgard, J. L., & Bursik, R. J. (1987). Extracommunity dynamics and the ecology of delinquency. *American Journal of Sociology, 92,* 775–787.

Herrnstein, R. J., & Murray, C. (1994). *The bell curve: Intelligence and class structure in American life.* New York: The Free Press.

Kitwana, B. (2003). *The hip hop generation: Young blacks and the crisis in African American culture.* New York: Basic Civitas Books.

Kornhauser, R. (1978). *The social sources of delinquency.* Chicago: University of Chicago Press.

Lilly, J. R., Cullen, F. T., & Ball, R. A. (2002). *Criminological theory: Context and consequences* (3rd ed.). Thousand Oaks, CA: Sage.

Lombroso-Ferrero, G. (1911). *Criminal man, according to the classification of Cesare Lombroso.* New York: Putnam.

Lowenkamp, C. T., Cullen, F. T., & Pratt, T. C. (2003). Replicating Sampson and Groves's test of social disorganization theory: Revisiting a criminological classic. *Journal of Research in Crime and Delinquency, 40,* 351–373.

Matza, D. (1969). *Becoming deviant.* Englewood Cliffs, NJ: Prentice Hall.

Merton, R. K. (1938). Social structure and anomie. *American Sociological Review, 3,* 672–682.

Merton, R. K. (1968). *Social theory and social structure.* New York: The Free Press.

Messner, S. F. (1988). Merton's "Social Structure and Anomie": The road not taken. *Deviant Behavior, 9,* 33–53.

Messner, S. F., & Rosenfeld, R. (1997). Political restraint of the market and levels of criminal homicide: A cross-national application of institutional anomie. *Social Forces, 75,* 1393–1416.

Messner, S. F., & Rosenfeld, R. (2001). *Crime and the American dream* (3rd ed.). Belmont, CA: Wadsworth.

Morenoff, J. D., & Sampson, R. J. (1997). Violent crime and the spatial dynamics of neighborhood transition: Chicago, 1970–1990. *Social Forces, 76,* 31–64.

Palen, J. J. (1981). *The urban world* (3rd ed.). New York: McGraw-Hill.

Pratt, T. C., & Cullen, F. T. (2000). The empirical status of Gottfredson and Hirschi's general theory of crime: A meta-analysis. *Criminology, 38,* 961–934.

Pratt, T. C., & Cullen, F. T. (2005). Assessing macro-level predictors and theories of crime: A meta-analysis. *Crime and Justice: A Review of Research, 32,* 373–450.

Pratt, T. C., & Godsey, T. W. (2003). Social support, inequality, and homicide: A cross-national test of an integrated theoretical model. *Criminology, 41,* 101–133.

Pratt, T. C., Maahs, J., & Stehr, S. D. (1998). The symbolic ownership of the corrections "problem": A framework for understanding the development of corrections policy in the United States. *Prison Journal, 78,* 451–464.

Pratt, T. C., Turner, M. G., & Piquero, A. R. (2004). Parental socialization and community context: A longitudinal analysis of the structural sources of low self-control. *Journal of Research in Crime and Delinquency, 41,* 219–243.

Rosenfeld, R. (1989). Robert Merton's contributions to the sociology of deviance. *Sociological Inquiry, 59,* 433–466.

Rothman, D. J. (1980). *Conscience and convenience: The asylum and its alternatives in progressive America.* Boston: Little, Brown.

Sampson, R. J., & Groves, W. B. (1989). Community structure and crime: Testing social disorganization theory. *American Journal of Sociology, 94,* 774–802.

Sampson, R. J., Raudenbush, S. W., & Earls, F. (1997). Neighborhoods and violent crime: A multilevel study of collective efficacy. *Science, 227,* 916–924.

Sampson, R. J., & Wilson, W. J. (1995). Toward a theory of race, crime, and urban inequality. In J. Hagan & R. D. Peterson (Eds.), *Crime and inequality* (pp. 37–54). Palo Alto, CA: Stanford University Press.

Shaw, C. R., & McKay, H. D. (1942). *Juvenile delinquency and urban areas.* Chicago: University of Chicago Press.

Steinbeck, J. (1947). *The wayward bus*. New York: Viking.
Wilson, J. Q., & Herrnstein, R. J. (1985). *Crime and human nature: The definitive study of the causes of crime*. New York: Simon & Schuster.
Wilson, W. J. (1987). *The truly disadvantaged*. Chicago: University of Chicago Press.
Wilson, W. J. (1996). *When work disappears*. New York: Knopf.

NOTES

1. This focus was based on Burgess's (1967) theory of urban development. The "zone in transition" was defined as the true "inner city," where residents were often displaced to live in slum-like conditions because of their inability to afford to live elsewhere.

2. As another testament to the influence of the work of Shaw and McKay, these two "prongs" of social disorganization theory provided the basis for individual-level theories such as social control/social bond theory and Sutherland's differential association theory (see Lilly et al., 2002).

3. This is not to say that Merton viewed the deviant rejection of middle-class values as unimportant for explaining crime. Instead, he provided an explanation as to why crime, although concentrated in urban slum areas, is still widely dispersed elsewhere (e.g., suburban or rural areas).

4. Although less obvious in Merton's discussion, he also raises the possibility that the intense emphasis on the goal of economic success, in and of itself, could cause anomie. Thus, his theory really specifies two potential pathways by which levels of anomie in society may result in high crime rates (Cullen, 1984).

5. Steinbeck is referring to the Teapot Dome scandal during the Harding administration, involving government corruption and bribery with regard to petroleum reserves in Wyoming (Bates, 1963).

6. The "reciprocal effects" mentioned by Bursik (1986, p. 64) have to do with the assumption that "within the context of ongoing urban dynamics, the level of delinquency in an area may also directly or indirectly cause changes in the composition of an area" due to "out-migration" (p. 64). Thus, Bursik estimated the simultaneous effects of social disorganization on crime, and crime on social disorganization. Similar approaches can be found in the work of Bursik and Webb (1982) and Morenoff and Sampson (1997), where changes in population characteristics were being predicted by changes in crime/delinquency rates.

7. Heitgerd and Bursik (1987) showed that a relatively socially organized community may experience high rates of delinquency simply by virtue of being located geographically adjacent to a socially disorganized community.

FIVE

KEY IDEA: HIRSCHI'S SOCIAL BOND/SOCIAL CONTROL THEORY

KEY WORK

Hirschi, T. (1969). *Causes of delinquency.* Berkeley: University of California Press.

Travis Hirschi's social bond/social control theory has remained a major paradigm in criminology since its introduction in 1969. To be sure, few theories have generated as much empirical attention, or have sparked as much debate within the field, as Hirschi's theory. It has been tested by scholars extensively (Akers & Sellers, 2008) and has been the source of heated disagreements among scholars on both theoretical and empirical grounds (Lilly, Cullen, & Ball, 2007). Hirschi himself has remained a leading figure in the discipline for over four decades now and continues to be among the most cited criminologists year after year (Wright, 2002). Indeed, few scholars can claim to have been this relevant to the field for this long. This was no accident—there's a reason why his ideas have "caught on" where other ideas (even those that seem to be eerily similar) have been ignored, and such is the focus of this chapter.

THE SOCIAL CONTEXT OF THE 1960s

The 1960s were an interesting time in American history for a variety of reasons. This was the decade of clashing values that brought us acid rock; police dogs and fire hoses set upon civil rights demonstrators in the South; Harper Lee's *To Kill a Mockingbird* and Ken Kesey's *One Flew Over the Cuckoo's Nest;* phrases like "free love" pitted against laws prohibiting the use of contraception; the burning of draft cards and the fleeing of draft dodgers to Canada; skateboards; miniskirts; the Black Panthers; the assassinations of John and Bobby Kennedy and of Martin Luther King, the presence of non-white athletes Roberto Clemente, Willie Mays, and Hank Aaron in major league baseball; the burning of bras by feminists, and the riots at the Democratic National Convention. It was also the decade that ushered in a number of new ways of thinking about crime and crime control, from the labeling perspective and its influence on juvenile justice system reforms (Lemert, 1967), to the early roots of Akers' social learning theory (Burgess & Akers, 1966), to the resurgence of the rational choice perspective (Becker, 1968) and the outright rejection of previous ways of thinking about crime such as social disorganization theory (Lilly et al., 2007). The late 1960s also contained two important demographic developments that occurred in concert and that became central to the introduction of Hirschi's social bond/social control theory.

First, there was a large maturing population of those who we would consider the World War II generation, starting to move into their 30s, 40s, and 50s—a time in life when, statistically speaking, people's political leanings tend to start creeping to the right, becoming more and more conservative (Franz, Freedman, Goldstein, & Ridout, 2007). At the same time, a second demographic shift was occurring: A youthful population, known as the "baby boomers" (people born shortly after the close of WWII), was entering late teens and early adulthood—a time in life when people's trajectories of antisocial behavior are at their peak (Blumstein, Cohen, Roth, & Visher, 1986) and their political leanings tend to be more liberal (Franz et al., 2007). Thus, at this time there was a generational imbalance in the United States that the country had never really experienced before, one that found two large groups of citizens at odds with one another—one struggling to gain independence and the other trying to reestablish the 1950s level of social order that they felt had been lost (Pratt, Maahs, & Stehr, 1998).

In addition, as the nation was riding a wave of post–Kennedy era political liberalism, the backlash against that movement gained steam. On one side we had the "summer of love" and Woodstock, which gave us the tradition-breaking music of The Grateful Dead, Jimi Hendrix, and Joan Baez, among others. It also saw the onset of a number of important legal developments such as the exclusionary rule, the 1964 Civil Rights Act, the 1965

Voting Rights Act, the 1968 Fair Housing Act, the expansion of inmates' rights, and the creation of a host of legal protections for juveniles.

On the other side, we had growing skepticism over the ability of the state to control crime benevolently through treatment, exemplified in films like *A Clockwork Orange;* a groundswell of anger over racial integration in the South; and a Nixon administration that was the first to formally adopt a "law and order" campaign strategy to combat crime (Baum, 1996) that served as the underpinning for the modern-day "get tough" movement (Pratt, 2009). This struggle between different ways of looking at the world was exacerbated by rising crime rates in the late 1960s—a problem that was blamed, at least in part, on what was perceived as an overly lenient criminal justice system (Cullen & Gilbert, 1982). As a result, society started to discuss seriously the potential problems of a culture of permissiveness (Currie, 1998).

This was the social and political climate that Travis Hirschi was operating within when he developed his theory. Hirschi grew up in rural Utah and attended the University of Utah, receiving an undergraduate degree in sociology in the early 1960s. Not known for being a progressive state either socially or politically, it was rather a culture shock for Hirschi when he moved to San Francisco to pursue graduate studies at the University of California, Berkeley, right in the middle of the psychedelic movement's epicenters off Berkeley's Telegraph Avenue and San Francisco's Haight-Ashbury (see Laub, 2002). It is not surprising that a kid who grew up in rural Utah in the 1950s would find 1960s San Francisco to be "out of control."

SOCIAL BOND/SOCIAL CONTROL THEORY

According to Hirschi (1969), virtually all existing criminological theories began with a faulty fundamental premise: that criminal behavior requires, in some form, the creation of criminal motivation. For example, strain theories that emerged out of Merton's (1938) work assumed that it was the pressure placed on social norms, due to a disconnect between youths' goals and aspirations and their ability to reach such goals through legitimate means, that created the motivation to offend—an assumption echoed by later versions of strain theory articulated by Cloward and Ohlin (1960). In addition, perspectives drawing on the differential association tradition (see Sutherland, 1939) assumed that the values and techniques associated with criminal behavior had to be learned—a process that occurred largely through exposure to deviant peers and to deviant value systems that created the motivation to offend (Akers & Sellers, 2008).

Hirschi, on the other hand, began with the opposite premise: that all of us, beginning at birth, possess the hedonistic drive to act in the kinds of selfish and aggressive ways that lead to criminal behavior. Indeed, it takes no disjunction between a child's long-term goals and his perception of blocked opportunities to meet those goals to steal another child's truck in a sandbox, nor does it take extended exposure to deviant peers or to deviant value systems for a child to impulsively and aggressively shove that child to the ground after swiping said sandbox truck without thinking about the long-term consequences of his actions. These behaviors, Hirschi contended, are part of our innate human nature—the important part, he argued, is that most of us control these "natural" urges. In short, Hirschi (1969) began his theory with the view that asking why offenders "do it" when it comes to crime and delinquency is, on its face, an irrelevant question. Instead, we should be asking, "why *don't* we do it?"

For Hirschi, the answer could be found in the bonds that people form to prosocial values, prosocial people, and prosocial institutions. It is these bonds, Hirschi held, that end up controlling our behavior when we are tempted to engage in criminal or deviant acts. Accordingly, these bonds come in four interrelated forms, the first of which is attachment. *Attachment,* according to Hirschi (1969), refers to the level of psychological affection one has for prosocial others and institutions. For Hirschi, parents and schools were of critical importance in this regard, where youths who form close attachments to their parents[1] and schools will, by extension, experience greater levels of social control. For example, in the movie *Scream* (Craven, 1996), when the two killers are unmasked, one of them laments that, once everyone finds out about them, "my mom is gonna be so mad at me." Although this particular fictional offender's maternal attachments obviously did not keep him from killing, it does point to the broader issue of how these attachments can control our behavior—of not wanting to disappoint those we love with our misbehavior.

The second type of bond is referred to as *commitment,* where Hirschi cited the importance of the social relationships that people value, which they would not want to risk jeopardizing by committing criminal or deviant acts. In essence, Hirschi noted that people are less likely to misbehave when they know that they have something to lose. For juveniles, this could mean not wanting to look bad in front of friends, parents, or teachers for having committed a crime—something for which shame from those whose opinion of them matters would be a likely consequence. The same would hold true for adults, Hirschi would argue, where people might refrain from engaging in deviant activities that may threaten their employment or marriage—bonds that, again, may serve as sources of social control.

The third type of social bond is known as *involvement,* which relates to the opportunity costs associated with how people spend their time. Specifically, Hirschi tapped into the old philosophy that "idle hands are the devil's workshop" in that if people are spending their time engaged in some form of prosocial activity, then they are not, by definition, spending their time engaged in antisocial activity. For example, youths who are heavily involved in legitimate school-related activities—either academically, socially, or athletically—will not be spending that same time destroying property, stealing things that don't belong to them, shooting heroin, and so on. This is not to say, of course, that such youths cannot engage in those behaviors *before or after* their legitimate activities. Nevertheless, Hirschi argued that, at least during that time, such youths will not be committing delinquent acts.

The final type of social bond identified by Hirschi is *belief,* which refers to the degree to which one adheres to the values associated with behaviors that conform to the law; the assumption being that the more important such values are to a person, the less likely he or she is to engage in criminal/deviant behavior. For example, youths who do not value the notion that it is a bad idea to skip school, and instead value spending the day playing the latest version of *Guitar Hero* (music video game) and smoking marijuana, are more likely to do just that. Conversely, youths who, for example, share the belief that using illegal narcotics is wrong are less likely to participate in such behavior. Although this relationship is quite simple, the underlying concept Hirschi was tapping into was that there is an important link between attitudes and behavior—not in the sense that attitudes motivate people to commit crime, but rather that prosocial attitudes constrain people from committing the crimes they otherwise would have in the absence of such social bonds (i.e., beliefs).

Perhaps the most significant element of Hirschi's theory is that, taken together, these social bonds coalesce in a way that controls our behavior indirectly—that is, we do not need to have these bonds directly present in our lives to keep our behavior in check. Instead, the prosocial bonds we have formed can control our behavior even when they are no longer there. To illustrate this point, ask yourself this question: Have you ever found yourself driving in the middle of nowhere and you encounter a four-way stop? You can see all around you and you know that nobody is coming, you don't need to yield to anyone, and there is no police officer camping out near the intersection to catch you if you were to just roll right through it. Yet what would many of us do? We would stop anyway (or come very close to it). Why do we do this? Our visual scan of the area says that it can't be because of the direct threat of getting a ticket or of getting into an accident. Hirschi would contend that it is instead the "indirect" psychological control exerted by our social bonds that causes us to stop at that intersection.

Relatedly, it is also important to note that Hirschi's social bonds represented, at least primarily, mechanisms of informal social control—that is, the bonds that control our behavior are typically social conventions rather than formally adopted laws. If you doubt the power of informal rules to guide what we decide to do or not do at any given moment, consider the example of elevator behavior. None of us has been given a pamphlet concerning how we should or should not behave when getting on an elevator, yet there are consistencies of action that all of us seem to follow: A little small talk is permissible, but keep it superficial; give everyone else adequate personal space; looking up at the light moving from floor to floor is the most common place to direct your visual attention. If you doubt the power of any of these informal norms, try violating them sometime and see just how uncomfortable you make those riding with you. Indeed, start a conversation about religion or politics with your elevator mates, or stand facing them while invading their space, or get on your hands and knees and closely examine a spot on the floor. You'll see just how quickly the discomfort level will rise, and you will know that your behavior has violated the rules that informally keep our behavior in check.

Perhaps a more criminologically relevant example would be how many of us handle holiday family get-togethers. We are there with family, whether we like it or not, and at times the veneer of civility starts to wear thin. When the uncle you may have loathed for your entire life takes the best piece of turkey right before you get to it, what stops you from beating him about the head with the gravy ladle? Is it because there are laws telling you that doing so is illegal—is that what stops you? Unlikely. The more likely explanation is that you have a set of bonds in the form of morals and values that tell you that bludgeoning someone with a serving implement is not an appropriate response to turkey pilfering—that is what keeps your behavior in line. Thus, the formal legal rule prohibiting assault-by-ladle likely plays little to no role in your decision to simply move on to the mashed potatoes.

In essence, Hirschi (1969) argued that juvenile delinquents and adult criminals lack these bonds to conventional society. Offenders behave the way they do because they are not controlled; their "natural instincts" are not curtailed. In taking this position, Hirschi created one of the deepest divisions within criminology—one where the very premise of all "motivational" theories was called into question. The legacy of this division is still with us today and can be seen, for example, in how vehemently scholars from the "control" versus "learning" camps disagree with one another (see McGloin, Pratt, & Maahs, 2004). This is a debate that has stayed with us for decades and is likely to continue well into the future. What is often overlooked, however, is the extent to which this debate was fueled not necessarily by Hirschi's idea itself, but rather the way in which Hirschi *presented* his theory. That is the subject of the following section.

THE MARKETING OF SOCIAL BOND/SOCIAL CONTROL THEORY

As Hirschi was developing his theory, it is important to note that "control theories" had been around in criminology for quite some time already. Shaw and McKay's (1942) social disorganization theory and the early perspectives of Reckless (1943) and Sykes and Matza (1957) all drew upon—at least to some degree—the notion of informal social control. What, then, made Hirschi's theory essentially unique and original even if the ideas underlying his theory weren't? We argue here that there were three properties of the way in which Hirschi's *Causes of Delinquency* was constructed—and therefore its ideas marketed—that aided considerably its impact on the field.

Reason #1: A New Approach to Theory Construction

Scholars have long held that, generally speaking, theory building in criminology has been a sloppy endeavor (see Gibbons, 1994). Rarely is a theory stated in one location (e.g., a book or a journal article) in its entirety, with clearly articulated, testable propositions. Instead, what we typically find is that theories are presented discursively over time, often involving multiple authors, over multiple publications, where elements are added, subtracted, and modified according to an ongoing dialogue with the field over the theory's relative strengths and weaknesses. Furthermore, until Hirschi came along, theoretical critiques were generally made on theoretical grounds; that is, ideas were debated among scholars according to criteria such as logical consistency and the clarity of the theory's key propositions. It wasn't until Hirschi entered the picture that the relationship between newly gathered empirical data and new theory construction would really get solidified. Indeed, Hirschi's 1969 book wasn't merely a theoretical critique of existing criminological paradigms on theoretical grounds—he went and got data to prove it!

To do so, as Hirschi was in the planning stages of his doctoral dissertation, he explored the option of using the data gathered by Sheldon and Eleanor Glueck, the authors of *Unraveling Juvenile Delinquency* (1950), who had a large longitudinal dataset containing 500 delinquent and 500 nondelinquent boys from Boston. His hopes were quashed, however, when Eleanor Glueck informed Hirschi's dissertation advisor, Charles Glock, that they were still using their data and weren't ready to share it with others yet (Laub, 2002). As Laub noted, "it is hard to imagine what criminology would have become in the latter part of the twentieth century if Hirschi had reanalyzed the Gluecks' data for his dissertation instead of writing *Causes* [*of Delinquency*]!" (p. xviii). In an odd twist of criminological history, along with Robert Sampson, John Laub himself would later use the Gluecks' data in the formulation of their life course theory of criminal behavior, which essentially affirmed the importance of Hirschi's original ideas (Laub & Sampson, 2003; Sampson & Laub, 1993).

So with the Gluecks' data off the table, as an alternative Hirschi was able to work with Alan B. Wilson—the principal investigator of the Richmond (California) Youth Project in 1964. Although this was not

Hirschi's study, Wilson made a deal with Hirschi that, in exchange for his work on the project, Hirschi would be allowed to develop questions that could be inserted into the survey instrument that he could then use for his dissertation work (Laub, 2002). Armed with data, Hirschi was ready to take the next step!

Reason #2: Operationalizing Theories

Drawing heavily upon an unpublished paper authored by Ruth Kornhauser—a paper that would be developed more fully into the influential *Social Sources of Delinquency* (1978)—Hirschi organized the field of criminology into three perspectives: his social bond theory, the "cultural deviance" theory most attributable to Sutherland (1939), and "strain theory" as articulated by Merton (1938) and more recently by Cloward and Ohlin (1960). Given this opportunity to create his own survey items, Hirschi then developed a set of direct, operational measures of the key concepts specified by each of these three theories. These items included questions tapping into each of the four bonds discussed above for social bond theory (items and scales that are still used today) and attitudes about the violation of laws according to the cultural deviance perspective. Yet what was perhaps most interesting was the measure of strain that he developed—one that would be used by researchers for many years after.

In particular, Hirschi faced the task of attempting to measure with survey items the disjunction between the intensity of one's goals of economic success (the goal integral to the American Dream, according to Merton) and the structural barriers to reaching those goals imposed by class inequalities. The difficulty of the task was compounded by the fact that these would be youths answering the surveys, yet Hirschi pressed on. He developed an indicator of "goals," which was youths' "educational aspirations," and then attempted to capture the structural barriers produced by differential opportunities by asking these youths about their "education expectations," the assumption being that such expectations tapped into what youths thought of as realistically possible (see Unnever, Cullen, Mathers, McClure, & Allison, 2009). He then created a new variable—the "aspiration-expectation gap"—that was his proxy for strain (the assumption being that those with larger gaps would be experiencing more strain).

This measure of strain that Hirschi constructed was important for two reasons. First, he found that, by and large, there really was no widespread aspiration-expectation gap among his respondents—in essence, the youths gave virtually the same responses to the aspirations and expectations questions on the survey. While it is possible that the youths participating in the survey didn't fully appreciate the linguistic difference between the two terms, Hirschi instead treated this finding as evidence that most kids simply don't experience that much strain. Second, and perhaps more important, Hirschi found that youths who had higher educational aspirations tended to have lower rates of juvenile delinquency. Hirschi interpreted this finding to mean that such aspirations are an indicator of commitment to conventional behavior. Thus, his strain measure became, by default, a social bond measure as well. In any event, now that the variables had been operationalized—something that hadn't really been attempted in criminology before when it came to a theoretical critique—the next step taken by Hirschi was perhaps the most critical.

Reason #3: Theoretical "Fight Club"

Some scholars hold that scientific knowledge can (and should) grow through theoretical integration, that by combining potentially compatible elements from alternative perspectives, a "better" understanding of criminal behavior could be reached (Tittle, 2000). Hirschi did not buy into this line of thinking at all. In fact, Unnever et al. (2009) stated that,

> For Hirschi, theories have incompatible core assumptions and should wage a contest to see which one, in the end, accounts more completely for the known empirical reality. As a result, in *Causes of Delinquency,* Hirschi was not seeking to uncover points of theoretical commonality but rather to show that the cultural deviance theory and strain theory were incorrect and should be relegated to the criminological dustbin. (p. 381)

If we were to make an analogy to a couple of recent films here, Hirschi's view of theory building was less like *The Sisterhood of the Traveling Pants* and more like *Fight Club.* Or, put differently, his theory leaned closer to being combative than it did to being inclusive.

So in the spirit of theoretical competition (or perhaps a theoretical brawl), Hirschi proceeded to test the measures derived from each of these theories against one another under the assumption that there would be a winner and perhaps multiple losers. For Hirschi, that was exactly the case. What he found was that, simply put, measures of social bonds "matter" when it comes to predicting delinquent behavior in youths. More important, measures derived from cultural deviance and strain theories—if they mattered at all—were rendered insignificant once statistical controls for the social bond measures were introduced. The clear "winner" in this contest, therefore, was social bond theory, or, put differently, cultural deviance and strain theories could consider themselves winners if social bond theory wasn't playing.

This approach that Hirschi took was new, and it fundamentally changed the game in criminology by introducing the "comparative test" that has been a staple of criminological theory and research ever since. No longer would it be good enough to merely develop measures of one theory and provide a test of its propositions. What made Hirschi's work so compelling was that he attempted to demonstrate empirically that not only was his theory "right," but the leading contenders were also "wrong," *within the same study.* This was no trivial matter, for it sealed Hirschi's theory in the minds of criminologists and radically changed the nature of "business as usual" in criminology.

THE LEGACY OF SOCIAL BOND/SOCIAL CONTROL THEORY

The impact of Hirschi's *Causes of Delinquency* is difficult to overstate. Accordingly, there are at least five tangible ways Hirschi's work has influenced the field of criminology. First, and as stated above, the "comparative test" between competing criminological ideas, using empirical data, has become commonplace in criminological research. Scholars see this approach as helping their chances at getting their work published in peer-reviewed journals, yet others have argued that this approach has actually hindered our understanding of criminal and deviant behavior because its outright rejection of theoretical integration is inconsistent with the body of empirical evidence pointing to its utility (McGloin et al., 2004). Either way, the comparative test is here to stay in criminology and, for better or for worse, we most certainly have Hirschi to thank for it.

Second, Hirschi (1969) provided the field with a set of operational measures for certain key variables specified by each of the major theoretical traditions in criminology. Not only did he develop social bond items that have been used in a number of subsequent studies (see Kempf, 1993), but he also provided indicators of cultural deviance and strain that researchers have used to some extent ever since. Even so, it is perhaps his measure of strain that proved to be the most controversial in the decades following the publication of *Causes of Delinquency.* In particular, not all scholars were fans of measuring strain through the "aspiration-expectation gap" that Hirschi developed. Citing the potential problem that youths are unlikely to make a cognitive distinction between the two terms—thus resulting in the measure failing to actually capture strain where it might exist—other scholars have used alternative measures, such as the perception of blocked opportunities, and have found considerably more support for strain theory than Hirschi did (see Burton & Cullen, 1992). Regardless, without the influence of Hirschi's strain measure—flawed or not—alternative approaches for assessing the merits of strain theory probably would not have been developed.

Third, Hirschi's theory sparked an enormous level of interest among scholars seeking to test his theory. In fact, social bond/social control theory is one of the most widely tested theories in criminology, with well over 100 published tests to its credit (Akers & Sellers, 2008). And while some reviews of the literature are rather equivocal concerning the theory's empirical status (Kempf, 1993), others are more firm in concluding that it is, on balance, one of the most well-supported criminological perspectives at work in the field today. Even some of Hirschi's competitors concede that the kinds of informal social control mechanisms specified by social bond theory are important to our understanding of criminal behavior (Andrews & Bonta, 1998).

Fourth, by pitting theories against one another, Hirschi's work has had the effect of creating theoretical "camps" within criminology. Most notably, there has emerged a duel over the "control versus learning" traditions in which scholars have "taken sides" (McGloin et al., 2004). For example, both Travis Hirschi and Ronald Akers (the respective primary architects of the control and learning criminological perspectives) have had numerous doctoral students over the last four decades, who have themselves gone on to train doctoral students, and so on. The result is large groups of criminologists who are loyal to their intellectual mentors and who regularly debate one another in this control versus learning fashion at professional conferences and in the peer-reviewed journals. Whether these arguments move the field forward or are merely entertaining for viewers and readers is debatable, yet there is no denying the fact that the legacy of Hirschi is alive and well, and that the control versus learning debate is still vigorous, entrenched, and ongoing in the field of criminology.

Finally, Hirschi's theory has served as the intellectual foundation for two subsequent criminological perspectives that have themselves become major traditions in the field of criminology. First, Sampson and Laub's (1993) life course theory drew heavily upon Hirschi's original notion of social bonds; specifically, Sampson and Laub noted that changes in criminal behavior over the life course could be explained by changes in age-graded informal social control mechanisms (a topic to be discussed at greater length in Chapter 11). In essence, this perspective holds that while the kinds of social bonds that constrain our behavior change as we age (e.g., parents are important for this task when we are young, but play less of a role as we age; bonds to employment are important for those in adulthood but not so much for children; and so on), it is still the principle of social bonding and the power of informal social controls that ultimately keep our behavior in check.

Equally as important is Hirschi's work with Michael Gottfredson in their self-control theory (Gottfredson & Hirschi, 1990). In this work, Hirschi retained the core notion that individuals are naturally predisposed toward criminal behavior and therefore need to be restrained from doing so, yet he rejected the notion of "indirect control" that had been a hallmark of his 1969 work. Instead, Gottfredson and Hirschi reconceptualized the control theory tradition as one of "direct control" involving individuals themselves. Viewed in this way, those who lack self-control (or, put differently, those whose parents failed to instill self-control in them; see Unnever, Cullen, & Pratt, 2003), will be impulsive, short-sighted, prone to risk taking, and will seek the very kind of immediate gratification (e.g., excitement, material goods) that criminal behavior provides. As such, the kinds of "bonds" that Hirschi specified in *Causes of Delinquency* are only important insofar as children are bonded enough to their parents for the kind of monitoring, supervision, and punishment of misbehavior that is necessary to result in the child's self-control being inculcated (Perrone Sullivan, Pratt, & Margaryan, 2004; Pratt, Turner, & Piquero, 2004). Given what is yet another provocative theoretical statement made by Hirschi (i.e., that virtually all other competing criminological theories are "wrong"), it is no surprise that self-control theory has attracted the attention of criminologists as well, and the result has been a high level of empirical support (Pratt & Cullen, 2000). It is clear, then, that Hirschi's influence has crept into nearly every corner of contemporary criminological thought.

CONCLUSION

In 1973, in response to slumping ticket sales and sagging profits, Major League Baseball instituted the "Designated Hitter" (DH) rule in the American League, whereby the pitcher's place in the batting order would be replaced by a hitter who himself would not have to face the responsibility of playing defense. The working assumption among the creators of this rule was that another "big bat" in the lineup would result in greater run production, which would be more exciting to fans, which would translate into increased revenue as more people filled the stadium seats. The DH rule did just that and a lot more: Yes, runs increased, yet time-honored strategies such as stealing bases, executing the "hit and run" and the "suicide squeeze" became virtually obsolete as teams instead organized their strategies around the home run, and aging players like Reggie Jackson could extend their careers as a DH and surpass the career home run totals of players like Mickey Mantle who didn't have the a luxury of being a DH. Thus, while the core of baseball remained the same, the DH rule changed the game in a number of extremely important ways.

Travis Hirschi's social bond/social control theory, as presented in *Causes of Delinquency,* was a similar kind of "game changer" in criminology. His work provided the field with a new idea and a new way of thinking about criminal behavior that "made sense" to the field at the time (Lilly et al., 2007). Equally important is the fact that the way he went about presenting that idea (and his attempt to dismantle the major competitors of the time) has fundamentally changed the way criminologists "do business" to this day. And much like the DH rule in baseball, his core message has proven to be both controversial and here to stay.

DISCUSSION QUESTIONS

1. How did Hirschi differ from other theorists with regard to his assumptions about criminal motivation? How did this difference in the initial premise inspire Hirschi to challenge the tradition of asking why people commit crime?
2. List and describe the four types of bonds, including the ways in which each bond militates against criminal conduct.
3. Describe the difference between formal and informal social control. Which type of control did Hirschi's theory pertain to? Explain your answer.
4. Explain the traditional methods of theory analysis and Hirschi's revolutionary method of comparative theory testing using empirical data. Which of these two methods ultimately became a staple of criminological research? Why?
5. List and summarize the five major influences that Hirschi's theory and methods have had on criminology.

REFERENCES

Akers, R. L., & Sellers, C. S. (2008). *Criminological theories: Introduction, evaluation, and application.* New York: Oxford University Press.

Andrews, D. A., & Bonta, J. (1998). *The psychology of criminal conduct* (2nd ed.). Cincinnati, OH: Anderson.

Baum, D. (1996). *Smoke and mirrors: The war on drugs and the politics of failure.* Boston: Little, Brown.

Becker, G. S. (1968). Crime and punishment: An economic approach. *Journal of Political Economy, 76*(2), 169–217.

Blumstein, A., Cohen, J., Roth, J., & Visher, C. (1986). *Criminal careers and "career criminals."* Report of the National Academy of Sciences Panel on Research on Criminal Care. Washington, DC: National Academies Press.

Burgess, R. L., & Akers, R. L. (1966). A differential association-reinforcement theory of criminal behavior. *Social Problems, 14,* 128–146.

Burton, V. S., & Cullen, F. T. (1992). The empirical status of strain theory. *Journal of Crime and Justice, 15*(2), 1–30.

Cloward, R. E., & Ohlin, L. E. (1960). *Delinquency and opportunity: A theory of delinquent gangs.* New York: The Free Press.

Craven, W. (Director). (1996). *Scream* [Motion picture]. New York: Dimension Films.

Cullen, F. T., & Gilbert, K. E. (1982). *Reaffirming rehabilitation.* Cincinnati, OH: Anderson.

Currie, E. (1998). *Crime and punishment in America.* New York: Henry Holt.

Franz, M. M., Freedman, P., Goldstein, K. M., & Ridout, T. R. (2007). *Campaign advertising and American democracy.* Philadelphia: Temple University Press.

Gibbons, D. C. (1994). *Talking about crime and criminals: Problems and issues in theory development in criminology.* Englewood Cliffs, NJ: Prentice Hall.

Glueck, S., & Glueck, E. (1950). *Unraveling juvenile delinquency.* New York: Commonwealth Fund.

Gottfredson, M. R., & Hirschi, T. (1990). *A general theory of crime.* Palo Alto, CA: Stanford University Press.

Hirschi, T. (1969). *Causes of delinquency.* Berkeley: University of California Press.

Kempf, K. L. (1993). The empirical status of Hirschi's control theory. In F. Adler & W. S. Laufer (Eds.), *New directions in criminological theory: Advances in criminological theory* (Vol. 4, pp. 143–185). New Brunswick, NJ: Transaction.

Kornhauser, R. R. (1978). *Social sources of delinquency: An appraisal of analytic models.* Chicago: University of Chicago Press.

Laub, J. H. (2002). Introduction: The life and work of Travis Hirschi. In J. H. Laub (Ed.), *The craft of criminology: Selected papers* (pp. vii–xlix). New Brunswick, NJ: Transaction.

Laub, J. H., & Sampson, R. J. (2003). *Shared beginnings, divergent lives: Delinquent boys to age 70.* Cambridge, MA: Harvard University Press.

Lemert, E. (1967). The juvenile court: Questions and realities. In the President's Commission on Law Enforcement and the Administration of Justice, *Task force report: Juvenile delinquency and youth crime* (pp. 91–106). Washington, DC: Government Printing Office.

Lilly, J. R., Cullen, F. T., & Ball, R. A. (2007). *Criminological theory: Context and consequences* (4th ed.). Thousand Oaks, CA: Sage.

McGloin, J. M., Pratt, T. C., & Maahs, J. (2004). Rethinking the IQ–delinquency relationship: A longitudinal analysis of multiple theoretical models. *Justice Quarterly, 21,* 601–631.

Merton, R. K. (1938). Social structure and anomie. *American Sociological Review, 3,* 672–682.

Perrone, D. M., Sullivan, C., Pratt, T. C., & Margaryan, S. (2004). Parental efficacy, self-control, and delinquent behavior: A test of a general theory of crime on a nationally representative sample. *International Journal of Offender Therapy and Comparative Criminology, 48,* 298–312.

Pratt, T. C. (2009). *Addicted to incarceration: Corrections policy and the politics of misinformation in the United States.* Thousand Oaks, CA: Sage.

Pratt, T. C., & Cullen, F. T. (2000). The empirical status of Gottfredson and Hirschi's general theory of crime: A meta-analysis. *Criminology, 38,* 961–934.

Pratt, T. C., Maahs, J., & Stehr, S. D. (1998). The symbolic ownership of the corrections "problem": A framework for understanding the development of corrections policy in the United States. *Prison Journal, 78,* 451–464.

Pratt, T. C., Turner, M. G., & Piquero, A. R. (2004). Parental socialization and community context: A longitudinal analysis of the structural sources of low self-control. *Journal of Research in Crime and Delinquency, 41,* 219–243.

Reckless, W. C. (1943). *The etiology of criminal and delinquent behavior.* New York: Social Science Research Council.

Sampson, R. J., & Laub, J. H. (1993). *Crime in the making: Pathways and turning points through life.* Cambridge, MA: Harvard University Press.

Shaw, C. R., & McKay, H. D. (1942). *Juvenile delinquency and urban areas.* Chicago: University of Chicago Press.

Sutherland, E. (1939). *Principles of criminology.* Chicago: University of Chicago Press.

Sykes, G., & Matza, D. (1957). Techniques of neutralization: A theory of delinquency. *American Sociological Review, 22*(6), 664–673.

Tittle, C. R. (2000). Theoretical developments in criminology. In G. LaFree, J. F. Short, R. J. Bursik, Sr., & R. B. Taylor (Eds.), *Criminal justice 2000, Vol. 1: The nature of crime* (pp. 51–101). Washington, DC: National Institute of Justice.

Unnever, J. D., Cullen, F. T., Mathers, S. A., McClure, T. E., & Allison, M. C. (2009). Racial discrimination and Hirschi's criminological classic: A chapter in the sociology of knowledge. *Justice Quarterly, 26*(3), 377–409.

Unnever, J. D., Cullen, F. T., & Pratt, T. C. (2003). Parental management, ADHD, and delinquent involvement: Reassessing Gottfredson and Hirschi's general theory. *Justice Quarterly, 20,* 471–500.

Wright, R. A. (2002). Recent changes in the most cited scholars in criminal justice textbooks. *Journal of Criminal Justice, 30*(3), 183–195.

NOTE

1. A criticism is often leveled against Hirschi that such attachments can be criminogenic if parents, for example, are deviant themselves (The same criticism could be made regarding forming attachments to deviant peers.). This should be considered an unfair critique of Hirschi's theory, however, since a close reading of his 1969 work clearly indicates that Hirschi was referring to prosocial attachments, not any and all attachments.

SIX

KEY IDEA: REHABILITATION IS DEAD

KEY WORK

Martinson, Robert (1974). What works? Questions and answers about prison reform. *The Public Interest, 35,* 22–54.

A glance into recent American history reveals a society characterized in part by lauded innovation and progressive development, but also one that has struggled to find answers to incessantly difficult questions. In both the academic and practical realm of criminology and criminal justice, one such struggle has surrounded the issue of *what,* exactly, states should do with law-violating members of society. In the words of Cullen and Gendreau (2000), "[t]his ostensibly simple question defies a simple answer" (p. 111). Should offenders simply be isolated from society for the longest reasonable time frame? Should the state organize its response to law violation around principles of retribution or delivering *harm* to seemingly deserving offenders? Or maybe states should focus their efforts around the principle of rehabilitation and changing offenders into law-abiding citizens? States have attempted each of these responses to one degree or another, but until relatively recently, the primary focus surrounded the effort to treat and correct offenders' undesirable behaviors. Principles of rehabilitation were the dominant response—or at least it was widely believed that these principles *should* be the dominant response (Cullen & Gilbert, 1982; Rothman, 1980). This was true for most of the 19th century, but the 1970s brought about dramatic reform to the correctional industry. Interestingly, this reform was closely linked to what is now a widely known article written by Robert Martinson (1974).

This chapter aims to inform the reader about the most important aspects of Martinson's (1974) influential work in the field of corrections. To fully understand its significance, however, it will be necessary to move beyond the substantive content of Martinson's article itself. Consequently, this chapter will examine, in some detail, the broader sociopolitical context during the time when Martinson's work was published as well as the manner in which Martinson "marketed" the content of his research. Once these factors are considered, it will then be possible to better understand and explain the powerful influence that a single article can wield under the right conditions.

THE MARTINSON REPORT

In 1974, an article written by Robert Martinson appeared in the *The Public Interest.* It was titled "What Works? Questions and Answers About Prison Reform." As the title implies, Martinson's work attempted to assess the effectiveness of various prison reforms, particularly those aimed at rehabilitating criminal offenders and reducing recidivism. To provide answers about what works in the way of correctional rehabilitation, Martinson reviewed the available evidence from existing studies of offender treatment. In the end, his essay painted a picture of modern rehabilitation that could only be characterized by widespread failure. In summarizing the literature, Martinson stated confidently that "with few and isolated exceptions, the rehabilitative efforts that have been reported so far have had no appreciable effect on recidivism" (p. 25).

Martinson's harsh assessment of correctional rehabilitation was delivered through his 1974 essay, which became known as the Martinson Report (see Pratt, 2009), though it was actually derived from a lengthy manuscript later published in book form by himself and his colleagues (Lipton, Martinson, & Wilks, 1975). In this coauthored work, Lipton et al. gathered all available studies of correctional treatment, including only analyses considered to be scientifically rigorous and excluding those that failed to meet this standard. For example, studies that reached their conclusions in the absence of a control group were rightfully considered methodologically weak and unfit for inclusion in their review. Their comprehensive search of the treatment literature netted 231 studies conducted between 1945 and 1967, which in essence contained everything that the scientific community knew about the effectiveness of offender rehabilitation. The only problem was that extracting all of the necessary knowledge from this large body of literature was a task that few academics had time for, let alone practitioners in the field of correctional treatment. A comprehensive synthesis of this research, then, had a very attractive benefit: It would allow correctional administrators, legislators, and any other interested parties to draw *scientifically* based conclusions about the success or failure of prison reform efforts. And of course, this science could then be used to drive the policies that determined how offenders should best be dealt with.

Basing his essay on this more comprehensive analysis, Martinson (1974) presented the reader with a series of questions—seven, to be precise—organized around the broad issue of "what works" in the context of prison reform. More specifically, Martinson posed an important question, followed by an answer, that was seemingly based on the best available empirical evidence at the time. For example, the first question posed to the reader asked,

> Isn't it true that a correctional facility running a truly rehabilitative program—one that prepares inmates for life on the outside through education and vocational training—will turn out more successful individuals than will a prison which merely leaves its inmates to rot? (p. 25)

Similarly phrased questions were not only asked about education and vocational training, but also about various forms of counseling, milieu therapy, medical treatment, community corrections, and even more traditional approaches such as increasing the level of security and length of sentence faced by inmates.

Time and again, Martinson's guided tour of the research wandered down a path ending with a similar conclusion: Prison reforms, as they existed, were quite simply unable to rehabilitate inmates in any consistent fashion. As mentioned, Martinson's tour began with an examination of the effectiveness of education and vocational training. Such training is commonplace in American prisons, and the assumption is that bettering inmates through education and providing them with skills to be employed in the marketplace will help them become a better fit in society, ultimately reducing future offending. This is certainly a worthy goal to be upheld by prisons seeking inmate reform, but can training of this nature truly reshape offenders and reduce recidivism? In reviewing the research, Martinson pointed to several studies that examined this question in the context of both young and adult males. Of the studies discussed, only one was able to demonstrate a reduction in recidivism, but this unique finding was quickly attributed to bias in the experimental group. Martinson (1974) was unable to explain why education and vocational programs were failing, but he was able to ensure the reader that "[w]hat we do know is that, to date, education and skill development have not reduced recidivism by rehabilitating criminals" (p. 28).

Working with the assumption that education and vocational training were not adequate methods for a truly rehabilitative approach, the reader was then assisted through the varied landscape of inmate counseling, including forms of psychotherapy, individual counseling, group counseling, and a form of counseling referred to as casework. At this juncture, Martinson put forth a similar view—one that appeared to reveal little success and much failure. Though Martinson noted that some studies reported positive findings (i.e., reduced recidivism), these effects appeared to be overshadowed by the fact that other studies found no effect at all or were considered too ambiguous to be useful. Considering the *inconsistent* findings, Martinson suggested that the empirical information was of little use to policy makers who were in need of generalizable results that could be readily applied with some certainty of success.

Of course, it was very possible that treatment effects were being compromised by the typical characteristics of prison environments (e.g., stressful inmate interactions, violence, participation in prison subcultures, gang activity, etc.), and if this was the case, it would be no surprise that rehabilitation did not seem to work. Considering this shortcoming, Martinson reviewed studies of milieu therapy, or therapy that was directed toward modifying the inmates' entire correctional environment, to sidestep the issue of negative prison influences. Here, the entire focus of the inmates' new environment was that of rehabilitation—maintaining security and doling out punishment took a backseat. This prevented the undesirable situation where inmates spent a few hours a day in a treatment program, only to be immediately released back into the criminogenic environment of the prison. But even this methodology fell short according to Martinson's review of the research—once again, the reader was presented with a body of literature that was described as inconsistent and lacking encouragement.

The same story is told of efforts to rehabilitate offenders through medical treatment, harsher sentencing, and community treatment. With regard to medical treatment, the only clearly positive finding reported by Martinson surrounded the castration of sex offenders in Denmark, but despite its supposed efficacy, this form of treatment was hardly considered mainstream. Placing offenders in higher-security institutions where the environment enforces stricter controls over the inmate and incarcerating offenders for longer periods of time were also unlikely to reduce recidivism according to Martinson's analysis. Here, too, the evidence was said to be mixed, leading Martinson (1974) to claim that "[n]o more than in the case of institution type can we say that length of sentence has a clear relationship to recidivism" (p. 38). In keeping with the theme of inconsistency, the effects of community-based treatments were also reported to be mixed. Martinson did, however, present some positive news regarding the treatment of offenders in the community: Even though it failed to lower recidivism, it was cheaper than traditional methods of imprisonment.

In sum, the evidence presented by Martinson clearly suggested that rehabilitation was ineffective for reducing future criminality. What was less clear, however, was exactly *why* rehabilitation was failing to show positive results in the literature. Martinson suggested that it was possible that the methods used to evaluate the treatment programs were simply not rigorous enough to capture their benefits. Or maybe the programs themselves, he proffered, were simply not being implemented as they were intended. These considerations were both recognized as potential candidates, but Martinson left his readers with an additional possibility—one that he appeared to subscribe to himself. Martinson (1974) suggested the following:

> It may be, on the other hand, that there is a more radical flaw in our present strategies—that education at its best, or that psychotherapy at its best, cannot overcome, or even appreciably reduce, the powerful tendencies for offenders to continue in criminal behavior. (p. 49)

SOCIAL CONTEXT

Before examining the influence that Martinson's research had in the field of corrections, a close consideration of the era's social and political climate is essential. In the years preceding the publication of Martinson's work, the nation as a whole was experiencing a troublesome crime problem. For reasons that were not entirely clear, both violent and property crimes had been on the rise throughout the 1960s, and this seemingly out-of-control crisis was propelled to the forefront of social thought, political campaigns, and certainly the American news media. During 1960, the Uniform Crime Reports indicated that there were approximately 9,110 homicides, or just over 5 per every 100,000 individuals in the United States. Over the next 15 years, the number of homicides literally doubled—more than 20,000 Americans (9.8 per 100,000) were murdered in 1974, the same year that Martinson's article appeared in print (Fox & Zawitz, 2007).

When examining other violent crimes, equally if not more troubling trends emerged. Throughout the 1960s and 1970s, the rates of aggravated assault, robbery, and rape more than tripled (see Gurr, 1981, for a historical review), striking fear into many law-abiding Americans. Concerns for public safety grew alongside the rising crime rates, and the severity of the situation was further exacerbated by the characteristics of these new crimes. When examining homicides, it was clear that dispute-related homicides, where the victim and offender knew one another, had remained relatively stable. Instead, it was robbery-related homicides, where the offender and victim had no relation at all, that were on the rise (Gurr, 1981). Crimes of this nature seemed to indicate that the crisis was not just affecting wayward, risk-prone individuals, but also undeserving, innocent bystanders—*anyone* could be a potential victim.

The dramatic increase in crime had captured the attention of the American people, and not surprisingly, crime control policies became a central component of the era's political campaigns and media coverage (Cavender, 2004). Since crime had recently spiraled out of control, it was apparent that the nation required immediate action in developing an effective response. Prompted by public concerns, politicians began to offer their views of promising solutions to the crime problem. It was during the 1964 presidential campaign that "street crime" first became such a dominant political issue—one that was introduced by Republican senator and presidential candidate Barry Goldwater (Simon, 2007). Though Goldwater's campaign was ultimately unsuccessful at gaining him the presidency, the concerns he expressed about the nation's rising crime rates resonated well with the American public—so well, in fact, that after defeating Goldwater in the presidential election, Lyndon Johnson officially declared a "war on crime." Since Johnson was unable to win the war during his years as president, when Richard Nixon took office in 1969, he too declared war on crime (Walker, 2006).

The nation's crime problem remained at center stage throughout much of the 1960s and persisted as a central issue into the 1970s. After witnessing the crime rates rise continuously throughout the previous decade, despite the proclaimed "war," the media began to take an even sharper interest in the nation's crime policies (Cavender, 2004). If crime could reach what appeared to be catastrophic levels in such a short period of time, it was reasoned, something *must* have been wrong with the criminal justice system. Not surprisingly, much of the crime control debate surrounded what exactly states were doing with criminals once they got their hands on them. At this point in time, the primary emphasis of the correctional system had been to provide *correction,* or treatment, for inmates. Consequently, the goal of correctional rehabilitation became central to the discussion of crime control.

Conservative critics honed their focus on what they believed to be a profound weakness in the rehabilitative ideal—convicted criminals were being released from prison *early* rather than serving the full length of their sentences. The fact was, rehabilitating inmates was no easy enterprise. It was not always clear what the best treatment approach should be, and it was certainly not clear how long it would take to rehabilitate any given inmate. Since there was no universal formula for treating offenders, the correctional system needed considerable leeway, or flexibility, to get the job done—this flexibility came in the form of *indeterminate sentencing* (Cullen & Gilbert, 1982; Spohn, 2000). Rather than sentencing offenders to a fixed or determined period of time within the correctional system, judges sentenced offenders to a possible range of time with a minimum and maximum length of stay. For example, a burglar might be sentenced to a term of 2–10 years in prison. The use of indeterminate sentencing allowed correctional agencies (through the use of parole boards) to keep treatment-resistant offenders for lengthy periods of time in the interest of successful rehabilitation. For the less difficult offenders, however, it was common practice to provide their supervised release shortly after they served the minimum length of stay.

Conservatives looked in on this process and saw a considerably flawed system—one that had the potential to keep criminals off the streets for longer periods of time, but deliberately chose not to. To conservatives, the rehabilitative ideal, which was largely born out of the liberal Progressive movement of the early 20th century, was far too lenient (see Cullen & Gilbert, 1982; Rothman, 1980). The aim of the system was all wrong—instead of focusing on fixing offenders, conservatives believed that a better system would focus its efforts on harsh punishment, deterrence, and incapacitation. To accomplish this, however, states would need to adopt harsher *determinate* sentencing structures where offenders served out a fixed term. Rehabilitation and its reliance on the indeterminate sentence stood directly in the way of these goals.

Since the heavy focus on correctional treatment was primarily the result of a liberal movement, it was not terribly surprising to see critiques leveled from conservative camps. Criticisms aimed at rehabilitation, however, were not limited to those from the right. Progressive liberals, who in the decades past had so proudly introduced the noble ideas underlying a rehabilitative correctional system, had also begun to see critical flaws (Cullen & Gilbert, 1982). It was not that the concept of rehabilitation itself was faulty, but rather the way that it was carried out in practice. Once offenders entered the correctional system, they fell squarely under the control of the government. Unfortunately, during the 1960s and 1970s a variety of events unfolded—events that caused many American citizens to lose faith in the very government that they had previously trusted to thoughtfully rehabilitate troubled offenders.

During the mid-1960s, the United States began to escalate its involvement in the ongoing Vietnam conflict, a decision that was not well received by many Americans at the time. As more and more soldiers lost their lives to a war that many failed to understand, public unrest began to grow (Heineman, 1993). Success in Vietnam had proven hard to come by, and Americans at home began to protest further involvement by the United States. By the end of Lyndon Johnson's presidency, thousands of Americans had lost their lives to the conflict. As the war continued on, in spite of growing disapproval, trust in the government to do the right thing began to dwindle.

The unpopularity of the Vietnam War had already left a sour taste in the mouths of many Americans, but the events that took place at Kent State

University on May 4, 1970, were even more troubling (Heineman, 1993). Many Americans wanted an end to the Vietnam War, and the government, led by the Nixon administration, had promised to bring this about. When news broke that the American military had expanded its efforts beyond the borders of Vietnam and into neighboring Cambodia, further protesting and public unrest broke out. At Kent State University, hundreds of students gathered to voice their antiwar opinions. When confronted by the National Guard, the students refused to end their protest and disperse, ultimately resulting in retaliation that shocked the conscience of America. Several National Guard members opened fire into the crowd, killing four unarmed students and wounding an additional nine. If Americans previously lacked a reason to distrust their government, it appeared that ample justification had been provided.

Governmental distrust also spilled over into the management of the criminal justice system itself. The very next year in 1971, the prisoners of New York's Attica Correctional Facility began rioting over what they felt to be poor living conditions. Within a short window of time, the inmates had taken complete control of the prison, holding several correctional officers hostage (see Useem & Kimball, 1991, for an overview). The initial takeover of the prison was followed by 4 days of negotiations, and Americans watched intently as state authorities struggled with the volatile situation. After several rounds of unsuccessful negotiations, it was decided that the prison would be retaken by force. On the morning of September 13, state police shot tear gas over the walls of the prison and followed up with a hail of bullets and shotgun blasts, indiscriminately killing dozens of inmates and even the correctional officers who were being held hostage. As reports of the death toll surfaced, Americans were, once again, shocked by the draconian response of their government.

The political turmoil spawned by the unpopular War in Vietnam, the Kent State massacre, and the Attica prison riot would seem to be troubling enough, but the years leading up to the mid-1970s were also characterized by a struggle for universal civil rights. During this era, the nation endured severe growing pains as citizens worked to eliminate various sources of discrimination. The aim of a more just society created a strong emphasis on fair and equal treatment for all citizens, despite their race, sex, or religion. Civil rights battles were fought and many were won, including the passage of the Civil Rights Act of 1964, yet the nation continued to struggle with issues of social justice. Throughout the 1960s and 1970s, questions about the treatment of poor minority offenders also began to garner attention. As Walker (2006) points out, "critics labeled America's jails the 'new poorhouses'" (p. 133). Money and status appeared to be more important than guilt or innocence.

By the time 1974 came around, many citizens had become disillusioned by the American government. Under the rehabilitative ideal, state and federal authorities had been given substantial discretion in the treatment of prison inmates, but the question of whether or not government officials could be trusted with this power was of serious concern (Cullen & Gendreau, 2000, Cullen & Gilbert, 1982). For many liberals—particularly *justice model* liberals who sought equality—the answer was an emphatic *no.* So, while conservatives believed that rehabilitation was too lenient, liberals of the era came to believe that it was a source of grave injustice. In the words of Cullen and Gendreau,

> For liberals, the discretion given to state officials was applied inequitably and coercively. In their eyes, judges were free to discriminate against poor and minority offenders, while parole boards used their discretion to punish offenders who challenged the status quo of an inhumane prison regime. (p. 122)

In the end, the social and political climate that emerged during the 1960s and 1970s cast considerable doubt over the appropriateness of correctional rehabilitation as the primary goal of American corrections. So, when Martinson's (1974) research announced that correctional treatment was essentially a defunct enterprise, the nation saw the perfect opportunity to legitimately sound the death knell for rehabilitation.

GETTING THE WORD OUT

There is no doubt that Martinson's research was released at a time when the nation was willing to listen, but this alone is rarely enough for most scientific endeavors—especially those of the social science flavor—to generate a powerful impact. Previous scholars reflecting on the influence of the Martinson Report have pointed out that his findings alone were not as revolutionary as one might think (Cavender, 2004; Cullen & Gendreau, 2000; Cullen & Gilbert, 1982). In fact, Martinson was not even the first social scientist of the era to publish research suggesting that rehabilitation did not work. A few years earlier, in 1966, Walter Bailey published a study summarizing 100 reports pertaining to correctional treatment. Ultimately, he drew very similar conclusions to Martinson, seriously questioning the effectiveness of rehabilitation programs. In 1971, two researchers by the names of James Robison and Gerald Smith published an assessment of treatment programs in California. Their findings also challenged the efficacy of rehabilitation programs, but it seemed that no one was listening. Like Bailey's work, theirs was also greeted with relative silence.

So why did Martinson, who essentially offered a similar view to prior researchers, gain so much attention for his work? Martinson's article appeared in print a few years later than the previously discussed works, and the social conditions were that much riper for change. Even so, it would appear that there was more to the story. Yes, Martinson drew similar conclusions to previous scholars, but he did do a few things differently.

First, he published his findings in a journal called *The Public Interest.* The journal was not heralded for its scientific objectivity, but it did carry the voice of prominent thinkers, including Harvard professor James Q. Wilson who also spoke out against the rehabilitation ideal. As such, *The Public Interest* was better poised to reach a larger audience and potentially yield a larger influence in the field. By way of contrast, Bailey's (1966) and Robison and Smith's (1971) research findings were published in more specialized academic journals. In fact, Robison and Smith's work appeared in *Crime & Delinquency,* a peer-reviewed journal that was, and remains, highly regarded in academia. However, even though the journal had an emphasis on publishing only the highest quality research, its audience was not as broad or far reaching as that of *The Public Interest.*

Martinson was successful in getting his findings out to a relatively large audience, but in this particular instance, he also avoided a shortcoming that is very prevalent in the world of academic research. Many social scientists work diligently to conduct studies and provide answers to important questions, but more often than not, their work is written for other academics. These researchers tend to get excited about advancing a particular body of knowledge, but frequently forget about connecting their research to the "real world" in any meaningful way. As Martinson drafted his manuscript for publication, it would seem that he deliberately avoided this shortcoming. Instead of filling his manuscript with technical jargon, he carefully crafted his thoughts around simple yet important questions that would generate the interest of not only specialists, but nearly any layperson as well. In addition, the mere fact that his research was organized around a series of questions meant that he was clearly providing the reader with a series of *answers.* This is exactly what practitioners desire when it comes to interpreting research—everything was clearly spelled out, and special skills were not required to decrypt the important information. Of course, if the questions are of significant importance and the answers are clearly provided, policy decisions are that much easier to make. Under these circumstances, study findings have a better chance of creating real-world impacts.

This strategy was fairly successful, as by the very next year, in 1975, Martinson's study had garnered so much attention that he was invited to appear on *60 Minutes* to share his findings with the nation. In a recent analysis of media effects on crime policy, researcher Gray Cavender (2004) recapped Martinson's appearance: The segment was placed in the context of the nation's rising crime rates, and Martinson was asked several questions about the effectiveness of rehabilitation. When asked whether or not these programs work, Martinson informed the host, Mike Wallace, along with millions of viewers, that treatment programs "have no fundamental effect" on offenders. In the end, Martinson was able to successfully disseminate his research among not only researchers, but also practitioners, policy makers, and even the general public.

THE INFLUENCE OF THE MARTINSON REPORT

Considering the social context of the 1960s and 1970s along with Martinson's strategy for disseminating his findings, it is clear that his work was well positioned to powerfully influence the world of offender rehabilitation. Correctional treatment had already developed a tarnished reputation and fallen from the favor of many Americans. Since it was not only disliked, but, according to the latest science, also ineffective, it seemed the perfect opportunity for many to abandon rehabilitation altogether. Of course, abandoning rehabilitation meant that there had to be some other more favorable strategy waiting in the wings to take its place. Remember, conservatives viewed rehabilitation as simply a slap on the wrist—criminals were getting out of prison too quickly and would-be criminals went undeterred by this unnecessary leniency. In the end, conservatives wanted harsher punishment for offenders, and this meant that indeterminate sentencing would need to be replaced by determinate sentencing where criminals were kept behind bars for fixed terms. Liberals were not seeking harsher punishment as much as they were seeking equity in the treatment of offenders, but as it turned out, determinate sentencing seemed to offer a solution to this as well. Criminals would be treated more harshly, but with predetermined sentences; judges would have far less discretion; and the seemingly discriminatory parole boards could be eliminated altogether. After all, if a precise sentence is determined ahead of time, what use would parole boards have? This approach, then, was able to simultaneously satisfy *both* conservatives and the justice model liberals (Cullen & Gendreau, 2000).

With a new vision in place, the criminal justice system was destined for serious reform, and this is precisely what took place in the years following Martinson's work. Rehabilitation was trumped by the desire for retribution and just deserts, and states began to rapidly adopt new laws with this aim in mind (Rothman, 1980; Spohn, 2000; Walker, 1993). These new regulations marked the end of the indeterminate sentence for many states and came in the form of sentencing guidelines, presumptive sentencing structures, mandatory minimum sentences, truth-in-sentencing statutes, and three-strikes laws. Sentencing guidelines, which were adopted by many of the states and the federal government, provided judges with a "grid" based on the offender's prior record and offense seriousness (Spohn, 2000). Using these two factors, the appropriate sentence could simply be "looked up" and applied to each offender that came before the court. Other similar presumptive sentencing structures also limited the options available to judges, substantially reducing their discretion.

Though both of these approaches were aimed at creating equity in the criminal justice system, most of the emphasis was placed on creating a system with more *bite.* Mandatory minimum sentencing statutes were passed by most states to ensure that offenders who engaged in certain crimes (usually violent or drug-related crimes) would receive more substantial sentences. These laws were successful at keeping prisoners behind bars for longer periods of time, but offenders were still able to earn an early release through "good time" or "good behavior," sometimes cutting their sentences in half or better. To limit the effect of good time incentives, "truth in sentencing" laws were enacted by many states to guarantee or mandate that offenders serve a certain portion of their sentence behind bars, typically 85 percent or more. Other states have gone even further by eliminating good time altogether, mandating that 100 percent of the sentence be served (Ditton & Wilson, 1999). "Three strikes" laws, which began to appear in the early 1990s, seemed to fully embody the powerful shift that had taken place in the criminal justice system. Washington State was the first to pass such a statute, but it was California's "three strikes and you're out" law that garnered national attention (Walker, 2006). These politically popular statutes put into place mandatory life sentences for offenders convicted of a third felony. Significant changes to the criminal justice system were clearly underway.

Parole, which had been integral to American corrections for most of the 19th century, rapidly transformed to accommodate the onslaught of new determinate sentencing laws. Prior to the mid-1970s, the process of inmate release was fairly universal in that states and the federal government relied on the decision making of parole boards (Rothman, 1980). Once an offender had served the minimum portion of his or her sentence, the individual became eligible for release, and parole boards held the authority to make this decision. The discretionary release of offenders by parole boards, however, quickly morphed into a mandatory release mechanism in many states, where offenders were automatically discharged, but only after they completed their full sentence (minus acquired good time), as prescribed by law. In 1977, approximately three-quarters of all offenders were released at the discretion of a parole board—this figure dropped to just under one-quarter by the late 1990s (Petersilia, 2003). Once released, the remainder of the sentence was carried out in the community under parole supervision, but this too began to take on a different form. Parole was originally designed to assist inmates with community reintegration, since transitioning out of prison was rarely an easy task. The prevailing social climate, however, refocused the emphasis of parole around more intense supervision for the purpose of catching recidivists and returning them to prison (Petersilia, 2003).

The abandonment of rehabilitation for the renewed goals of retribution, incapacitation, and deterrence has certainly yielded important procedural changes to the correctional arena, but probably the most pronounced effect of this movement has been the unprecedented growth of the prison industry (Austin & Irwin, 2001; Pratt, 2009). Prior to the reforms that began in the mid-1970s, the punishment trends in America had been relatively stable (Clear, 1994). However, when the new "get tough" policies began to take effect, this changed in dramatic ways. During the following decade, between 1980 and 1990, the incarceration rate more than doubled, from 139 to nearly 300 per 100,000 citizens, and it has currently risen to more than *500* per 100,000 citizens (West & Sabol, 2008). With more than 2.3 million people behind bars, the United States now operates the world's largest prison system (Pratt, 2009; Walker, 2006). In fact, the prison system has become so large that many states have considerable trouble housing their massive inmate populations (Franklin, Franklin, & Pratt, 2006).

It should be noted that these profound changes to the American criminal justice system did not go unchallenged. Very early on, several scholars directly confronted the notion that rehabilitation was a failed enterprise. The next year, Palmer (1975) published an article refuting Martinson's report. According to Martinson, none of the different treatment *types* (e.g., education, counseling, milieu therapy) were able to *consistently* reduce recidivism—within each of the different treatment modalities, some studies reported success while others did not. To Martinson, this indicated an overall failure. Palmer's reanalysis of the very same studies, however, revealed that nearly *half* of them demonstrated reductions in recidivism. Looked at this way, it was more difficult to argue that rehabilitation had *no fundamental effect* on offender behavior. If nothing worked, how could half of the studies mentioned in Martinson's (1974) article show reductions in recidivism? Although this was an important question, the prevailing social climate was not exactly demanding an answer. A few years later, even Martinson himself realized that his article had been somewhat exaggerated, and in a later work entitled *New Findings, New Views: A Note of Caution Regarding Sentencing Reform* (1979), he withdrew his heavy-handed "nothing works" position (see Cullen & Gendreau, 2000). Not surprisingly, even his recant was virtually ignored.

CONCLUSION

When Robert Martinson's (1974) article first appeared in print, it drew almost immediate attention from scholars, policy makers, practitioners, and even popular media outlets. His work provided the scientific foundation for what was to become one of the most significant shifts in modern American corrections. It is certainly rare for any single piece of research to mobilize such powerful changes, and in the case of Martinson's work, it has been demonstrated that there was much more to the situation than an important set of research findings. Instead, a combination of favorable factors had converged to elevate Martinson's work to one of the most important pieces of research in recent criminal justice history. In the mid-1970s, the social and political climate was ripe for change. Both conservatives *and* liberals were prepared to abandon rehabilitation, though for different reasons. Conservatives were fed up with rehabilitation because it was "soft on crime." Liberals, on the other hand, were angered by the excessive discretion afforded to less-than-trustworthy judicial and correctional officials in the name of rehabilitation. It was at this time that Martinson's article appeared in print, essentially claiming that "nothing works" in the realm of correctional treatment. Martinson was successful in communicating his findings, and once they reached the public domain, his results spread with intensity. As it turned out, his research was precisely what was needed by those who had already grown averse to the rehabilitative ideal, and in the end, it served as the *scientific justification* for both the abandonment of rehabilitation and the birth of the "tough on crime" criminal justice system of today.

DISCUSSION QUESTIONS

1. Why was it that during the 1970s many conservatives disliked rehabilitation and its reliance on the indeterminate sentence?
2. Why did many liberals, who have traditionally stood behind the use of rehabilitation, disfavor its use in the 1970s?
3. What was the impact of Martinson's (1974) work on the practice of corrections in America?

REFERENCES

Austin, J., & Irwin, J. (2001). *It's about time: America's imprisonment binge.* Belmont, CA: Wadsworth.

Bailey, W. (1966). Correctional outcome: An evaluation of 100 reports. *Journal of Criminal Law, Criminology, and Police Science, 57,* 153–160.

Cavender, G. (2004). Media and crime policy: A reconstruction of David Garland's *The Culture of Control. Punishment & Society, 6*(3), 335–348.

Clear, T. (1994). *Harm in American penology: Offenders, victims, and their communities.* Albany: State University of New York Press.

Cullen, F., & Gendreau, P. (2000). Assessing correctional rehabilitation: Policy, practice, and prospects. In J. Horney (Ed.), *Criminal justice 2000* (Vol. 3, pp. 109–176). Washington DC: National Institute of Justice, U.S. Department of Justice.

Cullen, F., & Gilbert, K. (1982). *Reaffirming rehabilitation.* Cincinnati, OH: Anderson.

Ditton, P., & Wilson, D. J. (1999). *Truth in sentencing in state prisons.* Washington, DC: U.S. Department of Justice, Bureau of Justice Statistics.

Fox, J., & Zawitz, M. (2007). *Homicide trends in the United States.* Washington, DC: U.S. Department of Justice, Bureau of Justice Statistics.

Franklin, T. W., Franklin, C. A., & Pratt, T. C. (2006). The effect of prison crowding on prison violence: A meta-analysis of conflicting empirical research results. *Journal of Criminal Justice, 34*(4), 401–412.

Gurr, T. (1981). Historical trends in violent crime: A critical review of the evidence. In M. Tonry (Ed.), *Crime and justice: A review of research* (Vol. 3, pp. 295–353). Chicago: University of Chicago Press.

Heineman, K. (1993). *Campus wars: The peace movement at American state universities in the Vietnam era.* New York: New York University Press.

Lipton, D. S., Martinson, R., & Wilks, J. (1975). *The effectiveness of correctional treatment: A survey of treatment evaluation studies*. New York: Praeger.

Martinson, R. (1974). What works? Questions and answers about prison reform. *The Public Interest, 35,* 22–54.

Martinson, R. (1979). New findings, new views: A note of caution regarding sentencing reform. *Hofstra Law Review, 7,* 243–258.

Palmer, T. (1975). Martinson revisited. *Journal of Research in Crime and Delinquency, 12*(2), 133–152.

Petersilia, J. (2003). *When prisoners come home: Parole and prisoner reentry.* New York: Oxford University Press.

Pratt, T. C. (2009). *Addicted to incarceration: Corrections policy and the politics of misinformation in the United States.* Thousand Oaks, CA: Sage.

Robison, J., & Smith, G. (1971). The effectiveness of correctional programs. *Crime & Delinquency, 17*(1), 67–80.

Rothman, D. (1980). *Conscience and convenience: The asylum and its alternatives in progressive America.* Boston: Little, Brown.

Simon, J. (2007). *Governing through crime: How the war on crime transformed American democracy and created a culture of fear.* New York: Oxford University Press.

Spohn, C. (2000). Thirty years of sentencing reform: The quest for a racially neutral sentencing process. *Criminal Justice 2000, 3,* 427–501.

Useem, B., & Kimball, P. (1991). *States of siege: U.S. prison riots, 1971–1986.* New York: Oxford University Press.

Walker, S. (1993). *Taming the system: The control of discretion in criminal justice, 1950–1990.* New York: Oxford University Press.

Walker, S. (2006). *Sense and nonsense about crime and drugs: A policy guide.* Belmont, CA: Wadsworth.

West, H., & Sabol, W. (2008). *Prisoners in 2007.* Washington DC: U.S. Department of Justice, Bureau of Justice Statistics.

SEVEN

KEY IDEA: CRIME CONTROL THROUGH SELECTIVE INCAPACITATION

KEY WORKS

Wilson, J. Q. (1975). *Thinking about crime.* New York: Basic Books.

Wilson, J. Q. (1983b). *Thinking about crime* (2nd ed.). New York: Vintage Books.

James Q. Wilson has been and continues to be a prolific presence in criminal justice and criminology. He ranks among the most oft-cited people in the field (Cohn & Farrington, 1994; Wright, 1995). Wilson is not—and candidly admits as much—a criminologist; he is a political scientist and policy scholar. He is today considered one of the most influential persons in 20th-century criminal justice and criminology, and this fame is attributed largely, though not solely, to his 1975 book *Thinking About Crime* (Laub, 2003). This book became a key work in criminology and criminal justice because it advocated the use of selective incapacitation to paralyze high-rate, recidivistic offenders. Wilson argued that prisons can reduce crime and that society can protect itself from chronic criminals by using institutional space strategically and targeting the "worst of the worst." Policy makers and the public were instantly seduced by this purported solution to crime, and academics launched a campaign of research into the issue that continues to this day. This chapter is devoted to Wilson's selective incapacitation thesis and the reasons why this idea became a turning point in the history of criminal justice and criminology.

THE CONTEXT: CRIMINOLOGY, CRIMINAL JUSTICE POLICY, AND SOCIETY IN THE 1970s

Criminological research progressed through many stages during the 1900s, each of which can be loosely characterized as an "era" (Laub, 2003). At the turn of the 20th century, criminologists' attention was on individual behavior patterns. Although Cesare Lombroso's ideas had been discarded (see Chapter 3 of this book), focus was still on individual-level analyses and longitudinal data-collection methods. Researchers tracked groups of people over time to study their behavior throughout their lives. This person-focused paradigm lost favor in the first few decades of the 1900s, though. By the end of the 1930s, an era of macro-level criminology—helmed by Merton's strain theory and Shaw and McKay's theory of social disorganization—had arisen (Lilly, Cullen, & Ball, 2007; see also Chapter 4 of this book). The macro-level tradition attributed crime to poverty, the chaos of explosive urbanization, and the fact that the American "Dream" was a living nightmare for the scores of immigrants, rural farmers, and Southern blacks who flocked to cities in search of better lives only to be met with crushing labor, low wages, and slum tenements. Beginning in the 1930s and continuing for the next several decades, criminology was dominated by sociological theories of crime (Laub, 2003).

In 1972, though, something happened that would fracture criminologists and send some of them off in a different direction. This was the year that Marvin Wolfgang and his colleagues published the now-famous Philadelphia study, *Delinquency in a Birth Cohort* (Wolfgang, Figlio, & Sellin, 1972), and longitudinal research was thus reinvigorated and ready to recapture its venerated position in the field (Laub, 2003; Lilly et al., 2007). The most famous and influential of Wolfgang et al.'s findings was the fact that a large portion of the total crime committed by the cohort was produced by a very small number of people in the group. Criminologists had known about the existence of habitual offenders for decades (Gottfredson & Hirschi, 1986), but Wolfgang et al. reintroduced the idea and renewed interest in it with the level of detail and insight they offered (Barnett & Lofaso, 1985; Walker, 2001). This study provided a crucial piece of information about the distribution of criminal offending that would become the foundation of the concept of "career criminals" in the ensuing years (Laub, 2003). Such was the state of criminology in the 1970s.

Criminal justice policy, for its part, has also followed a life course trajectory throughout the past century. Its history is characterized by fads about crime and punishment that arrive suddenly, become wildly popular almost overnight, and then flicker out as interest wanes. Each one has promised great things in the areas of crime control, fairness, and fiscal responsibility, and each one has failed, on the whole, to deliver (Blackmore & Welsh, 1983). The Classical School of criminology (see Chapter 2 of this book), which began in the late 1700s, dominated the original construction of criminal sentencing policy in the United States and helped the penitentiary rise as a predominant method of criminal punishment. Incarceration replaced corporal penalties (e.g., whipping) as a more humane alternative.

By the turn of the 20th century, prisons came to be seen as conduits through which reform could be delivered to its occupants, and during the first half of the 1900s, penology was devoted to the rehabilitation ideal (see Chapter 6). Correctional policy employed indeterminate sentencing to accommodate the perceived need for judges and parole boards to wield tremendous discretion (Clear, 1994). In the 1960s, though, a steady stream of research seeming to show no relationship between rehabilitation and subsequent criminal behavior eroded public and academic confidence in the system's ability to furnish effective interventions for prisoners (Blumstein, 1983a, 1983b; Martinson, 1974; for a review, see Pratt, 2009). The country again turned to sentence length as a solution to crime under the assumption that the amount of time offenders spent in prison was more important than what they did while awaiting the expiration of their sentence (Rothman, 1983; see also Blumstein & Nagin, 1978). The rehabilitation model and indeterminate sentencing were on the chopping block.

The social context of the 1970s is also important to understand in order to fully appreciate the reasons for *Thinking About Crime*'s popularity. The 1960s and 1970s were tumultuous years in the United States. The government faced a crisis of legitimacy. The civil rights movement, the feminist movement, the deinstitutionalization movement, and the Vietnam debacle resulted in an outpouring of people's grievances against the government. At the same time, crime was on an upward trend. Violent crime in particular started to ravage inner-city areas and take a toll on youth and young adult populations across the nation (Blumstein, 2000). The public blamed policy makers for failing to protect society.

Policy makers were unsure what to do. In the decades leading up to the 1960s, experts in criminology, psychology, social work, and other academic fields were considered the preeminent authorities on policy (Rothman, 1983; see also Wilson, 1975, 1983b). During this time period, it was generally agreed upon in the academic community that crime resulted from systemic problems like poverty, joblessness, and lack of funding for inner-city schools. When asked for policy advice, criminologists advocated strategies to address macro-level criminogenic conditions like poverty and low education, and politicians responded by endorsing antipoverty campaigns (Wilson, 1983b). Crime rates, though, kept rising. Nothing seemed to be working.

The presidency of Richard Nixon—followed by that of Ronald Reagan—spawned fundamental and lasting change in the politics of crime control. Under the banner of laissez-faire capitalism and governmental minimalism, these presidents gutted social welfare programs and demanded more punitive criminal sanctions. Individual choice became the country's new idol. The belief began spreading that people who committed crimes did so because they were selfish and immoral and because they believed the benefits of crime outweighed the costs. In somewhat of a historical irony, then, popular views on crime came full circle and landed right where they had been 200 years prior—at the micro level (Lilly et al., 2007; see also Garland, 2001). The stage was set for someone to step in and offer a new anticrime proposal that reflected the fervent individualism that now dominated political and policy arenas.

JAMES Q. WILSON'S *THINKING ABOUT CRIME*

James Q. Wilson was a recognized name in many crime policy circles by the time the first edition of *Thinking About Crime* appeared in 1975. He had written the influential book *Varieties of Police Behavior* (1968) and had served on various government-sponsored crime policy panels. When his 1975 book hit the shelves, people bought it.

The cover of the revised and expanded second edition of Wilson's *Thinking About Crime* (1983b) bears a quote from *Fortune* magazine describing the book as "A powerful indictment of the American criminal-justice system," but this description is not entirely accurate. Wilson certainly heaped criticism upon existing criminal justice system policies, but his real indictment was of criminologists as sources of crime policy that, in his view, had been nothing short of abject failure. In both editions of *Thinking About Crime,* Wilson blamed criminologists and uncritical politicians for what he claimed was a single-minded (even downright opinionated) focus on poverty and social inequality as the primary driving forces behind crime. He declared himself a staunch critic of criminological theories of crime (1975, 1983b; see also 1983a; Wilson & Petersilia, 2004), and he adopted a vehemently antiacademic stance (see also Laub, 2003; Zimring, 1995). He alleged that a devastating paucity of empiricism rendered criminologists' input into public policy virtually useless and that the rising crime rate could be stemmed only by a policy-driven proposal that dispensed with the sticky issues of crime causation (see also Wilson, 2004) and instead concentrated on the question of what to do about those individuals who break the law. The recurring theme was that the so-called "root causes" of crime were irrelevant and that what was needed were practical public policies.

Wilson's policy essays in *Thinking About Crime* are topically diverse, but the element that ultimately fascinated the public most was his conviction that incarceration reduces crime. He justified incarceration on grounds of incapacitation, though he stated that it also served the ends of deterrence and retribution as well. Incapacitation theory holds that crime can be reduced by physically preventing offenders from recidivating. Although incapacitation can be effected with strategies ranging from intensive-supervision probation to chemical restraints to lobotomies, imprisonment is the most popular and mainstream modality (Clear & Barry, 1983).

Incapacitation (via imprisonment) is a seemingly simple, straightforward, and intuitive theory of crime reduction. Wilson's choice of imprisonment as his favored crime-reduction policy was deliberate—it comported perfectly with his assertion that effective crime policy need not be concerned with the root sources of crime. Under the rubric of incapacitation, offenders' criminality can be quelled without ever broaching the issue of the source(s) of their offending. Wilson touted the findings of Wolfgang et al. (1972) and other researchers who had offered evidence of the existence of career criminals who offend repeatedly and contribute disproportionately to the crime problem. The 1975 edition of *Thinking About Crime* promised crime reductions of up to two-thirds if incapacitation were used to physically put an end to criminals' careers. This proposition got people's attention and sparked further research into the idea that these criminals might be identified early on in their careers and targeted for incapacitation. One of the most influential of these research efforts was that by RAND Corporation researchers (see, e.g., Chaiken & Chaiken, 1983, 1984; Greenwood, 1983). Under the auspices of RAND and inspired in part by *Thinking About Crime,* these researchers set out to gather more information about habitual offenders (Walker, 2001). Wilson used the findings by RAND and other groups (e.g., the Institute for Law and Social Research, or INSLAW) as a springboard for expanding his selective incapacitation thesis in the second edition of *Thinking About Crime* (1983b).

There are two types of incapacitation—collective and selective—and Wilson considered both of them. *Collective incapacitation* entails the incarceration of all offenders under the assumption that they are likely to continue offending. Wilson was quick to reject this model. He explained that collective incapacitation has several problems that limit its usefulness and feasibility as crime policy. The foremost downfall is that an indiscriminant incarceration policy that imprisons all manner of offenders would require exponential increases in prison populations in order to achieve even modest drops in crime. Prisons would have to be stuffed full, which would be cost-prohibitive and would raise serious human rights objections. Wilson (1983b) argued that blunt, unrefined strategies like collective incarceration are unnecessary because the Wolfgang et al. (1972) study, the RAND and INSLAW teams' findings, and other criminal career research offered promise of a more sophisticated and effective sentencing policy: *selective incapacitation.* Wilson contended that honing in on high-rate offenders would allow scarce prison space to be used strategically so as to maximize the crime-reduction potential of every precious cell.

The obvious next question was how these high-rate offenders would be identified so that selective incapacitation could be parlayed from a neat idea into actual policy. Wilson had an answer ready based on the findings of RAND and INSLAW. Each group had identified sets of factors that they believed distinguished high-rate from low-rate offenders. The items comprising the two prediction scales differed somewhat but overlapped in the themes that high-rate offenders tend to be young, often have a history of drug use, and probably started offending as juveniles (Wilson, 1983b; see also Chaiken & Chaiken, 1983, 1984; Greenwood, 1983). Some RAND researchers—most notably, Peter Greenwood—announced unequivocally (and prematurely, it later turned out) that these correlates could be used to identify the high-rate offenders who generated the most crime (Blackmore & Welsh, 1983; von Hirsch, 1984; see also Barnett & Lofaso, 1985). Wilson (1983b) was somewhat more circumspect about the issue. He noted that more research would be needed before selective incapacitation could be translated into policy, but he endorsed the idea nonetheless.

WHY IT CAUGHT ON

There are many reasons why *Thinking About Crime* was so influential, and they can be grouped into six themes. First, as described above and in Chapter 6, the country was disillusioned with correctional rehabilitation. The collapse of the rehabilitation regime was a vital force in *Thinking About Crime*'s rise to fame because it created an opportunity for Wilson and other conservative commentators, analysts, and politicians to push for expanded use of punitive sanctions (Cullen, 2004). While criminologists, by and large, thought the premise that crime could be effectively managed through the manipulation of sanctions ranked only slightly above voodoo on the list of plausible solutions to the problem (see Lilly et al., 2007), policy makers assured the public that the national volume of offending was indeed amenable to change via the shaping of penalty structures.

During the 1960s, too, prisons were becoming crowded, wardens' and guards' institutional control over inmates was slipping, and prisoner litigation concerning conditions of confinement was on the rise (Gottfredson & Gottfredson, 1985; von Hirsch, 1984). The country was in the market for a new sentencing scheme, and Wilson's selective incapacitation thesis was timed perfectly to capitalize on this transition. Had *Thinking About Crime* appeared just a few years earlier when rehabilitation still reigned or a few years later after some other sentencing plan had taken rehabilitation's place, selective incapacitation might have slipped quietly and unceremoniously into the waters of public opinion. Due to optimal timing, though, Wilson's thesis cannonballed smack into the middle of a paradigm shift, virtually guaranteeing itself a good deal of attention.

A second reason for the success of the selective incapacitation thesis was that Wilson (1975, 1983b) recognized and addressed the nation's desire for short-term solutions to the crime problem. He spoke directly to the private citizens, political officials, and other nonexperts who were waiting impatiently for fast results (see Blackmore & Welsh, 1983; Chaiken & Chaiken, 1984). Criminologists have always attempted to reason with policy makers and the public by saying that it takes time for long-term, large-scale crime reduction strategies like social welfare programs and offender rehabilitation efforts to produce visible signs of success. Some have also argued that true crime reduction can come only with fundamental changes in the social, economic, and political landscape. Appeals to complex, long-term solutions do not go over well with a country itching for quick fixes, though. Wilson dismissed criminologists' assertions on the matter and proclaimed that success is within reach. Prisons, he said, already exist, and sentencing structures are in place to send people there. His was an immediate solution designed to reap benefits *now,* not at some unspecified time in the possibly distant future.

A third reason for Wilson's popularity lies in the distinctly "everyman" appeal of selective incapacitation. The policy is intuitive and seems to make perfect sense; in Wilson's (1983b) words, incapacitation "works by definition" (p. 145). If a small proportion of all offenders are responsible for a disproportionately large chunk of crime, then locking them away would make society safer (see also Greenwood, 1983). It was not, moreover, just sentencing decisions to which the thesis could be applied—selective incapacitation could be used by police making arrest decisions, by prosecutors making charge decisions, and by judges making bail decisions (Forst, 1983; Greenwood, 1983). To critical academic audiences, selective incapacitation is based on dubious—even faulty—assumptions (see the following section), but to the lay public, selective incapacitation is a self-evident solution to crime.

Fourth, Wilson (1975; 1983b) framed selective incapacitation as being palatable to people of all political orientations. Political conservatives had (and still have) a penchant for believing that incarceration reduces crime and is therefore worthy policy (Cullen, 2007; see also Lilly et al., 2007), so a proposal premised on an incarcerative strategy had innate appeal to that group. Wilson (1983b) claimed, though, that it was not just conservatives who would support selective incapacitation—prison critics would support it, too, because it would ensure long prison sentences for those high-rate, dangerous offenders that "even the most determined opponents of prison would probably concede should be behind bars" (p. 158). He sweetened the deal even further by explaining that if high-rate offenders were put behind bars for long stretches of time, low-rate offenders could start being offered shorter prison sentences in order to control institutional populations, keep correctional costs manageable, and make sentencing more just. Selective incapacitation seemed to offer crime control, cost control, and greater fairness all at once.

A fifth selling point was that selective incapacitation offers a veneer of scientific validity (Mathiesen, 1998). Some proponents spun selective incarceration as the only sentencing strategy that does not require the application of morals, ethics, opinions, or other fallible human value judgments; to the contrary, they argued, it is a science-based system in which penalties can be computed numerically using statistical models to make neutral, detached, rational sentencing decisions (see von Hirsch, 1984). Sentencing could be based upon objective criteria rather than upon the idiosyncratic morality of the masses or the whimsical, discretionary, and possibly biased predilections of judges and parole boards (Greenwood, 1983; see also Clear, 1994). As Peter Greenwood, one of the original and most avid proponents of selective incapacitation put it, "[O]f course courts and parole boards have always in practice considered future dangerousness in sentencing and release decisions. . . . Selective incapacitation does not alter this practice; it merely seeks to base predictions on objective evidence" (p. 263). It seemed to many that selective incapacitation did away with fluffy philosophy about the nature and ethics of punishment in favor of empirical, fact-based sentencing.[1]

A final reason that Wilson's selective incapacitation thesis gained widespread popularity and credibility is that no one from the academic community openly challenged it. In *Thinking About Crime* and in his other books and essays, Wilson threw several punches at criminologists, but criminologists never punched back (Laub, 2003). Internally, the scientific field of criminology and criminal justice bustled with activity pertaining to Wilson's selective incapacitation thesis, and knowledgeable experts immediately identified numerous devastating flaws in selective incapacitation. Their analyses and critiques, though, were couched in jargon and tucked away in academic journals rather than packaged in a parlance and medium accessible to the public. Nobody offered the criminological counter-thesis to *Thinking About Crime* or publicly dismantled the selective incapacitation argument. They very well could have, but they did not, and their silence permitted Wilson's thesis to go unchallenged in the mass media, political discussions, and other public policy forums.

SELECTIVE INCAPACITATION'S EFFECT ON CRIMINAL JUSTICE AND CRIMINOLOGY: EMPIRICAL TESTS, EMPIRICAL CRITIQUES, AND ETHICAL DILEMMAS

The two releases of *Thinking About Crime* (1975 and 1983) helped kill the already exsanguinated rehabilitation ideal and usher in the conservative crime control movement that still dominates in the United States today.

Wilson's (1975, 1983b) strong stance against academia (Laub, 2003; Zimring, 1995) also contributed to and seemed to offer validation for the anti-intellectualism prevalent among the lay public and politicians, whom academics have criticized for routinely eschewing scientific findings in favor of anecdotes and personal opinions (Cullen, 2004; Laub, 2003). Wilson assisted conservative lawmakers' efforts to eject criminology experts from the policy realm.

Despite its initial popularity, Wilson's thesis ultimately became fodder for the get-tough, pro-prison movement. He argued for the superiority of selective incapacitation over its collective counterpart, but even as policy makers and the public voiced support for the former, they adopted the latter. Selective incapacitation is a punitive strategy, but apparently it was not punitive enough to satisfy public demands for ever-harsher criminal penalties. Wilson's proposed strategy offered a bridge between rehabilitation and mass incarceration—he legitimized the use of prison as a crime-control strategy and helped shift penology away from rehabilitation and toward punishment, but once policy makers and the public had tasted punishment, they wanted more than selective incapacitation could give them.

In fact, so-called "wars" on crime and drugs have supplanted anything resembling selectivity in sentencing. The number of crimes for which prison is an authorized penalty skyrocketed during the 1980s and 1990s, sentences for all prison-eligible crimes increased dramatically, and drug offenders took center stage as targets for harsh incarceration policies (Blumstein, 2004; Clear, 1994) that utilize mandatory minimums and conspiracy laws (Gaskins, 2004). Mass—not selective—incarceration is the sentencing strategy the United States uses today (see, for example, Clear, 1994; Currie, 1998; Garland, 2001; Lilly et al., 2007; Pratt, 2009).[2] When the subject of prison crowding arises before legislative bodies, the proposed solution is almost always to build more correctional facilities rather than to reduce the number or length of prison sentences (Sherman & Hawkins, 1981). Policy makers still talk about career criminals and selective incapacitation, and these concepts have become ingrained in crime policy (Walker, 2001), but use of these terms to refer to current sentencing policies is misleading. True selective incapacitation of the sort Wilson envisioned never came to fruition.

The attention that academics in criminal justice and criminology paid to Wilson's selective incapacitation is best described as preemptive. In the years following the publication of *Thinking About Crime,* the popular media, political reports, and other policy voices expressed enough interest in Wilson's ideas to give academics the impression that selective incapacitation just might gain a foothold and become official sentencing policy (Blumstein, 1983b; von Hirsch, 1984). Federal dollars from numerous agencies initially poured into selective incapacitation research (Clear, 1994; see also Gottfredson & Hirschi, 1986), and incapacitation was at the forefront of stated penological goals (Galvin, 1983; Walker, 2001).

Entranced by the career criminal concept and anticipating the potential policy impact of Wilson's thesis, academics launched investigations and produced a frenzy of research and commentary. For a time, career criminals and selective incapacitation dominated the criminological research agenda to the near exclusion of every other topic. The career criminal concept reached the level of dogma in the discipline, primarily because it had direct policy implications and academics were trying to stay ahead of the curve and secure as much government grant money as possible (Gottfredson & Hirschi, 1986).

Selective incapacitation's impact on criminal justice and criminology is highlighted most poignantly in the ongoing search for the Holy Grail of selective incapacitation—a number called "lambda" (e.g., Copas & Tarling, 1988; Horney & Marshall, 1991; Loeber & Snyder, 1990; Marvell & Moody, 1994). Lambda (λ) is the rate at which an individual criminal offends and it is used to estimate the crime-reduction effect of incapacitating that person. If λ is the number of crimes someone perpetrates per year and "Z" is the number of years for which that person is incarcerated, then the incapacitation effect "I" for that person is: $I = Z\,\lambda$.[3] The incapacitative effect is maximized when both λ and Z are high.

It seems simple enough, but crippling pitfalls are encountered when one starts digging. The first vexing issue is how to find out what λ really is, as its definition has thus far evaded the grasp of even the most sophisticated statistical models; quite simply, nobody knows how many crimes offenders commit per year (e.g., Blumstein, 1983a, 1983b; Clear & Barry, 1983; Gottfredson & Hirschi, 1986; Piquero, Farrington, & Blumstein, 2003). Lambda's elusiveness hinders efforts to estimate the effect of incarceration on crime (Gottfredson & Hirschi, 1986; Miles & Ludwig, 2007; Spelman, 2000; see also Rosenfeld, 2000).

Measurement problems have impeded the search for λ. One source of confusion concerns whether lambda should be measured using official arrest records, conviction data, or offenders' self-reports (e.g., Chaiken & Chaiken, 1984; Maxwell & Maxwell, 2000; von Hirsch, 1984). Another issue revolves around the fact that the RAND study and similar investigations into offenders' crime commission rates employed self-report data (see Wilson, 1983b), which has prompted the criticism that these studies used *postdiction* rather than prediction; that is, they were entirely past-oriented and said nothing about what the interviewed offenders might do in the future (Blumstein, 1983b; Clear & Barry, 1983; see also Maxwell & Maxwell, 2000). As always, hindsight is 20/20: It becomes clear in interviewing incarcerated adults which ones had the highest lambdas and which had the lowest.

Postdiction, however, does not translate into prediction, and there is no way to tell in advance whether a given individual will be a high-rate or a low-rate offender (e.g., Barnett & Lofaso, 1985). Certainly, there are warning signs. Being young, having prior criminal convictions, having a juvenile record, being unemployed, being unmarried, and having a history of drug abuse (Chaiken & Chaiken, 1983, 1984; Greenwood, 1983; see Wilson, 1983b) are some of the prominent risk factors for future offending. The problem is that these are merely macro-level correlates of high-rate offending in aggregate samples and are poor indicators of individual-level behavior (Blumstein, 1983b; Chaiken & Chaiken, 1983, 1984). Predictions about future criminality are notoriously inaccurate (e.g., Auerhahn, 1999; Gottfredson & Gottfredson, 1985), particularly with regard to low base-rate crimes like serious violence (Blumstein, 1983b).The most common error is that of false positives, where a person is predicted to be recidivistic but in fact never reoffends (Blumstein, 1983b; Chaiken & Chaiken, 1983, 1984; Clear, 1994; Clear & Barry, 1983; Pratt, 2009; von Hirsch, 1984). Put simply, most predictions about future dangerousness are wrong.

The issue of criminal career length adds another twist. The age-crime curve was one of the first major discoveries in longitudinal research and has been the focus of many theories of crime (Lilly et al., 2007). The majority of crime is committed by juveniles and young adults, and most youthful offenders eventually age out of criminal activity (e.g., Sampson & Laub, 1993; see Chapter 11 of this book). The age-crime curve produces the problem of diminishing marginal returns. Putting a repeat offender behind bars during the peak of his or her criminal career will prevent many crimes, but as the offender begins the negatively sloping journey on the downward side of the age-crime curve, his or her offending rate will plummet and it will no longer be worthwhile, from an incapacitation standpoint, to incarcerate the individual (Blumstein, 1983b; Piquero et al., 2003; von Hirsch, 1988; for a review, see Piquero & Blumstein, 2007). What is needed, then, is information not just on rates of offending but on the duration of criminal careers.

Researchers have noted many other problems with selective incapacitation as well. Replacement effects are a concern for drug crimes and crimes committed by gangs and other groups. If a low-ranking drug runner or gang member is imprisoned, a new person will simply be recruited to take his place (Blumstein, 1983b, 2004; Miles & Ludwig, 2007; Piquero & Blumstein, 2007). Another limitation is that most high-rate offenders commit the majority of their crimes in their teens and early 20s but are not incarcerated until they are in their mid-20s and have built up a criminal record that is sufficiently serious to warrant a prison sentence. This means that by the time most high-rate offenders are incarcerated, they might already be well into their criminal career. This delay suppresses the incapacitation effect of imprisonment (Blumstein, 1983a).

Beyond the technical problems outlined above are issues of ethics. The United States Constitution, Bill of Rights, and common law make it clear that people can be punished only when they have committed an offense against society (see Packer, 1968). Preemptive incarceration for crimes that have not been committed runs afoul of the heralded precept of "no punishment without a crime." Critics of incapacitation view this penological theory as irreconcilable with the rule of law and notions of justice in sentencing (Blumstein, 1983b; Mathiesen, 1998; von Hirsch, 1984, 1988).

Another ethical roadblock concerns sentencing disparities. An official selective incapacitation policy would require inequities in sentencing because penalty severity would be based only partially on the offense a person committed—the real consideration would be that person's score on a predictive instrument showing his or her likelihood of future offending (Piquero & Blumstein, 2007). One robbery offender, for instance, whose score indicated a low likelihood of recidivism might get a fairly short prison sentence while another robbery offender whose score indicated a high likelihood would be given a far longer sentence (von Hirsch, 1984). Given that the U.S. legal system has from its inception subscribed to the tenet that punishment should be predicated upon the offense for which a person was convicted (see Chapter 2 of this book), a punishment system that hands down very different sentences to persons convicted of the same crime seems ethically indefensible.

Concerns have also been raised with regard to the prediction criteria advocated by selective incarceration proponents. High-rate offenders are disproportionately young, poor, unemployed or underemployed, and unmarried (e.g., Chaiken & Chaiken, 1984; Greenwood, 1983). If selective incapacitation is indeed a strategy that reduces the sentencing decision to a transparent, value-free mathematical computation based on preset risk-prediction criteria, then extralegal factors such as an offender's race and socioeconomic status would be perfectly acceptable characteristics upon which to premise prison sentence length (Blumstein, 1983a). Could the courts, criminal justice system, and people of the United States today stomach a sentencing structure like this? Certainly not. A major mark against the policy, then, is that to be effective, selective incapacitation would require unconscionable use of extralegal characteristics (Gottfredson & Hirschi, 1986; Mathiesen, 1998; von Hirsch, 1984; see also Monahan, 1981).

CONCLUSION

James Q. Wilson is one of the leading names in criminal justice policy. He earned his fame in large part by vociferously rejecting the complexities and nuances of criminological inquiry into the causes of crime and insisting instead that the focus of policy should be on what can be done about those individuals who break the law. His selective incapacitation thesis resounded through policy and academic circles, though it was ultimately trumped by the collective version of incapacitation as prison advocates clamored for ever more severity in sanctioning. Given the statistical and ethical dilemmas with selective incapacitation, it is unlikely that the strategy would have worked even if policy makers had given it a legitimate effort. Wilson's influential book *Thinking About Crime* was a lesson to criminologists about the power of marketing: Even flawed arguments about the nature of crime and purposes of punishment can make a major splash if they are communicated in a way that is broadly accessible to a nonacademic audience. Wilson's selective incapacitation thesis marked a major turning point in the life course of criminal justice and criminology (Laub, 2003) and is appropriately listed among the ranks of the most important ideas in the history of the field.

DISCUSSION QUESTIONS

1. Trace the shift of criminological theories over time with regard to the transitions between macro-level and micro-level theories.
2. What was it about the criminological context of the 1970s that created an opening for the selective incapacitation thesis?
3. Identify the statistical and ethical problems with selective incapacitation.

REFERENCES

Auerhahn, K. (1999). Selective incapacitation and the problem of prediction. *Criminology, 37*(4), 703–734.

Barnett, A., & Lofaso, A. J. (1985). Selective incapacitation and the Philadelphia cohort data. *Journal of Quantitative Criminology, 1*(1), 3–36.

Blackmore, J., & Welsh, J. (1983). Selective incapacitation: Sentencing according to risk. *Crime & Delinquency, 29*(4), 504–528.

Blumstein, A. (1983a). Prisons: Population, capacity, and alternatives. In J. Q. Wilson (Ed.), *Crime and public policy* (pp. 11–29). San Francisco: ICS Press.

Blumstein, A. (1983b). Selective incapacitation as a means of crime control. *American Behavioral Scientist, 27*(1), 87–109.

Blumstein, A. (2000). Disaggregating the violence trends. In A. Blumstein & J. Wallman (Eds.), *The crime drop in America* (pp. 13–44). Cambridge, UK: Cambridge University Press.

Blumstein, A. (2004). Prisons: A policy challenge. In J. Q. Wilson & J. Petersilia (Eds.), *Crime: Public policies for crime control* (pp. 451–482). San Francisco: ICS Press.

Blumstein, A., & Nagin, D. (1978). On the optimum use of incarceration for crime control. *Operations Research, 26*(3), 381–405.

Chaiken, J. M., & Chaiken, M. R. (1983). Crime rates and the active criminal. In J. Q. Wilson (Ed.), *Crime and public policy* (pp. 11–29). San Francisco: ICS Press.

Chaiken, J. M., & Chaiken, M. R. (1984). Offender types and public policy. *Crime & Delinquency, 30*(2), 195–226.

Clear, T. R. (1994). *Harm in American penology.* New York: State University of New York Press.

Clear, T. R., & Barry, D. M. (1983). Some conceptual issues in incapacitating offenders. *Crime & Delinquency, 29*(4), 529–544.

Cohn, E. G., & Farrington, D. P. (1994). Who are the most influential criminologists in the English-speaking world? *British Journal of Criminology, 34*(2), 204–225.

Copas, J. B., & Tarling, R. (1988). Stochastic models for analyzing criminal careers. *Journal of Quantitative Criminology, 4*(2), 173–186.

Cullen, F. T. (2004). Rehabilitation and treatment programs. In J. Q. Wilson & J. Petersilia (Eds.), *Crime: Public policies for crime control* (pp. 253–289). Oakland, CA: ICS Press.

Cullen, F. T. (2007). Make rehabilitation corrections' guiding paradigm. *Criminology & Public Policy, 6*(4), 717–728.

Currie, E. (1998). *Crime and punishment in America.* New York: Owl Books.

Forst, B. (1983). Prosecution and sentencing. In J. Q. Wilson (Ed.), *Crime and public policy* (pp. 165–182). San Francisco: ICS Press.

Galvin, J. (1983). Introduction—Special issue: Prisons and sentencing reform: Prison policy reform ten years later. *Crime & Delinquency, 29*(4), 495–503.

Garland, D. (2001). *The culture of control.* Chicago: University of Chicago Press.

Gaskins, S. (2004). "Women of circumstance"—the effects of mandatory minimum sentencing on women minimally involved in drug crimes. *American Criminal Law Review, 41,* 1533–1553.

Gottfredson, S. D., & Gottfredson, D. M. (1985). Selective incapacitation? *Annals of the American Academy of Political and Social Science, 478,* 135–149.

Gottfredson, M., & Hirschi, T. (1986). The true value of lambda would appear to be zero: An essay on career criminals, criminal careers, selective incapacitation, cohort studies, and related topics. *Criminology, 24*(2), 213–234.

Greenwood, P. W. (1983). Controlling the crime rate through imprisonment. In J. Q. Wilson (Ed.), *Crime and public policy* (pp. 251–269). San Francisco: ICS Press.

Horney, J., & Marshall, I. H. (1991). Measuring lambda through self-reports. *Criminology, 29*(3), 471–495.

Laub, J. H. (2003). The life course of criminology in the United States: The American Society of Criminology 2003 Presidential Address. *Criminology, 42*(1), 1–26.

Lilly, J. R., Cullen, F. T., & Ball, R. A. (2007). *Criminological theory: Context and consequences* (4th ed.). Thousand Oaks, CA: Sage.

Loeber, R., & Snyder, H. N. (1990). Rate of offending in juvenile careers: Findings of constancy and change in lambda. *Criminology, 28*(1), 97–109.

Martinson, R. (1974). What works? Questions and answers about prison reform. *The Public Interest,* 22–54.

Marvell, T. B., & Moody, C. E., Jr. (1994). Prison population growth and crime reduction. *Journal of Quantitative Criminology, 10*(2), 109–140.

Mathiesen, T. (1998). Selective incapacitation revisited. *Law and Human Behavior, 22*(4), 455–469.

Maxwell, S. R., & Maxwell, C. D. (2000). Examining the "criminal careers" of prostitutes within the nexus of drug use, drug selling, and other illicit activities. *Criminology, 38*(3), 787–810.

Miles, T. J., & Ludwig, J. (2007). The silence of the lambdas: Deterring incapacitation research. *Journal of Quantitative Criminology, 23,* 287–301.

Monahan, J. (1981). *Predicting violent behavior.* Beverly Hills, CA: Sage.

Packer, H. L. (1968). *The limits of the criminal sanction.* Palo Alto, CA: Stanford University Press.

Piquero, A. R., & Blumstein, A. (2007). Does incapacitation reduce crime? *Journal of Quantitative Criminology, 23,* 267–285.

Piquero, A. R., Farrington, D. P., & Blumstein, A. (2003). Criminal career paradigm: Background, recent developments, and the way forward. *International Annals of Criminology, 41,* 243–269.

Pratt, T. C. (2009). *Addicted to incarceration.* Thousand Oaks, CA: Sage.

Rosenfeld, R. (2000). Patterns of adult homicide: 1980–1995. In A. Blumstein & J. Wallman (Eds.), *The crime drop in America* (pp. 130–163). Cambridge, UK: Cambridge University Press.

Rothman, D. J. (1983). Sentencing reforms in historical perspective. *Crime & Delinquency, 29*(4), 631–647.

Sampson, R. J., & Laub, J. H. (1993). *Crime in the making.* Cambridge, MA: Harvard University Press.

Sherman, M., & Hawkins, G. (1981). *Imprisonment in America.* Chicago: University of Chicago Press.

Spelman, W. (2000). The limited importance of prison expansion. In A. Blumstein & J. Wallman (Eds.), *The crime drop in America* (pp. 97–129). Cambridge, UK: Cambridge University Press.

von Hirsch, A. (1984). The ethics of selective incapacitation: Observations on the contemporary debate. *Crime & Delinquency, 30*(2), 175–194.

von Hirsch, A. (1988). Selective incapacitation reexamined: The National Academy of Sciences' report on criminal careers and "career criminals." *Criminal Justice Ethics, 7*(1), 19–35.

Walker, S. (2001). *Sense and nonsense about crime and drugs* (5th ed). Belmont, CA: Wadsworth.

Wilson, J. Q. (1968). *Varieties of police behavior.* New York: Atheneum.

Wilson, J. Q. (1975). *Thinking about crime.* New York: Basic Books.

Wilson, J.Q. (1983a). Preface. In J. Q. Wilson (Ed.), *Crime and public policy* (pp. 3–8). San Francisco: ICS Press.

Wilson, J. Q. (1983b). *Thinking about crime* (2nd ed.). New York: Vintage Books.

Wilson, J. Q. (2004). Crime and public policy. In J. Q. Wilson & J. Petersilia (Eds.), *Crime: Public policies for crime control* (pp. 537–557). San Francisco: ICS Press.

Wilson, J. Q., & Petersilia, J. (2004). Introduction. In J. Q. Wilson & J. Petersilia (Eds.), *Crime: Public policies for crime control* (pp. 1–3). San Francisco: ICS Press.

Wolfgang, M., Figlio, R. M., & Sellin, T. (1972). *Delinquency in a birth cohort.* Chicago: University of Chicago Press.

Wright, R. A. (1995). The most-cited scholars in criminology: A comparison of textbooks and journals. *Journal of Criminal Justice, 23*(4), 303–311.

Zimring, F. E. (1995). Recent books: Will success spoil James Q. Wilson? *Journal of Criminal Law and Criminology, 85*(3), 828–832.

NOTES

1. The extent to which Wilson himself has subscribed to this view over the years is unclear. In *Thinking About* Crime, he vacillated between implying that selective incarceration was a value-free approach and claiming that retribution and deterrence were also laudable goals of correctional policy. Recently, he argued more explicitly that policies must account for the public's desire to see people punished for bad deeds and that to this end, sentencing cannot be based upon purely rational calculations to the exclusion of moral judgments about offenders' blameworthiness (Wilson, 2004).

2. This is not to say, by any means, that modern sentencing makes no use of predictions about future offending; quite to the contrary, prediction is and has been for the last century a staple of sentencing. In the early 1900s, Progressive reformers took up the issue of prediction and tried to make sentencing more rational and scientific. The presentence investigation and report that are still used today are a product of this movement (Rothman, 1983). Judges typically consider a variety of factors ranging from prior record to employment status to community ties when attempting to craft an appropriate sentence for a given offender. Prediction is embedded in the sentencing process (Monahan, 1981; Wilson, 1983b) and to this extent, all sentences contain an element of attempted selective incapacitation. This is not attributable to Wilson, however, since these ideas preceded him.

3. This equation is a dramatically simplified version of the very complex formulas proposed in the selective incapacitation measurement literature. It is used here for illustrative purposes only.

EIGHT

KEY IDEA: THE POLICE CAN CONTROL CRIME

KEY WORK

Wilson, J. Q., & Kelling, G. L. (1982, March). The police and neighborhood safety: Broken windows. *Atlantic Monthly,* 29–38.

Broken windows theory has profoundly impacted the way that police and city-level political officials view crime and disorder and has fundamentally altered the role of the beat cop in modern cities. Broken windows theory and the policing strategy to which it gave rise have been incorporated into police agency mission statements from coast to coast. Proponents claim that broken windows has caused dramatic improvements in the quality of life in urban areas and has spurred unprecedented reductions in violent crime. Many academics in criminology and criminal justice, however, believe that the theory is fatally flawed and that its associated policing strategy does not reduce crime and can damage police–community relationships. This chapter examines the reasons why broken windows theory caught on, why its popularity continues, and the impact it has had on the way academics, the public, and the police themselves view the law enforcement function.

THE CONTEXT OF CRIMINOLOGY AND POLICING

By the mid-1970s, individual-level explanations for criminal offending had eclipsed macro-level, sociological theories in the public eye. Gone were the ideas that crime could be quelled by improving the lot of the most misfortunate echelons of society (see Chapter 4) or that rehabilitation could help offenders turn their lives around (see Chapter 6). Academics were divided as to the most plausible causes of and solutions to crime (Laub, 2003), but the public and policy makers were not: The latter groups adopted a conviction that crime was the product of personal choice and that the only way to deal with selfish, amoral criminals was to make sanctions harsh to either deter them from committing crime (see Chapter 2) or incapacitate them once they had proven themselves unworthy of living in society with good people (see Chapter 7).

There is a conflict, though, inherent in the belief that crime is the product of individual choice alone. That conflict springs from the fact that crime is concentrated in disadvantaged urban areas. The ecological patterning of crime makes it undeniable that there is something about certain environments that makes crime more or less likely to occur. Social disorganization theory (see Chapter 4) and rational choice theory (see Chapter 2) are not necessarily incompatible insofar as available choices and incentive structures are a function of the sociostructural conditions that characterize a person's environment and affect individual decision making (see generally Nagin, 2007). Even in the heyday of the get-tough movement, then, the ecology of crime could not be brushed aside as easily as some would have perhaps liked.

The institution of policing is, of course, an individual-level mechanism of crime control because an officer's job is not to figure out where crime comes from but, rather, to identify and apprehend those who do bad things. It might seem, then, that social disorganization, as a macro-level theory of crime, would have little or no bearing on police work. In the late 1970s, however, changes began to happen in policing that would soon bring this field to an intersection with social disorganization. Since the 1930s (Langworthy & Travis, 2003), policing had been dominated by an emphasis on the apprehension of serious criminal offenders. Various methods were employed to enable police to react quickly when crimes were reported and to identify and arrest the culprits (Kelling & Moore, 1988). The late 1970s saw this so-called "professional model" of policing gradually replaced by a more "community-based" or "order maintenance" model, which stressed the role of police as agents of *social* control, not just *crime* control (see Kelling & Moore, 1988; Walker, 1984). Social disorganization theory was back but, as will be seen, in a quite different form.

The changes in policing reflected a changing society that required police to reassess their approach (Kelling & Coles, 1996). The civil rights movement, race riots, and the escalating Vietnam conflict inflamed the country's passions and caused intense violence and widespread fear in some cities. At the same time, the deinstitutionalization movement was spawned by the development of new, highly effective psychotropic medication and civil libertarians' push for less government control over individual liberty. State psychiatric hospitals gradually emptied their wards and closed their doors. Many of the former patients had nowhere to go and no way to care for themselves, and they were simply funneled—some of them in the throes of untreated psychological illnesses—onto the streets to begin lives of begging by day and sleeping in alleys by night. The sociopolitical unrest resulting from the public's disenchantment with current government policies and the increasing visibility of disheveled, ill, and sometimes pushy or even violent vagabonds generated mass unease. To many observers, this general malaise seemed symptomatic of a deep crumbling in society's ability to exercise control over its wayward members and to keep its more "conventional" citizens safe. The public's fear of crime hit record highs (Lewis & Salem, 1986).

Enter the criminologists at this point. Until the 1960s, criminologists did not concern themselves much with empirical testing. During this decade, though, theory testing took off (Laub, 2003). Criminologists were armed with brand-new statistical techniques and the computer software to use them. The public's fear of crime and rising discontent about the government's response to crime and criminality inspired criminologists to analyze policing's effect on crime. The results were almost unanimously depressing: Police, it seemed, had negligible power over crime rates. Focusing solely on serious crimes and responding to these crimes reactively by emphasizing rapid response to calls for service did not appear to exert a material impact on public safety (Sherman, 1997; see also Sherman & Weisburd, 1995).

BROKEN WINDOWS THEORY: REVAMPING THE POLICE ROLE

By the 1980s, social and economic conditions had degraded in inner-city communities ripped apart by drugs, guns, unemployment, and a general sense of hopelessness. City dwellers with the financial means to do so fled to the suburbs, leaving the poor, the unhoused, and the mentally ill in slums and other areas of economic woe (W. J. Wilson, 1987). Violent crime rates were at an all-time high and were still rising (Blumstein, 2000). All across the country, cries went out for better public safety.

Yet some began voicing the idea that crime itself was not the problem. While violence and the fear of violent victimization are central to Americans' fear of crime (Zimring & Hawkins, 1997), many scholars in the 1970s and 1980s pointed out that relatively few people in the United

States are ever victimized and fewer still are violently attacked. What people are exposed to on a regular basis, they argued, are obnoxious structural conditions. Researchers dubbed these irritants "incivilities" or "disorder" (Lewis & Salem, 1986) and proposed that vandalism, graffiti, prostitution, aggressive panhandling, and other socially undesirable conditions and behaviors were the true forces behind people's fear of crime.

It was at this point that broken windows theory arrived. In 1983, James Q. Wilson (of *Thinking About Crime* fame; see Chapter 7) and George L. Kelling released an article entitled "Broken Windows: The Police and Neighborhood Safety." The authors' central thesis was that disorder, if left unchecked, causes serious crime. Disorder encompasses many conditions and behaviors (see Skogan, 1990). Physical disorder includes litter in public areas, dilapidated or abandoned buildings, graffiti, vandalism, vacant lots, unkempt yards, and other physical conditions that contribute to a generally run-down atmosphere in a neighborhood or community. Social disorder involves activities such as panhandling, prostitution, sale and use of illegal drugs, public urination, and public drinking and intoxication. In its most basic definition, "disorder" is any condition or behavior that fails to conform to traditional standards of decency, cleanliness, and proper conduct (see also Duneier, 1999).

Disorder, so the theory goes, is a visible indicator that a community is out of control. The presence of disorder in an area signals to residents and to criminals that this community cannot regulate itself and that it cannot (or will not) control noxious sociostructural conditions. This perceived absence of control causes fear among residents of disorderly areas because they no longer believe the streets are safe. If nobody can stop gangs from tagging buildings or prostitutes from peddling their "wares" in broad daylight, then who can possibly keep innocent people from falling victim to violent predators? Fear, according to Wilson and Kelling, causes social withdrawal as citizens who once used public spaces for a variety of purposes now stay indoors. They do not socialize with their neighbors and they spend minimal time walking on public sidewalks, visiting public parks, or engaging in other activities outside their homes.

At the heart of broken windows theory is a self-fulfilling prophecy wherein what at the outset had been merely a *perceived* loss of social control becomes an *actual* loss because there are no longer law-abiding citizens monitoring public areas and discouraging criminal activities. Private citizens going about their business in urban centers serve a peace-keeping function by providing "eyes upon the street" (Jacobs, 1961, p. 45). Even though these people may have nothing in common with one another and may never have met before and will probably never meet again, the mere presence of large groups of people means that everyone has one or more guardians. Each and every person in that crowd possesses a pair of "eyes upon the street," and criminals shy away from victimizing people upon whom several pairs of eyes are trained.

Broken windows theory concerns itself with what could happen when disorderly conditions drive these eyes indoors. Criminals supposedly take the desertion of public spaces to mean that their chances of apprehension are low. There may be no one to witness crimes and, if someone does see something happening, that bystander will be unlikely to intervene and might even be loathe to call the police. Criminals see these areas as perfect places to execute serious criminal activity like street robbery. Wilson and Kelling (1982) referred to the influx of motivated criminals into a disorderly area as a "criminal invasion" (p. 32). It is at this point that the broken windows process has actualized and there is a serious crime problem in a once-safe neighborhood or community.

Broken windows theory bears a strong resemblance to social disorganization theory (see Chapter 4) and can be seen as a modern offshoot of its predecessor. Social disorganization theory links crime to macro-level disadvantage; in particular, low socioeconomic status, ethnic or racial heterogeneity, and high rates of residential mobility are linked to crime via the debilitating impact these structural conditions have on community networks, schools, and other mechanisms and institutions of informal social control (see, e.g., Bursik & Grasmick, 1993; Kornhauser, 1978; Lowenkamp, Cullen, & Pratt, 2003; Sampson & Groves, 1989). As Bursik (1988) described it, area levels of (dis)organization affect "the strength of the commitment of the residents to group standards" (p. 521). Where this commitment is strong, crime is kept in check; where it is deficient, crime spirals out of control.

Broken windows posits a process of community decline that is quite similar to that proposed by social disorganization theory, but the former breaks sharply from its parent theory by characterizing disorder as the true villain that sparks community downfall. Disorder, in the broken windows framework, is a manifestation of structural disadvantage; that is, things like graffiti, vandalism, and prostitution symbolize deep and powerful disruptions to the community fabric. Whereas social disorganization theory would seem to suggest that it is the underlying conditions causing disorder that need to be disrupted in order to help repair the community and bring crime down,[1] Wilson and Kelling (1982) argued that the exact same outcome could be achieved by taking the less labor-intensive route of snuffing out disorder. In this way, broken widows theory boils a macro-level process down to the micro level—by targeting *this* panhandler and *that* loiterer, the entire criminogenic "cloud" can supposedly be dispersed (Pratt & Gau, 2010).

So, who keeps disorder in check? According to Wilson and Kelling (1982), the police do. They wrote that, "Though citizens can do a great deal, the police are plainly the key to order-maintenance" (p. 36). This claim was a sharp departure from the conventional image of police as crime fighters who are far too busy collaring bad guys to bother with graffiti and panhandlers (but see Walker, 1984, who refutes this position); however, Wilson and Kelling argued that this departure was justified.

They took the view that residents of inner-city neighborhoods feared encountering unruly troublemakers just as much as they feared predatory street criminals because the existence of the former is an indication of the prevalence of the latter. Wilson and Kelling argued that police should act *proactively,* not reactively, and should stop crime before it starts by taking control of the streets and sending the message that deviant or threatening behavior of any variety will not be tolerated. Quashing the behavior of teenage hooligans, pushy panhandlers, and other miscreants would, the argument went, send the message to serious criminals that the police are in charge and that order reigns.

Wilson and Kelling contended that order maintenance policing would also jumpstart informal social control in areas where it had broken down. Once neighborhood residents saw the police enforcing codes of conduct and norms of order, they wrote, these private citizens would be emboldened and would embark on their own agenda of order restoration and maintenance. Wilson and Kelling believed that police intervention in disorder would churn the wheels of informal social control mechanisms so that eventually, once-downtrodden neighborhoods would regain the capacity to self-regulate.

HOW BROKEN WINDOWS THEORY REACHED ITS AUDIENCE

Broken windows theory quickly attached itself to the public's imagination for several reasons. Chief among these reasons was the form and outlet in which it originally appeared. The debut article was a small, unassuming piece in the popular magazine the *Atlantic Monthly.* This article had no statistics, no criminological jargon, and no talk of theories. It was even illustrated with little drawings of prostitutes and car vandals. Compared to the theory-laden, statistics-based format of standard criminological articles, Wilson and Kelling's piece looked almost absurdly simplistic.

The simplicity of its presentation turned out to be its greatest strength in gaining popular appeal. Police practitioners do not generally make a habit of combing criminological journals—they do, however, read mainstream magazines like the *Atlantic Monthly.* Academics have a poor track record of communicating effectively to policy makers and others outside scholarly circles (see Cullen, 2007). People not trained in theories of crime, not schooled in statistics, and not familiar with the principles of social science have a difficult, if not impossible, time comprehending most criminology and criminal justice research. Rarely do people in academic circles deliberately reach out to practitioners and try to speak in a language that makes sense to them the way Wilson and Kelling did.

Another reason why police administrators liked broken windows theory was that it conceptualized police as being central to crime prevention and reduction. There was mutual animosity between criminologists and police at the time. Practitioners resented the ivory-tower academics for their snooty mantra about the ineffectiveness of police, and academics saw practitioners as knuckle-dragging dullards who could only understand simple concepts and tiny words. Not surprisingly, police do not like hearing about their ineffectiveness nearly as much as they like hearing what they *can* do. Wilson and Kelling were the first people from the academic sphere to publicly espouse the belief that the police are vital to community safety and can have a dramatic impact on crime. Disorder, according to Wilson and Kelling, was the main cause of serious crime, and police were the only ones who could do anything about disorder.

Broken windows theory was in many respects a reification of what many practitioners already believed: The legalistic style of policing was a fiction. Practitioners had for some time wanted policy makers and the public to adopt a more realistic picture of the police function. Wilson and Kelling offered a way to do this and, even better, a way to do it using a veneer of scientific validity because Wilson and Kelling were academics. James Q. Wilson had already achieved the status of expert in policing and crime policy due in large part to his famous books *Varieties of Police Behavior* (1968) and *Thinking About Crime* (1975; see also 1983; see Chapter 7 of this book).[2] Few in policy circles questioned his wisdom—if James Q. Wilson said that disorder causes crime, then there was probably something to it.

Police officials also delighted in the straightforwardness of the theory. Practitioners generally found macro-level theories of crime (e.g., social disorganization theory) that focused on criminogenic conditions to be useless because these theories had no direct implications for police policy. Broken windows offered police a refreshingly simple formula they could follow to reduce serious crime (Bratton, 1999): Keep disorder in check. This was something police felt they could do.

THE INFLUENCE OF BROKEN WINDOWS THEORY

Broken windows was a success because it hit multiple facets of public policy in ways that proved productively symbiotic. It provided a way for police to "do something" about disorder and crime, and it fueled the urban renewal movement spearheaded by business improvement districts. Each of these topics is treated in turn below.

Policing, Broken Windows Style

Broken windows theory pandered to popular sentiment about the conditions of urban areas in the 1980s and early 1990s. The theory's statement regarding the deleterious effects of disorder on people's quality of life was an echo of the opinion that was becoming more and more prevalent among the citizenry (Duneier, 1999). The due process and civil rights revolution in the 1960s and early 1970s had left some fringe segments of the population with what many people believed were too many rights; specifically, at the same time that mentally ill persons were pouring into the streets from the closing psychiatric hospitals, laws and ordinances prohibiting panhandling, vagrancy, and loitering were being strongly limited and even struck down by the courts (e.g., *Papachristou v. City of Jacksonville,* 1972; for a modern example, see *City of Chicago v. Morales,* 1999; see also Kelling & Coles, 1996). The police felt helpless as the public became more and more insistent that something be done about the squalor and veritable anarchy that had come to characterize many urban areas.

Wilson and Kelling's thesis solved the dilemma by providing a scholarly basis that police could rely upon to justify widening the category of deviant behaviors that warranted official intervention. By positing a causal relationship between disorder and crime, broken windows theory legitimized an expansion of the police role from the narrow focus on serious crime to a broader, more comprehensive concern with general neighborhood conditions. Prior researchers had linked disorder to the fear of crime (see Perkins & Taylor, 1996), but police are supposed to concentrate on actual crime, not people's fear of it, so these earlier theories did not implicate the police in order maintenance. Broken windows theory went a step further than prior theories had when named crime as the ultimate outcome in the disorder-fear process (Taylor, 2001)—crime is the realm of police, so if disorder causes crime, then disorder is part of the police realm, too. Wilson and Kelling neatly brought disorder under the police umbrella and in so doing equipped police with a justification for interjecting when they saw disorderly behaviors.

Broken windows-style policing owes its popularity in large part to one person: William Bratton, formerly of the New York City Transit Authority (NYTA; 1993–1994) and the New York City Police Department (NYPD; 1994–1996). In these positions and later, as head of the Los Angeles Police Department (LAPD), Bratton displayed antipathy toward criminology and criminologists. He painted himself as a sort of "rogue" who was going to prove everyone wrong and show once and for all that the police can reduce crime (Bratton, 1999; Bratton & Knobler, 1998). He gave broken windows theory trial runs first in the subways and then on the streets of New York City. During his tenure as NYTA chief, he made disorder reduction the primary task of the subway police. With George Kelling as a consultant, Bratton pinpointed what he thought were the most problematic types of disorder in the subway and then formulated plans to rid the system of these problems (see Kelling & Coles, 1996).

At about the same time that Bratton launched his broken windows campaign in the city, violent crime took a sharp downward turn. Bratton and Kelling were quick to credit broken windows policing for the crime drop (Bratton, 1999; Kelling, 2000; Kelling & Bratton, 1998). After all, street crimes—robberies, muggings, murders—were precisely what broken windows policing was supposed to reduce. Bratton had radically altered the focus and function of the cops on the streets of New York and, as predicted, crime had fallen.

Convinced that what Bratton said must be true and taking the New York City example of broken windows in action as conclusive proof of the theory's validity, police officials across the nation scrambled to install their own broken windows efforts. Though broken windows had only been tried out in one city, two circumstances made the theory and policing strategy uniquely attractive to police officials. First, New York City was infamous for its seemingly intractable crime problems—anything that worked to reduce crime in that city must have potential. Second, the theory aligned very well with popular beliefs at the time—broken windows came along right as the public was clamoring for the police to do something about disorder. This second point segues into the next subsection.

The Economics of Order Maintenance: The Rise of the Business Improvement District

The police were not the only ones who seized upon broken windows theory; small businesses in the commercial centers of cities immediately recognized the theory's financial potential. Broken windows theory hit just at the time that business improvement districts (BIDs) were taking off and, not surprisingly, New York City was the first U.S. jurisdiction to embrace the idea. In 1982, the same year Wilson and Kelling's thesis appeared, the New York City Council adopted local laws making it easier for businesses to form BIDs (Ward, 2006) and in 1984, the first BID in New York City was formed in the Union Square Park commercial district.

BIDs are the product of decades of economic depression in inner-city areas. Booming industry and the rapid growth of cities in the mid- to late 1800s brought jobs and wealth to city dwellers (Frost, 1991). In the 1930s and 1940s, however, large and upper-scale businesses began drifting into the suburbs (Walsh, 2006), following the out-migration of the middle classes into these areas. Smaller businesses were left behind. These businesses floundered. Many of them went under because the residents with disposable incomes had moved away, and the people who remained did not have enough money to spend to keep the local economy moving.

Business improvement districts began as an effort by small, local businesses to stay afloat in inner-city commercial areas. BIDs are created when businesses in a downtown center or other commercial district voluntarily band together. The primary goal of BIDs is to attract business, and the most common strategy is neighborhood cleanup BIDs set goals and standards in terms of expectations for each business owner and collective goals for the group. Members often pay extra property taxes to the city in exchange for enhanced public services (e.g., sanitation, graffiti removal, police coverage). BIDs employ private security guards or contract with the city for enhanced police services in their districts so that laws against activities like public urination, aggressive panhandling, and loitering can be strictly enforced. BIDs are thus a nexus where public and private governance of public spaces come together (Justice & Goldsmith, 2006). There are currently over 400 BIDs in the United States (Levy, 2001), and 16 countries around the world have implemented BID or BID-like programs (Ward, 2006).

Proponents of BIDs applaud the public services they provide, such as the installation of more street lighting and the closing off of vacant lots. Fundamentally, though, the BID is a profit-generating entity, and the uplifting effects it has on its surrounding community are really nothing more than positive externalities (Levy, 2001). The "zero tolerance" attitude BIDs adopt toward disorder (Ward, 2006) and the fact that it is the middle class that BIDs try to lure in (Stokes, 2006) set the stage for potential authoritarian rule against lower-class city dwellers who do not conform to middle-class suburban shoppers' standards of appearance or conduct (see Ward, 2006). Critics of BIDs have charged these agencies with the "Disneyfication" of inner-city areas that were once tolerant of diverse people, activities, and lifestyles but have been forcefully morphed into racially and financially homogenous areas that adhere to narrow norms of "acceptable" behavior (Reichl, 1999; Sites, 2003; see also Duneier, 1999).

Broken windows did not ignite the BID movement, but it greased the wheels and put nitrous in the engine. Broken windows theory armed BIDs with a defense against charges of discrimination and intolerance: Thanks to Wilson and Kelling (1982), BIDs could argue that disorder is not merely in the eye of the beholder, but rather, it actually causes crime and is therefore unquestionably a bad thing. Like the NYPD and other police agencies, business owners and local city councils were legitimized in their order maintenance efforts by this seemingly scholarly delineation of the causes of crime. BID proponents had long believed that disorder hindered business, but now they had what they considered solid evidence that disorder also causes crime. This gave them extra incentive to fight physical and social disorder and left them with an even stronger sense that what they were doing was right.

EMPIRICAL TESTS AND CRITIQUES OF BROKEN WINDOWS THEORY AND POLICING

Broken windows theory continues to be tested, and the results are calling its validity into question. Some studies (Skogan, 1990; Xu, Fiedler, & Flaming, 2005) have shown support for the theory, while others show either minimal support or none at all (Armstrong & Katz, 2010; Gau & Pratt, 2008; Harcourt, 2001; Sampson & Raudenbush, 1999, 2004; Taylor, 2001; Worrall, 2006a). Disorder and crime are related, but the precise nature of the connection is unclear.

One potential explanation is that broken windows theory made the age-old mistake of confusing correlation with causation. Disorder and crime could be co-occurring problems in areas characterized by a general state of sociostructural malaise, and they may both be outcomes of underlying breakdowns in social ties and informal control (Sampson & Raudenbush, 1999). Both phenomena would, then, bloom simultaneously in certain neighborhoods, but only because they are both produced by the same underlying problem and not because one causes the other.

Another problem that researchers have uncovered is that the early scholars who assumed that disorder and crime were separate, distinct phenomena (e.g., Lewis & Salem, 1986; Wilson & Kelling, 1982) were quite possibly wrong; people may, in fact, not draw a clear mental distinction between these two categories of offenses (Armstrong & Katz, 2010; Gau & Pratt, 2008; Worrall, 2006a). In addition, there are striking differences between the actual prevalence of disorder and citizens' *perceptions* of prevalence (Piquero, 1999)—the level of racial heterogeneity and poverty a neighborhood experiences is a better predictor of people's perceptions of disorder than are the true area rates of disorder (Franzini, Caughy, Nettles, & O'Campo, 2008; Sampson & Raudenbush, 2004). These findings indicate that the logical foundations upon which broken windows theory rests are shaky at best.

Order maintenance policing, the policy arm of broken windows theory, has also met with lukewarm support in empirical tests. There are evaluations that indicate that disorder-based policing approaches can reduce crime (Braga et al., 1999; Corman & Mocan, 2005; Kelling & Sousa, 2001; Sampson & Cohen, 1988; Smith, 2001; Worrall, 2006b), but there are also many studies that find no such effect (Harcourt & Ludwig, 2006; Katz, Webb, & Schaefer, 2001; Novak, Hartman, Holsinger, & Turner, 1999; see also Eck & Maguire, 2000; Fagan & Davies, 2000; Greene, 1999). There is no conclusive empirical evidence supporting broken windows advocates' (e.g., DiIulio, 1995; Kelling, 2000) claims that the strategy was the driving force behind the precipitous New York City crime drop (Fagan, Zimring, & Kim, 1998; Harcourt & Ludwig, 2006; see also Blumstein & Rosenfeld, 1998; Blumstein & Wallman, 2000; Eck & Maguire, 2000; Heymann, 2000).

Broken windows theory and policing both suffer from definitional ambiguity. "Disorder" has never been empirically defined (Gau & Pratt, 2008; Kubrin, 2008) and, similarly, it is unclear just what "order maintenance" means in the context of policing. There is a general ambiguity about what types of conditions or behaviors pose threats to communities and should be the targets of police efforts (Manning, 2001; see also Roberts, 1999). Failing to explore the multiple layers and facets of disorder also poses the risk that police, BIDs, and other anti-disorder forces will unwittingly invite unforeseen consequences. Breaking up groups of homeless persons, for instance, fits with an order maintenance agenda but puts these people at terrible risk of victimization because they banded together for safety and now must navigate the streets alone (Duneier, 1999). It is hard to implement and evaluate order maintenance policing if there is no solid definition of the concept.

Finally, broken windows–type policing has received criticism for being a threat to police–community relations, particularly in impoverished, high-crime areas where police–citizen relationships are already strained (see Brunson, 2007, 2010; Brunson & Miller, 2006). At the core of many departments' order maintenance strategies is an emphasis on the use of stop-and-frisks to root out disorderly behavior. Anyone acting "suspiciously" is a target for police scrutiny. This version of order maintenance policing potentially threatens police legitimacy via the resentment it evokes from the people who are subject to police scrutiny and restrictions upon their movement and use of public space (Gau & Brunson, 2010; Solis, Portillos, & Brunson, 2009; Weitzer & Brunson, 2009). Order maintenance can impose a heavy cost on police and on society.

CONCLUSION

Broken windows theory (Wilson & Kelling, 1982) has had far-reaching effects in criminal justice and criminology and, particularly, on police policy. The notion that police could control crime by tackling physical and social disorder was a novel idea and one that caught on quickly, especially with the help of the New York City experience. It is, indeed, hard to find a contemporary police agency that does not practice (or at least claim to practice) some version of order maintenance. Academics, though, have been less enthusiastic about the theory than practitioners have been. The future of broken windows theory is uncertain. Empirical testing continues, and while it appears clear at this point that Wilson and Kelling's original version of the theory has a lot of problems, it remains to be seen whether those problems can be addressed or whether the theory is irredeemable and must be scrapped. Hopefully, the upcoming years will find academics and police practitioners coming together so that policy and theory can be integrated to eventually produce a policing initiative that carries promise for improving communities and enhancing public safety.

DISCUSSION QUESTIONS

1. Explain the similarities and differences between social disorganization theory and broken windows theory. Which one seems like it holds better promise for reducing crime? Explain your answer.

2. What characteristics of Wilson and Kelling's (1982) original article helped broken windows theory reach a practitioner audience?

3. How did broken windows theory fit in with the urban renewal movement promulgated by business improvement districts? Why did BID leaders like this theory?

4. Explain the role of informal social control in broken windows theory and the way in which the theory argues for the use of formal social control to supplement informal control.

REFERENCES

Armstrong, T., & Katz, C. (2010). Further evidence of the discriminant validity of perceptual incivilities measures. *Justice Quarterly, 27*(2), 280–304.

Blumstein, A. (2000). Disaggregating the violence trends. In A. Blumstein & J. Wallman (Eds.), *The crime drop in America* (pp. 13–44). Cambridge, UK: Cambridge University Press.

Blumstein, A., & Rosenfeld, R. (1998). Explaining recent trends in U.S. homicide rates. *Journal of Criminal Law and Criminology, 88*(4), 1175–1216.

Blumstein, A., & Wallman, J. (2000). *The crime drop in America.* Cambridge, UK: Cambridge University Press.

Braga, A. A., Weisburd, D. L., Waring, E. J., Mazerolle, L. G., Spelman, W., & Gajewski, F. (1999). Problem-oriented policing in violent crime places: A randomized controlled experiment. *Criminology, 37*(3), 541–580.

Bratton, W. J. (1999). Great expectations: How higher expectations for police departments can lead to a decrease in crime. In R. H. Langworthy (Ed.), *Measuring what matters: Proceedings from the Policing Research Institute meetings* (pp. 11–26). Washington, DC: National Institute of Justice.

Bratton, W. J., & Knobler, P. (1998). *Turnaround: How America's top cop reversed the crime epidemic.* New York: Random House.

Brunson, R. K. (2007). "Police don't like black people": African-American young men's accumulated police experiences. *Criminology & Public Policy, 6*(1), 71–102.

Brunson, R. K. (2010). Beyond stop rates: Using qualitative methods to examine racially biased policing. In S. K. Rice & M. D. White (Eds.), *Race, Ethnicity and Policing: New and Essential Readings* (pp. 221–238). New York: New York University Press.

Brunson, R. K., & Miller, J. (2006). Gender, race, and urban policing: The experience of African American youths. *Gender & Society, 20*(4), 531–552.

Bursik, R. J. (1988). Social disorganization and theories of crime and delinquency: Problems and prospects. *Criminology, 26,* 519–551.

Bursik, R. J., Jr., & Grasmick, H. G. (1993). *Neighborhoods and crime.* Lanham, MD: Lexington.

Carr, P. J. (2003). The new parochialism: The implications of the beltway case for arguments concerning informal social control. *American Journal of Sociology, 108(6),* 1249–1291.

City of Chicago v. Morales, 527 U.S. 41 (1999).

Corman, H., & Mocan, N. (2005). Carrots, sticks, and broken windows. *Journal of Law and Economics, 48,* 235–266.

Cullen, F. T. (2007). Make rehabilitation corrections' guiding paradigm. *Criminology & Public Policy, 6*(4), 717–728.

DiIulio, J. J., Jr. (1995). Arresting ideas. *Policy Review, 74,* 12–17.

Duneier, M. (1999). *Sidewalk.* New York: Farrar, Straus and Giroux.

Eck, J. E., & Maguire, E. R. (2000). Have changes in policing reduced violent crime? An assessment of the evidence. In A. Blumstein & J. Wallman (Eds.), *The crime drop in America* (pp. 207–265). Cambridge, UK: Cambridge University Press.

Fagan, J., & Davies, G. (2000). Street cops and broken windows: Terry, race, and disorder in New York City. *Fordham Urban Law Journal, 28,* 457–504.

Fagan, J., Zimring, F. E., & Kim, J. (1998). Declining homicide in New York City: A tale of two trends. *Journal of Criminal Law and Criminology, 88*(4), 1277–1323.

Franzini, L., Caughy, M. O., Nettles, S. M., & O'Campo, P. (2008). Perceptions of disorder: Contributions of neighborhood characteristics to subjective perceptions of disorder. *Journal of Environmental Psychology, 28,* 83–93.

Frost, L. (1991). *The new urban frontier: Urbanisation and city building in Australasia and the American West.* Sydney, Australia: University of New South Wales Press.

Gau, J. M., & Brunson, R. K. (2010). Procedural justice and order maintenance policing: A study of inner-city young men's perceptions of police legitimacy. *Justice Quarterly, 27*(2), 255–279.

Gau, J. M., & Pratt, T. C. (2008). Broken windows or window dressing? Citizens' (in)ability to tell the difference between disorder and crime. *Criminology & Public Policy, 7*(2), 163–194.

Greene, J. A. (1999). Zero tolerance: A case study of police policies and practices in New York City. *Crime and Delinquency, 45*(2), 171–187.

Harcourt, B. E. (2001). *Illusion of order: The false promise of broken windows policing.* Cambridge, MA: Harvard University Press.

Harcourt, B. E., & Ludwig, J. (2006). Broken windows: New evidence from New York City and a five-city social experiment. *University of Chicago Law Review, 73*(1), 271–320.

Heymann, P. B. (2000). The new policing. *Fordham Urban Law Journal, 28,* 407–454.

Jacobs, J. (1961). *The death and life of great American cities.* New York: Random House.

Justice, J. B., & Goldsmith, R. S. (2006). Private governments or public policy tools? The law and public policy of New Jersey's special improvement districts. *International Journal of Public Administration, 29,* 107–136.

Katz, C. M., Webb, V. J., & Schaefer, D. R. (2001). An assessment of the impact of quality-of-life policing on crime and disorder. *Justice Quarterly, 18*(4), 825–876.

Kelling, G. L. (2000). Why did people stop committing crimes? An essay about criminology and ideology. *Fordham Urban Law Journal, 28,* 567–586.

Kelling, G. L., & Bratton, W. J. (1998). Declining crime rates: Insiders' view of the New York City story. *Journal of Criminal Law and Criminology, 88*(4), 1217–1231.

Kelling, G. L., & Coles, C. M. (1996). *Fixing broken windows.* New York: Simon & Schuster.
Kelling, G. L., & Moore, M. H. (1988). The evolving strategy of policing. *Perspectives on policing* (Vol. 4, pp. 1–15). Washington, DC: National Institute of Justice.
Kelling, G. L., & Sousa, W. H., Jr. (2001). *Do police matter? An analysis of the impact of New York City's police reforms.* New York: The Manhattan Institute.
Kornhauser, R. (1978). *The social sources of delinquency.* Chicago: University of Chicago Press.
Kubrin, C. E. (2008). Making order of disorder: A call for conceptual clarity. *Criminology & Public Policy, 7*(2), 203–214.
Langworthy, R. H., & Travis, L. F., III. (2003). *Policing in America* (3rd ed.). Upper Saddle River, NJ: Pearson.
Laub, J. H. (2003). The life course of criminology in the United States: The American Society of Criminology 2003 Presidential Address. *Criminology, 42*(1), 1–26.
Levy, P. R. (2001). Paying for the public life. *Economic Development Quarterly, 15*(2), 124–131.
Lewis, D. A., & Salem, G. (1986). *Fear of crime: Incivility and the production of a social problem.* New Brunswick, NJ: Transaction.
Lowenkamp, C. T., Cullen, F. T., & Pratt, T. C. (2003). Replicating Sampson and Groves's test of social disorganization theory: Revisiting a criminological classic. *Journal of Research in Crime and Delinquency, 40,* 351–373.
Manning, P. K. (2001). Theorizing policing: The drama and myth of crime control in the NYPD. *Theoretical Criminology, 5,* 315–344.
Nagin, D. (2007). Moving choice to center stage in criminological research and theory: The American Society of Criminology 2006 Sutherland Address. *Criminology, 45*(2), 259–272.
Novak, K. J., Hartman, J. L., Holsinger, A. M., & Turner, M. G. (1999). The effects of aggressive policing of disorder on serious crime. *Policing: An International Journal of Police Strategies & Management, 22*(2), 171–190.
Papachristou v. City of Jacksonville, 405 U.S. 156 (1972).
Perkins, D. D., & Taylor, R. B. (1996). Ecological assessments of community disorder: Their relationship to fear of crime and theoretical implications. *American Journal of Community Psychology, 24*(1), 63–107.
Piquero, A. (1999). The validity of incivility measures in public housing. *Justice Quarterly, 16,* 793–818.
Pratt, T. C., & Gau, J. M. (2010). Social disorganization theory. In H. Copes & V. Topalli (Eds.), *Criminological theory: Readings and retrospectives* (pp. 104–112). New York: McGraw-Hill.
Reichl, A. J. (1999). *Reconstructing Times Square.* Lawrence: University Press of Kansas.
Roberts, D. E. (1999). Race, vagueness, and the social meaning of order-maintenance policing. *Journal of Criminal Law and Criminology, 89*(3), 775–836.
Sampson, R. J., & Cohen, J. (1988). Deterrent effects of the police on crime: A replication and theoretical extension. *Law & Society Review, 22*(1), 163–189.

Sampson, R. J., & Groves, W. B. (1989). Community structure and crime: Testing social disorganization theory. *American Journal of Sociology, 94*(4), 774–802.

Sampson, R. J., & Raudenbush, S. W. (1999). Systematic social observation of public spaces: A new look at disorder in urban neighborhoods. *American Journal of Sociology, 105*(3), 603–651.

Sampson, R. J., & Raudenbush, S. W. (2004). Seeing disorder: Neighborhood stigma and the social construction of "broken windows." *Social Psychology Quarterly, 67*(4), 319–342.

Sampson, R. J., Raudenbush, S. W., & Earls, F. (1997). Neighborhoods and violent crime: A multilevel study of collective efficacy. *Science, 277*(5328), 918–924.

Sherman, L. W. (1997). Policing for crime prevention. In L. W. Sherman, D. Gottfredson, D. MacKenzie, J. Eck, P. Reuter, & S. Bushway (Eds.), *Preventing crime: What works, what doesn't, what's promising: A report to the United States Congress* (pp. 8-1–8-67). Washington, DC: National Institute of Justice.

Sherman, L. W., & Weisburd, D. (1995). General deterrent effects of police patrol in crime "hot spots": A randomized, controlled trial. *Justice Quarterly, 12*(4), 625–648.

Sites, W. (2003). *Remaking New York: Primitive globalization and the politics of urban community.* Minneapolis: University of Minnesota Press.

Skogan, W. G. (1990). *Disorder and decline: Crime and the spiral of decay in American neighborhoods.* Berkeley: University of California Press.

Smith, R. (2001). Police-led crackdowns and cleanups: An evaluation of a crime control initiative in Richmond, Virginia. *Crime & Delinquency, 47*(1), 60–83.

Solis, C., Portillos, E. L., & Brunson, R. K. (2009). Latino youths' experiences with and perceptions of involuntary police encounters. *Annals of the American Academy of Political and Social Science, 623,* 39–51.

Stokes, R. J. (2006). Business improvement districts and inner city revitalization: The case of Philadelphia's Frankford Special Services District. *International Journal of Public Administration, 29*(1), 173–186.

Taylor, R. B. (2001). *Breaking away from broken windows.* Boulder, CO: Westview Press.

Walker, S. (1984). "Broken windows" and fractured history: The use and misuse of history in recent police patrol analysis. *Justice Quarterly, 1,* 77–90.

Walsh, R. W. (2006). Union Square Park: From blight to bloom. *Economic Development Journal, 5*(2), 38–46.

Ward, K. (2006). "Policies in motion," urban management and state restructuring: The trans-local expansion of business improvement districts. *International Journal of Urban and Regional Research, 30*(1), 54–75.

Weitzer, R., & Brunson, R. K. (2009). Strategic responses to the police among inner-city youth. *Sociological Quarterly, 50,* 235–256.

Wilson, J. Q. (1968). *Varieties of police behavior.* New York: Atheneum.

Wilson, J. Q. (1975). *Thinking about crime.* New York: Basic Books.

Wilson, J. Q. (1983). *Thinking about crime* (2nd ed.). New York: Vintage Books.

Wilson, J. Q., & Kelling, G. L. (1982, March). The police and neighborhood safety: Broken windows. *Atlantic Monthly,* 29–38.

Wilson, W. J. (1987). *The truly disadvantaged: The inner city, the underclass, and public policy.* Chicago: University of Chicago Press.

Worrall, J. L. (2006a). The discriminant validity of perceptual incivility measures. *Justice Quarterly, 23*(3), 360–383.

Worrall, J. L. (2006b). Does targeting minor offenses reduce serious crime? A provisional, affirmative answer based on an analysis of county-level data. *Police Quarterly, 9*(1), 47–72.

Xu, Y., Fiedler, M. L., & Flaming, K. H. (2005). Discovering the impact of community policing: The broken windows thesis, collective efficacy, and citizens' judgment. *Journal of Research in Crime and Delinquency, 42*(2), 147–186.

Zimring, F. E., & Hawkins, G. (1997). *Crime is not the problem: Lethal violence in America.* New York: Oxford University Press.

NOTES

1. There is also much literature pertaining to the ways in which the criminogenic effects of structural deficiencies can be ameliorated by informal controls such as local friendship ties, shared expectations for control, community-based organizations, and a neighborhood's ability to secure external resources (Bursik & Grasmick, 1993; Carr, 2003; Sampson, Raudenbush, & Earls, 1997).

2. In the 1983 edition of *Thinking About Crime,* J. Q. Wilson reprinted the original broken windows article. Those who missed it in the *Atlantic Monthly* thus had an opportunity to catch a rerun in Wilson's book.

NINE

KEY IDEA: THE WAR ON DRUGS

KEY WORK

Nancy Reagan's "Just Say No" campaign

During the 1980s, America found itself deeply engaged in two very profound wars—they were not, however, wars in the traditional sense of the word. Instead of battling a clearly defined foreign enemy, America was battling two of its own internal problems—crime and drugs. After the Johnson and Nixon administrations of the 1960s both declared a "war on crime," it eventually made sense that a "war on drugs" was also necessary if the nation was to eradicate the problem of illegal substance abuse. To this end, the Reagan administration declared a "war on drugs" in the mid-1980s, which was followed by President George H. W. Bush who declared his own war in 1989 (see Shoemaker, 1989; Walker, 1998), though the war itself had already been well underway by this point.[1] The United States government did, in fact, direct some of its efforts toward foreign countries identified as major drug suppliers (see Bagley, 1988), but much of the battle played out on the streets and in the homes and schools of America itself—these were the primary battlegrounds of the "war on drugs."

America's drug war adopted a multifaceted approach, but, as the *war* metaphor implies, much of the efforts were punitive in nature. Harsh punishments, deterrence, and a focus on incarceration were key mechanisms in the battle against drugs. This approach, of course, was very consistent with the "get tough" movement that had swept throughout the nation during the 1980s, and consequently America's prisons became home to more drug offenders than ever before (Tonry, 1995). But this does not tell the whole story of the drug war, as incarceration was focused more heavily on the *supply,* rather than the *demand* for drugs. To battle the demand side of the equation, the U.S. government adopted a variety of educational approaches, of which one achieved a level of cultural significance and has earned the focus of the current chapter—Nancy Reagan's "Just Say No" campaign to stop substance abuse among America's youth.

The key work discussed in this chapter diverges from the others in this text, as it falls beyond the bounds of traditional academic works. Each of the other works was introduced by scholars in the fields of criminology and criminal justice, whereas the "just say no" approach to drug use was, instead, introduced by a prominent public figure. As will be made clear, however, characterizing America's drug problem as a simple, albeit bad, choice made by individuals was rooted in notions of rational choice theory—a perspective that fueled much of the "get tough" movement. A close examination of Nancy Reagan's "just say no" campaign, along with the social context of the era, will demonstrate why this simple idea became a dominant strategy to resolve an issue that had become central to American criminal justice and the war on drugs.

WINNING THE WAR IS EASY—JUST SAY NO!

A brief examination of recent history reveals that First Ladies of the United States customarily adopt humanitarian or philanthropic causes for bettering the nation. More recently, this can be seen in Michelle Obama's 2010 announcement of the "Let's Move" campaign to eliminate childhood obesity in a single generation. Nearly three decades earlier, Nancy Reagan took up her own equally ambitious cause to rid the nation of a menacing social ill of a different sort—substance abuse by America's youth. And just as the recent campaign to end childhood obesity is characterized by a catchy slogan, Nancy Reagan's antidrug campaign was captured through the simple concept of "Just Say No." In a February 18, 2004, interview with Katie Couric on NBC's *Today Show,* Nancy Reagan recalled the birth of the "Just Say No" campaign:

> I was in California and I was talking to, I think, fifth graders, and one little girl raised her hand and said, "Mrs. Reagan, what do you do if somebody offers you drugs?" And I said, "well, you just say no." And there it was born.

> I think people thought that we had an advertising agency over who dreamed that up—not true.

Shortly after the First Lady made these comments, the "Just Say No" antidrug campaign took off and by the mid-1980s, advertising was widespread (Forman & Lachter, 1989).

The purpose of the "Just Say No" campaign was to employ public education as a means for reducing the demand for illicit drugs. As discussed by Walker (2006), Nancy Reagan's approach relied primarily on two tactics: *fear arousal* and *moral appeal.* The former approach simply attempts to convince its target audience that a particular behavior—in this case, illegal drug use—has frightening consequences. In essence, the goal here is to scare people into "just saying no." The latter approach attempts to convince its target audience that certain behaviors are inherently wrong—because illegal drug use is morally unacceptable, the *right* choice is to "just say no." These messages were delivered to the public through media advertisements, popular television shows, multiple public appearances by Nancy Reagan herself, and the emergence of "Just Say No" clubs for children.

The message to America's youth was clear, but it is important to understand the theoretical reasoning underlying the "just say no" mantra. Despite the complexity surrounding illegal drug use, abuse, and addiction, Nancy Reagan's solution to the problem took a very simplified approach—each individual will either choose to use drugs or, alternatively, choose not to use drugs. Further, this choice is largely considered to be rational: If the individual believes that using drugs will provide some sort of benefit—be it social acceptance, an exhilarating high, or an escape from the problems of everyday life—and the perceived benefit appears to outweigh the potential costs (e.g., being expelled from school, getting kicked off a sports team, or running the risk of health problems), the end result will be drug use. In essence, individual choices are preceded by a cost-benefit analysis that ultimately leads to a decision outcome.

Thinking of this sort is not uncommon, and in the world of criminology, this framework is referred to as *rational choice theory* (see Clarke & Cornish, 2001; Cornish & Clarke, 1986). The implication of this theory is that individual choices can be altered in the desired direction through the use of *deterrence* (see Chapter 2). By informing actual or potential drug users of the negative consequences associated with drug use, the rational choice will be to "just say no." This assumes, of course, that the negative consequences will tip the scale in such a manner that the costs will be perceived to outweigh the benefits. While this perspective is not free of criticism (see Cullen, Pratt, Miceli, & Moon, 2002; Lilly, Cullen, & Ball, 2007), particularly when dealing with potential youth drug users who may feel invincible (Walker, 2006), the "just say no" message has, at times, become a bit disconnected from criminological theory.

For example, Nancy Reagan threw out the first pitch during the 1988 World Series where she also made a short announcement to bolster her campaign against drug use. Rather than focusing on the negative consequences of consuming illegal substances (though she did quickly mention the possibility of withdrawals), the focus was dedicated to informing parents of the imperative need to tell their children to "just say no" if they are ever offered drugs. Similarly, the Ad Council of the National Institute on Drug Abuse also aired short announcements on television displaying adolescents of various ages refusing menacing attempts by shady drug dealers to push their products—each of the scenarios ended with a forceful "No!" shouted out by the potential youth victims. In these instances, the "Just Say No" campaign did not even offer a reasonable deterrent or convincing argument that "no" was the best response to drug use. Instead, the message was simply reduced to "just say no." Not surprisingly, research suggests that public service announcements delivering the "just say no" approach, without actually going a step further and explaining why "no" is the best answer, are unlikely to be effective (Fishbein, Hall-Jamieson, Zimmer, Haeften, & Nabi, 2002).

Even when grounded in notions of rational choice and deterrence, Nancy Reagan's approach suffers from a variety of additional critiques. First, by assuming that children are rational actors who make rational choices, the actual *root causes* of drug abuse frequently go unaddressed. Imagine the adolescent who suffers from sexual, physical, or emotional abuse in the home and ultimately "chooses" to escape his or her intolerable reality through drug abuse. Advising such an individual to avoid the pains of drug use by "just saying no" is hardly useful for addressing the conditions, or criminogenic needs (see Chapter 10 for a related discussion), that may have led to drug abuse in the first place.

Second, the very assumption that youth reach decisions through a rational choice framework is subject to scrutiny. If youth tend to be oriented toward short-term satisfaction rather than potential long-tem consequences of their behavior, then efforts to deter may be unlikely to affect their decisions (Walker, 2006). Along these lines, Bouffard (2007) found that younger individuals were less likely to consider the social consequences of their actions and the potential harm to others when deciding whether to engage in certain offenses. This is hardly the image of the rational calculator in the traditional sense.

Third, fear arousal strategies do not always have their intended consequences, a fact that has become exceedingly clear in the evaluation of efforts to *scare* kids straight. The now infamous Scared Straight programs—where hardcore offenders or "lifers" set out to "teach" juveniles about the horrifying realities of prison life—have been proven not only to be ineffective, but actually *harmful.* Several evaluations of this fear arousal tactic unveiled catastrophic results: Juveniles that were exposed to the "scared straight" sessions were, on average, *more likely* to engage in crime than those who did not participate in the program (Petrosino, Turpin-Petrosino, & Finckenauer, 2000). Nearly eight decades ago, Franklin D. Roosevelt famously told a suffering nation that "the only thing to fear is fear itself." With some contextual adjustment and a bit of a twist, it would seem that the same advice may well ring true in the case of fear arousal strategies. As Walker (2006) suggests, the bottom line is that fear arousal strategies aimed at reducing drug use may "backfire by glamorizing the forbidden behavior" (p. 274).

Despite these shortcomings, Nancy Reagan's "Just Say No" to drugs campaign emerged as a central component to America's drug war in the early 1980s; the simple message soon became a catch phrase that permeated public discourse on drug abuse. Certainly, the vessel by which this message was delivered—the First Lady of the United States—was influential in its adoption as a drug-reduction strategy, but, as will be made clear, the social context of the era also created an atmosphere that was highly conducive to the ideology underlying the "Just Say No" movement.

THE 1980s IN CONTEXT

During the 1980s, the United States transitioned into a new era where the overarching sociopolitical climate was dominated by conservative thought, or what some even referred to as conservative *theology*—a term indicating the staunch commitment to certain "truths" about social reality and human behavior held by conservative proponents (Walker, 2006). Lilly, Cullen, and Ball (2007) make clear that the onset of conservative thought in the 1980s was in part an "ideological reaction against (a) the moral decadence and distain for faith of the hedonistic secular culture and (b) the liberal welfare state whose policies were seen to make social dependents out of the poor and minorities" (p. 234). Elements of conservative thought were by no means absent during the 1960s and 1970s, but during that era, some of the more prominent critiques of the American social system focused on issues of inequality—especially racial inequality as seen through the civil rights movement. Recognizing the social ills facing America, criminologists frequently traced ideas about crime and its causation to the broader social structure. But soon, this thinking became inconsistent with the dominant viewpoint of Americans.

Moving into the 1980s, the United States was beginning to suffer from an economic downturn, and at the same time, was just exiting a period of tumultuous social unrest that represented a departure from the flourishing years that followed World War II. Longing for the peace, prosperity, and stability of the 1950s, the American mood began to shift toward the conservative end of the spectrum. In a way, the conservative framework offered many Americans a sense of relief, and this was particularly true when it came to understanding the causes of crime. While the previous decades had unraveled a variety of criminogenic conditions rooted within U.S. society, and the general population had ultimately blamed unjust social conditions for crime (as well as inequality and poverty), conservatives were dissatisfied with this assessment and instead placed the blame squarely on the individual. For many conservatives, the root cause of criminal behavior essentially boiled down to *bad people* making *bad choices.* Armed with this understanding, conservatives could proudly embrace American society—and with a clear conscience, since social conditions were not to blame but rather the *individual.*

By shifting the source of undesirable behavior off of society and onto the individual, the solution to America's social problems took on a new form: Poverty was not seen as the result of broad structural inequalities rooted in American society, but rather as the absence of appropriate values among the poor. Any American had the opportunity to be well off, but it required citizens to take personal responsibility for their condition, to work hard, and to ultimately take their lives into their own hands. Those who remained members of the lower class did so as a consequence of their own choices. Even further, it was not the government's responsibility to provide for citizens unwilling to provide for themselves. Likewise, since crime was not caused by social injustice, but rather the bad choices made by people, it made sense to adopt harsh punishments to encourage lawful decision making. If this failed, then individuals would be forced to take personal responsibility for their criminal behavior through the stiff sanctions that awaited them.

Conservative ideology provided the framework for "getting tough" on offenders, and not surprisingly, the get tough movement intensified considerably during the 1980s. During this era, it seemed to make more sense than ever before to rely on incarceration as a solution to the crime problem. If individuals' choices were at the heart of the crime problem, then imprisonment seemed a reasonable solution—and if people were not deterred by the threat of punishment, they could be removed from society instead. In accordance with this perspective, the incarceration rate skyrocketed throughout the 1980s, reaching levels never before seen in history (Austin & Irwin, 2001; Pratt, 2009).

America's war on drugs fit nicely into this conservative crime control model. If Americans refused to stop buying, selling, using, and possessing drugs, they would have to be punished, and more severely than in the past. Here, too, the problem was clearly rooted in *individuals* who *chose* to make bad decisions related to drugs. Consequently, the conservative administrations led by Reagan and Bush, Sr. during the 1980s ramped up the war on drugs beyond the efforts of their predecessors and considerably enhanced punishments for drug-related offenders. Some of the most notable changes entailed the adoption of the Anti-Drug Abuse Acts of 1986 and 1988. As a result of these and similar laws, Americans for the first time were facing *mandatory* prison sentences for merely possessing illegal substances (Gray, 2001).

But Nancy Reagan's "Just Say No" campaign was not calling for draconian punishments to deter illegal drug use. In fact, by comparison, her response seemed a bit soft for the conservative approach that was largely embodied in the rhetoric of "war." So how is it, then, that the social context of the 1980s favored the "just say no" strategy? The answer to this question does not require one to dig too deeply. As discussed previously, the "just say no" crusade very much embodied an *individualistic* approach to understanding drug use. Drug users, like any other criminals, were seen as rational individuals who simply made bad decisions. They either needed to have their moral compasses adjusted, or they needed to be educated about the fearful consequences of drug use—once accomplished, they would "just say no." Either way, the roots of drug use were clearly traced to the individual, fully bypassing the possibility that complex structural conditions within society might be at play. Whether or not drug use was more heavily concentrated in poverty-stricken, urbanized communities was of no concern. Ultimately, such explanations had no place in the conservative theology that began to permeate American thought during the 1980s.

THE MAGIC IN "JUST SAY NO"

The "Just Say No" movement certainly caught on with some ferocity during the 1980s, and as demonstrated, much of the reasoning behind the onset of this movement was linked to the social context of the time. But it was more than just social context that fueled the popularity of "just say no." To be sure, scholars writing during this era and in the years prior had begun to argue that criminals were simply rational thinkers that could be deterred from engaging in illegal behavior, whether it be drug use or other crimes—that they simply made choices based on assessment of costs and benefits (e.g., Becker, 1968; see also Gibbs, 1975). It was not their writings, however, that popularized the rational choice perspective and placed it at the forefront of American thought. The academic debates about the utility of rational choice in understanding criminal behavior largely remained confined to the arena of scholars (primarily sociologists and economists), but beyond that had little influence on public perceptions. Conservative opinions about crime causation had certainly begun to sweep the nation, but it was Nancy Reagan who packaged the idea of rational choice and delivered it to the American public through her "Just Say No" campaign in a way that had not been previously accomplished.

In some cases, the messenger is just as important as the message itself—and sometimes even more important. Certainly this phenomenon played a significant role in the rising popularity of the key idea discussed in this chapter. Fortunately for Nancy Reagan, the nature of the news media is such that high-profile individuals like the First Lady generate substantial media attention. Whereas criminologists often find themselves in the dissatisfying position of being wholly ignored by the American public, Nancy Reagan was perfectly positioned to deliver her message in a way that would be difficult for Americans to miss. Only a few years into the "Just Say No" campaign, Nancy Reagan had already appeared on numerous talk shows where her ideas about drug use were championed to a receptive American public (Benze, 2005). Without doubt, the First Lady's audience included a large portion of the American people. As illustrated in Chapter 6, the media can play a central role in popularizing ideas about criminal justice issues, and this was surely an advantage afforded to the "just say no" message.

The media certainly provided coverage of Nancy Reagan's "just say no" efforts, but exposure was not limited to press attention. The very nature of the "Just Say No" campaign itself was geared toward informing the public and as a result, considerable resources were allocated to this end. "Just Say No" was plastered across billboards and worked into public service announcements that appeared on television and were aired over the radio (Forman & Lachter, 1989). In 1986, President Reagan established Just Say No Week to help bolster national attention to the campaign, and by this time, "Just Say No" clubs were being established across the nation. Consequently, it is not surprising that Nancy Reagan's solution to the drug problem was able to reach such a large audience, and this is central to understanding how this key idea became so dominant during the 1980s.

The popularity of the "just say no" message can also be traced to the simplicity of the idea itself. Imagine for a minute that Nancy Reagan had delivered a different message, one that was more complex in nature. She could have attempted to unpack the multifaceted nature of drug addiction and the various individual and structural correlates of drug abuse, but this would have been tough to sell. First, it would be exceedingly difficult to capture the nature of a complex problem within the confines of short speeches, quick public service announcements, and billboard messages. But even more important is the fact that complex problems almost always require complex solutions—and complex solutions are much less likely to convey the message that victory is within reach. Even when disconnected from reality, a simple solution can be much more appealing, despite the complicated nature of the problem. By adopting an overly simplistic, though seemingly genuine, understanding of the drug problem, Nancy Reagan's "Just Say No" campaign had a flavor with widespread appeal to Americans. After all, if kids "just say no," the drug problem will eventually cease to exist. Even when solutions seem to rely more on magic than reality, it is not uncommon for people to gravitate toward positive messages that offer hope, and "just say no" did just that.

THE IMPACT OF "JUST SAY NO"

To date, there is no convincing evidence that Nancy Reagan's efforts were able to reduce illegal drug use in the United States. If anything, evidence suggests that efforts aimed to convince children to "just say no" are ineffective (Fishbein et al., 2002; Walker, 2006). Even so, the "Just Say No" campaign had a powerful influence on the U.S. approach to the drug problem. As will be made clear, the popularity of "just say no" created an environment that supported an onslaught of media attention to the drug problem and sparked a variety of efforts that paralleled the strategy embodied by Nancy Reagan's movement.

In 1986, only a few years after Nancy Reagan began her campaign, the Partnership for a Drug-Free America (PDFA) emerged as a nonprofit organization that aimed to "unsell" narcotics to the American public, a mission that it continues to date (www.drugfree.org). The organization's approach was very similar to that of the "Just Say No" campaign—simple public service announcements were aired with the intention of "educating" the public about the harms of drug use. The most famous of these advertisements relied on an egg and a frying pan to deliver a fear-inspiring message about the effects of drug use. In the short advertisement, a man held up an egg and said, "This is your brain." Pointing to a searing hot frying pan, he then said, "This is drugs." Without delay, he cracked open the egg, spilled its contents onto the scalding pan where they quickly began to fry, and announced, "This is your brain on drugs." To end the segment, the "educator" stared into the camera and asked, "Any questions?" Later versions of the egg advertisement targeted heroin use, and featured a woman who smashed an egg with a frying pan and then proceeded to violently destroy the entire kitchen, demonstrating that the effects of drug use went beyond the individual (egg) to destroy families, friends, and futures (kitchen). The message was clear—the costs of drug use clearly outweigh any potential benefits. Who could possibly have questions? But in the end, these and similar fear-inspiring efforts appeared more useful for generating a laugh than a reduction in drug use (Walker, 2006).

Around the same time, the National Institute on Drug Abuse (NIDA) also took advantage of the groundwork laid by the "Just Say No" movement to introduce a national advertising campaign targeting the "lies" of cocaine use (Forman & Lachter, 1989). NIDA consulted the same agency that helped bring popularity to Nancy Regan's effort, the Ad Council, and launched its first public service announcement: "Cocaine, The Big Lie" (Shoemaker, 1989). The short advertisements featured once-successful adults who shared their stories of loss as a result of cocaine abuse. The purpose of the message was to demonstrate the damaging effects of the drug and to convince the public that cocaine was a highly addictive substance—if anyone suggested otherwise, it was a "big lie."

Other drug-reduction strategies also capitalized on the publicity of Nancy Reagan's "just say no" message. Throughout the 1980s and 1990s, programs such as D.A.R.E (Drug Abuse Resistance Education), Project SMART, Project ALERT, and many others flourished. Though somewhat different in their approaches, each of these efforts contained strong elements of the "just say no" ideology. The primary prevention mechanism was to teach kids to abstain from drug use. As these efforts became popularized, D.A.R.E. emerged at the forefront of drug education strategies. The attention that Nancy Regan had brought to the issue placed D.A.R.E. in the perfect position for federal funding, and during the 1980s, the program took off. It eventually spread throughout the nation, appearing in classrooms in every state, and even made its way to foreign countries who were hoping to combat their drug problems (Midford, 2000). Although the effects of educational programs are somewhat varied, the overwhelming evidence pertaining to the efficacy of D.A.R.E suggests that it was a failed attempt. As it turned out, D.A.R.E. kids were no more likely to "say no" to drugs than non-D.A.R.E. kids (Clayton, Catterello, & Johnstone, 1996; Ennett, Tobler, Ringwalt, & Flewelling, 1994; Midford, 2000). With a bit of irony, these and other findings have prompted scholars to offer candid advice: "Just say no to D.A.R.E." (see Rosenbaum, 2007). But the scientific community was not enough to overcome the sheer popularity of the program—currently, D.A.R.E. continues to receive funding nationwide.

Nancy Reagan's high-profile "Just Say No" campaign set the stage for the United States to bombard its children with messages about the frightening consequences of drug use. In doing so, it also played a role in striking a "moral panic" among the American public (Goode, 1990; Kerr, 1986). Writing of the drug problem during the 1980s, Goode (1990) explained,

> In short, by every conceivable criterion, drug use emerged as a major social problem—indeed, some say, *the* social problem—during the 1980s. So intense and widespread was (and is) this concern that it is fair to say that the country experienced and is experiencing something of a *moral panic.* (p. 1089, emphasis original)

The efforts of "Just Say No," along with similar efforts that paralleled this basic message, brought considerable attention to the issue of drug abuse—so much attention, in fact, that the problem itself became disconnected from reality. Indeed, the drug use/abuse problem was being framed politically as "out of control" at a time when overall drug use in the country had been dropping steadily for nearly two decades (see Baum, 1996). Looking back on this issue, scholars such as Goode (1990) suggested that the drug problem was not fully grounded in reality, but rather was in part *constructed* by the media. Such overreactions may not be healthy for the psyche of the American public, but were certainly helpful in furthering America's war on drugs.

CONCLUSION

The "Just Say No" campaign emerged as a popular approach for managing drug abuse during the 1980s and was an integral part of the "war on drugs." As was demonstrated in this chapter, the way in which Nancy Reagan marketed the idea, along with the social context of the 1980s, created the perfect conditions for "Just Say No" to flourish. The mood of the American public had undergone a very evident shift as the nation transitioned out of the turbulent 1960s and 1970s and into the 1980s. Conservative ideology had become more dominant during this era, and this was reflected in the elections of Republican presidents Ronald Reagan and George H. W. Bush. Popular among conservatives was the notion that human behavior was largely rational, and consequently, the root of many social problems could be traced to individuals and their bad choices.

Consistent with this ideology, some scholars during the late 1960s and 1970s attempted to promote rational choice perspectives of crime causation. This was particularly true of economists who developed an interest in criminal behavior (see, for example, Becker, 1968; Ehrlich, 1973). Even though the social context of the 1980s had become very favorable to these ideas, scholars were not responsible for popularizing the rational choice theory of offending among the American people. This was largely accomplished by Nancy Reagan, who was much better positioned to influence public discourse about human behavior, and particularly drug use.

Armed with a simple message that was easy for the public to swallow and the media to market, the First Lady invented the "rational" drug user who could "just say no." Because this message fit well with the conservative climate in America, the "Just Say No" campaign was able to shape the country's response to illicit drug use in powerful ways. Despite its overly simplistic conception of the drug problem and lack of scientific support, elements of Nancy Reagan's antidrug ideology permeated the era's drug-reduction strategies in the form of various educational programs and advertisements demonstrating the fearful consequences of drug use in the hopes that children would "just say no."

DISCUSSION QUESTIONS

1. What theoretical perspective of crime causation was Nancy Reagan's "Just Say No" message predicated on?
2. How did Nancy Reagan's "just say no" message fit in with the "get tough" approach to the war on drugs?
3. What effect did the "Just Say No" campaign have on the public's perception of the extent of America's drug problem during the 1980s?

REFERENCES

Austin, J., & Irwin, J. (2001). *It's about time: America's imprisonment binge.* Belmont, CA: Wadsworth.

Bagley, B. (1988). The new hundred years war? US national security and the war on drugs in Latin America. *Journal of Interamerican Studies and World Affairs, 30*(1), 161–182.

Baum, D. (1996). *Smoke and mirrors: The war on drugs and the politics of failure.* New York: Little, Brown.

Becker, G. (1968). Crime and punishment: An economic approach. *Journal of Political Economy, 76*(2), 169–217.

Benze, J. (2005). *Nancy Reagan: On the White House stage.* Lawrence: University Press of Kansas.

Bouffard, J. (2007). Predicting differences in the perceived relevance of crime's costs and benefits in a test of rational choice theory. *International Journal of Offender Therapy and Comparative Criminology, 51*(4), 461–485.

Clarke, R. V., & Cornish, D. B. (2001). Rational choice. In R. Paternoster & R. Bachman (Eds.), *Explaining criminals and crime: Essays in contemporary criminological theory* (pp. 23–42). Los Angeles: Roxbury.

Clayton, R., Catterello, A., & Johnstone, B. (1996). The effectiveness of Drug Abuse Resistance Education (Project DARE): 5-year follow-up results. *Preventative Medicine, 25*(3), 307–318.

Cornish, D. B., & Clarke, R. V. (1986). *The reasoning criminal: Rational choice perspectives on offending.* New York: Springer.

Cullen, F. T., Pratt, T. C., Miceli, S. L., & Moon, M. M. (2002). Dangerous liaison? Rational choice theory as the basis for correctional intervention. In A. R. Piquero & S. G. Tibbetts (Eds.), *Rational choice and criminal behavior: Recent research and future challenges* (pp. 279–296). New York: Routledge.

Ehrlich, I. (1973, May/June). Participation in illegitimate activities: A theoretical and empirical investigation. *Journal of Political Economy, 81*(3), 521–565.

Ennett, S., Tobler, N., Ringwalt, C., & Flewelling, R. (1994). How effective is drug abuse resistance education? A meta-analysis of Project DARE outcome evaluations. *American Journal of Public Health, 84,* 1394–1401.

Fishbein, K., Hall-Jamieson, K., Zimmer, E., Haeften, I. von, & Nabi, R. (2002). Avoiding the boomerang: Testing the relative effectiveness of antidrug public service announcements before a national campaign. *American Journal of Public Health, 92,* 238–245.

Forman, A., & Lachter, S. (1989). The National Institute on Drug Abuse cocaine prevention campaign. In P. Shoemaker (Ed.), *Communication campaigns about drug use: Government, media, and the public.* Hillsdale, NJ: Erlbaum.

Gibbs, J. (1975). *Crime, punishment, and deterrence.* New York: Elsevier.

Goode, E. (1990). The American drug panic of the 1980s: Social construction or objective threat? *International Journal of the Addictions, 25*(9), 1083–1098.

Gray, J. (2001). *Why our drug laws have failed and what we can do about it.* Philadelphia: Temple University Press.

Kerr, P. (1986, November 17). Anatomy of an issue: Drugs, the evidence, the reaction. *New York Times,* pp. A1, B6.

Lilly, R., Cullen, F. T., & Ball, R. (2007). *Criminological theory: Context and consequences* (4th ed.). Thousand Oaks, CA: Sage.

Midford, R. (2000). Does drug education work? *Drug and Alcohol Review, 19,* 441–446.
Petrosino, A., Turpin-Petrosino, C., & Finckenauer, J. (2000). Well-meaning programs can have harmful effects! Lessons from experiments of programs such as Scared Straight. *Crime & Delinquency, 46*(3), 354–379.
Pratt, T. C. (2009). *Addicted to incarceration: Corrections policy and the politics of misinformation in the United States.* Thousand Oaks, CA: Sage.
Rosenbaum, D. (2007). Just say no to D.A.R.E. *Criminology & Public Policy, 6*(4), 815–824.
Shoemaker, P. (1989). *Communication campaigns about drugs: Government, media, and the public.* Hillsdale, NJ: Erlbaum.
Tonry, M. (1995). *Malign neglect—Race, crime, and punishment in America.* New York: Oxford University Press.
Walker, S. (1998). *Popular justice: A history of American criminal justice* (2nd ed.). New York: Oxford University Press.
Walker, S. (2006). *Sense and nonsense about crime and drugs: A policy guide.* Belmont, CA: Thomson Wadsworth.
Whitford, A., & Yates, J. (2003). Policy signals and executive governance: Presidential rhetoric in the war on drugs. *Journal of Politics, 65*(4), 995–1012.

NOTE

1. It is worth noting that Nixon was the first president to use the phrase "war on drugs" (Whitford & Yates, 2003), though the most substantial policy changes came from the Reagan and Bush, Sr., administrations.

TEN

KEY IDEA: REHABILITATION—NOT DEAD YET

KEY WORK

Andrews, D. A., Zinger, I., Hoge, R. D., Bonta, J., Gendreau, P., & Cullen, F. T. (1990). Does correctional treatment work? A clinically relevant and psychologically informed meta-analysis. *Criminology, 28,* 369–404.

In the decades following the Martinson Report (discussed in Chapter 6), the world of American corrections underwent monumental changes. The onslaught of new laws targeting criminals for lengthier, determinate prison terms signaled a new era where rehabilitation took a distant backseat to deterrence, punishment, and incarceration. Prisons began to abandon treatment programs that "didn't work," and both the states and the federal government engaged in a variety of sentencing reforms that aimed at cracking down on offenders. American corrections had officially transitioned from the medical model of diagnosis and treatment to the "get tough" model of fear and punishment. Though policy makers had clearly made up their minds, to which the growing prison industry could undoubtedly attest, researchers continued to debate the efficacy of rehabilitation and whether or not it had a meaningful place in the future of correctional practice. Much of this debate went unheard by the American public (after all, in their minds, the debate was settled) and fell short of offering practitioners real-world guidance that might alter their course of action.

Rehabilitation had only recently succumbed to a very public death, and few, it would seem, were willing to entertain the idea of resuscitating an old practice that was "proven" to be ineffective. Over time, however, key researchers chipped away at the flawed reputation of the rehabilitation ideal, pointing out that *some types* of programs did appear to be effective, at least for *some types* of offenders. The obvious question to be answered was, which programs were best for which offenders? In recognizing the complexity of this simple question, Ted Palmer (1975) noted that,

> lest we think that a complete answer lies just around the corner, the following "reminder" may not be entirely amiss: The history of science teaches that all-encompassing solutions are seldom to be found and that neither "breakthroughs" nor "comprehensive approaches" emerge without careful preparation. . . . Despite its understandable pressures and frustrations, corrections will have to cultivate not just imagination but, above all, patience and precision. (p. 150)

Palmer was correct in identifying the need for patience and precision, as it was not until 15 years later that Don Andews and his colleagues (Ivan Zinger, Robert Hoge, James Bonta, Paul Gendreau, and Francis Cullen) introduced and tested the principles of risk, need, and responsivity, which marked a notable advance toward understanding the ingredients of effective rehabilitation. While not an "all-encompassing solution" to the problem of offender recidivism, Andrews, Zinger, et al.'s (1990) work breathed new life into the rehabilitative approach.

This chapter identifies the most important elements of Andrews, Zinger, et al.'s (1990) article. In doing so, it demonstrates how these researchers were able to successfully communicate a message to a field that was, at least initially, less than willing to listen. The success of their work was not independent of the prevailing social context, and as such, the state of crime and corrections in America are also addressed in this chapter. Finally, this chapter concludes with a discussion of the overall impact that this work has had in the quest to lower offender recidivism.

THE PRINCIPLES OF RISK, NEED, AND RESPONSIVITY

While U.S. criminologists, policy makers, and correctional officials used Martinson's (1974) "proof" that rehabilitation was a failed concept to segue into the new "tough on crime" era, a few scholars remained skeptical of the primary justification for change. Simply put, they were not convinced that "nothing works" to rehabilitate offenders. As noted by Cullen and Gendreau (2001), these scholars were primarily operating from outside of the United States, and equally critical, from outside the field of criminology. It is important to recognize—and this will be further discussed in the following section—that these Canadian psychologists had not accepted the "conventional wisdom" in America that positive behavioral changes were impossible, or at least too improbable, to instill in criminal offenders. As we will see, these individuals were far enough removed from the prevailing social context of the United States that they remained particularly immune to the dominant belief that rehabilitation had ultimately failed. In their minds—and this is exceedingly clear in Andrews, Zinger, et al.'s (1990) work—conventional wisdom suggested that some attempts at rehabilitation were more successful than others. To be sure, some programs were so poorly thought out and executed that their effects were even harmful (see Petrosino, Turpin-Petrosino, & Finckenauer, 2000). But ultimately, there was a meaningful explanation for *why* some programs failed and why others were quite successful.

However, this sentiment, that certain programs worked and worked well, was not shared by the majority of American criminologists. For this reason, researchers such as Palmer (1975) and Gendreau and Ross (1979) attempted to demonstrate that some correctional treatment programs did work to lower recidivism. Palmer reanalyzed Martinson's (1974) data and reported that nearly half of the evaluation studies discussed by Martinson demonstrated positive effects (see Chapter 6 for further discussion). In an attempt to refute the common belief that rehabilitation was hopeless when pitted against hardened criminals, Gendreau and Ross published a provocative article entitled "Effective Correctional Treatment: Bibliotherapy for Cynics." In their article, they provided the reader with "bibliotherapy," or more specifically, findings from a long list of recently conducted studies that demonstrated positive outcomes. Moreover, these researchers also offered some insight into the question of why particular programs were better than others. Even so, it would seem that a more concrete or usable explanation of quality programs was needed. It was this void that Don Andrews and his colleagues attempted to fill.

In 1990, Andrews and his coauthors, Zinger, Hoge, Bonta, Gendreau, and Cullen, published the findings of their research in an article entitled "Does Correctional Treatment Work? A Clinically Relevant and Psychologically Informed Meta-Analysis." As the title suggests, the researchers were attempting to provide practitioners with information that could be used in the "real world" for enhancing clinical practice. In essence, what Andrews, Zinger, et al. offered was a theoretical perspective that explained which programs were likely to succeed and which were likely to fail. The researchers set out to test their hypothesis about effective correctional treatment through the use of meta-analysis, a technique that was relatively new to the field of American corrections and a methodology that some claim is in part responsible for saving rehabilitation (Cullen & Gendreau, 2000).

Before delving into the theoretical perspective offered by Andrews, Zinger, et al., a few words about meta-analysis are necessary. As mentioned, the technique itself was fairly new to correctional research, though its utility had been previously established in other fields such as education, medicine, and psychology. Meta-analysis has gained popularity largely as a result of the critiques associated with narrative literature reviews. When undertaking a narrative review, the researcher gathers all available evidence on a topic of interest (e.g., the effect of treatment programs on offender recidivism), wades through the studies, and provides a subjective summary of the "overall" findings and patterns that emerge. This is particularly useful for those interested in the general status of a given subject matter, but the shortcoming is that the reader must rely primarily on the judgment of the reviewer. In the end, narrative reviews can be beneficial, but suffer from a lack of transparency—it is not always clear how exactly the narrative reviewer derived his or her conclusions. What is considered successful to some may indeed appear to be a failure to others.

While not a wholesale solution to the potential subjectivity of narrative reviews, meta-analysis is able to offer a *quantitative* and *transparent* summary of the literature. Rather than simply summarizing trends and patterns, the meta-analyst extracts the statistical "effect size" for the relationship of interest from each qualifying study. In the context of our discussion here, the effect size would represent a treatment program's effect on recidivism (compared to a nontreatment or control group), as reported in each study gathered by the meta-analyst. The effect size could take the form of a positive, negative, or zero value, indicating a reduction in recidivism, an increase in recidivism, or no effect on recidivism, respectively. The effect sizes provided by the research studies included in the meta-analysis are averaged to determine the overall effect size across all studies. This process provides the reader with a fairly precise estimate of the relationship of interest—something that the narrative reviewer is forced to speculate about, usually with a bit of generality and vagueness. Not only that, but the meta-analyst can also extract other important information from the studies that might have a bearing on the average effect size. Since no two studies are exactly the same, study characteristics such as sample size, geographic location, type of offender, type of treatment, and various other factors can each be coded and controlled in the analysis. This approach allows the meta-analyst to answer important questions about the factors associated with effective treatment (i.e., a larger average effect size). All of this can be accomplished in a way that provides the reader with the precise methodology employed by the meta-analyst, eliminating much of the subjective mystery that often accompanies a traditional narrative review. (For more about meta-analysis, see Lipsey & Wilson, 2001.)

Using this technique, Andrews and colleagues set out to test what they believed to be important elements of successful rehabilitative treatment—namely, adherence to the principles of risk, need, and responsivity. According to these researchers, programs designed around these three principles would be more effective than those programs that failed to recognize their importance.

Risk

The principle of *risk,* as indicated by Andrews, Zinger, et al. (1990), "suggests that higher levels of service are best reserved for higher risk cases and that low-risk cases are best assigned to minimal service" (p. 374). This relatively straightforward principle is based on the fact that higher-risk offenders have more "room for improvement" than lower-risk offenders, and that lower-risk offenders, quite simply, are less likely to reoffend to begin with. Even so, it is not uncommon for practitioners to assume that the best approach is to find those offenders who appear "easiest" to fix. These individuals are frequently believed to be amenable to change, while the high-risk individuals are viewed as hardened criminals who cannot be helped. Moreover, such an approach can "appear" effective from a practitioner's standpoint, since adequate control groups are not always used to draw conclusions about the efficacy of treatment programs. Instead, as long as the number of offenders who do not reoffend "looks good," then the program may be considered a success. Unfortunately, as Andrews and colleagues point out, taking such an approach is not only misguided, but is an unfortunate waste of precious resources. Once an appropriate control group is introduced, the "apparent success" of the program can quickly dwindle. In the end, higher-level treatment must be reserved for high-risk offenders to produce the largest reductions in recidivism.

Need

According to Andrews, Zinger, et al. (1990), the principle of *need* must also be recognized and explicitly addressed by treatment programs. The authors identified two types of risk factors that relate to criminal offending: static risk factors and dynamic risk factors. The former entails various characteristics of the offender that are unchangeable, such as being raised by a single mother or having a criminal history. While these may be factors that place an individual at risk for future criminality, there is nothing that can be done to change them. Dynamic risk factors, on the other hand, include offender characteristics that can, in fact, be changed. These dynamic risk factors are referred to as "criminogenic needs" and represent the characteristics of the offender that should ideally be targeted by treatment for successful rehabilitation. In some detail, Andrews, Zinger, et al. describe that,

> The most promising intermediate targets include changing antisocial attitudes, feelings, and peer associations; promoting familial affection in combination with enhanced parental monitoring and supervision; promoting identification with anticriminal role models; increasing self-control and self-management skills; replacing the skills of lying, stealing and aggression with other, more prosocial skills; reducing chemical dependencies; and generally shifting the density of rewards and costs for criminal and noncriminal activities in familial, academic, vocational, and other behavioral settings. (p. 375)

The dynamic risk factors, or criminogenic needs, represent various factors identified by criminologists as important to understanding criminal behavior. If such factors are at the root cause of crime and delinquency, they must be targeted for effective change.

While this principle may seem to offer nothing more than common sense, it, too, has been frequently underutilized by practitioners responsible for designing treatment programs. Instead of creating programs that cater to the offender's specific criminogenic needs, many programs take a "one-size-fits-all" approach, rendering the same treatment to all offenders despite variation in their underlying needs. At best, this strategy may only work for a very small proportion of offenders. Other programs, such as those based on the boot camp prison or "scared straight" models, target few, if any, criminogenic needs. Instead, they rely on assumptions that harsh discipline and fear will be enough to instill lasting change in offenders. This strategy may provide momentary satisfaction to a public frustrated by crime and delinquency, but it relies on a methodology that does not exactly garner the criminologists' "stamp of approval." In the end, addressing this simple principle of need, as Andrews, Zinger, et al. argue, offers real value to the field of corrections, and implies substantial change for many correctional programs.

Responsivity

The final principle that Andrews, Zinger, et al. (1990) introduced was *responsivity,* a principle that, in their words, "has to do with the selection of styles and modes of service that are (a) capable of influencing the specific types of intermediate targets that are set with offenders and (b) appropriately matched to the learning styles of offenders" (p. 375). In short, the authors suggest that treatment programs must adopt methods that are appropriate for addressing the underlying causes of undesirable, wayward, or criminal behaviors. In many instances, this might include a form of behavioral or cognitive treatment that is specifically adapted to the *learning styles* of the offender. It is now common knowledge among educators that individuals learn in different ways, with some individuals being more responsive to one method but less so to another. Andrews and his colleagues suggest that programs designed to be "highly verbal, evocative, and relationship dependent" seem to work best with offenders that possess a high level of verbal skills, the ability to engage in deep self-reflection, and an attachment to others. This approach is expected to work well with offenders of this type since it attempts to specifically address their learning styles. Applying this method of treatment to individuals with poor verbal skills and an inability to relate well to others should be less likely to proffer the desired results. Thus, a successful rehabilitative program must consider the responsivity of its clients.

Putting the Principles to the Test

It should be noted that the principles of risk, need, and responsivity had been introduced in an earlier work by Andrews, Bonta, and Hoge (1990), but had not stood the test of empiricism. Past criticisms of rehabilitative programs ranged from "nothing works" (e.g., Martinson, 1974; Whitehead & Lab, 1989) to "we don't really know what works." While the more extreme "nothing works" mantra eventually dissipated, the remaining question of what works and for whom became increasingly important to answer. Of course, Andrews, Zinger, et al. (1990) believed a good portion of this answer was found in their principles of effective rehabilitation. If they were right, a meta-analysis of the research would demonstrate considerable differences in the effectiveness of programs that adhered to the principles as compared to those programs that failed to do so.

Consequently, Andrews and his colleagues gathered the relevant studies (80 in total, yielding 154 effect sizes), many of which were conducted in the years following Martinson's (1974) report, and conducted a meta-analysis. The studies were divided into four categories: (1) criminal sanctions, (2) inappropriate correctional service, (3) appropriate correctional service, and (4) unspecified correctional service. In their study, criminal sanctions included typical punitive dispositions such as using custody in lieu of probation. This category of studies provided the reader with the ability to compare the reductions in recidivism (presumably) gained by enhancing criminal sanctions versus reductions gained by relying on correctional treatment. The inappropriate correctional service category included those programs that ignored the principles of risk, need, and responsivity. The appropriate correctional service category, on the other hand, included those programs that adhered to the risk, need, and responsivity principles. The last category of studies addressed programs in which the studies did not make it explicitly clear as to whether issues of risk, need, and responsivity were addressed.

The findings of Andrews, Zinger, et al.'s (1990) meta-analysis were supportive of their conceptual framework. As they expected, the type of treatment was highly correlated with the magnitude of the effect size estimates, and programs that fell into the appropriate correctional service category provided the most substantial reduction in recidivism rates—an average decrease of 53 percent. The average reduction in recidivism for the studies falling into the unspecified correctional treatment category was much smaller, but the effect of these programs was still in the desired direction. In sharp contrast, however, the studies included in the criminal sanctions and inappropriate correctional treatment categories failed to reduce recidivism rates. In the end, their study offered strong empirical evidence supporting the principles of risk, need, and responsivity, and ultimately provided a solid foundation for answering the questions of what works and for whom.

SOCIAL CONTEXT

The social context that led to the death of rehabilitation played a very strong and clear role—both conservatives and liberals were disillusioned by rehabilitation, though for different reasons, and ultimately pushed for its demise. Martinson's (1974) "nothing works" assessment fit nicely into this sociopolitical climate by providing the scientific justification needed to abandon the failed rehabilitative ideal. Though social context is important for understanding the eventual impact of Andrews, Zinger, et al.'s (1990) research, the link between the two is somewhat less obvious. As will be seen, the public was not exactly begging for the return of rehabilitation, and ultimately, its reemergence was far slower than its comparatively abrupt death. Even so, an examination of what was going on in the United States in the years leading up to Andrews and colleagues' work helps to clarify why it eventually had a powerful influence among scholars and correctional practitioners.

During the post-rehabilitation years that preceded the 1990s, the nation remained rather tightly focused on "get tough" policies. Crime rates were on the rise, and this was especially true with regard to violent crimes during the late 1980s. Reintroducing rehabilitation in this context was not likely to succeed (critics of rehabilitation commonly characterize it as "soft on crime"), nor was there a particularly strong core of proponents within the United States that was willing to do so. Instead, conventional U.S. wisdom prescribed even harsher punishments with a continued emphasis on incarceration—in the decade prior to Andrews, Zinger, et al.'s (1990) article alone, the incarceration rate literally doubled, demonstrating the narrow and intense focus of correctional policy (Snell, 1995). Consequently, it was not surprising, as Cullen and Gendreau (2001) explain, that the primary force behind the reaffirmation of rehabilitation was centered squarely *outside* of the United States.

In Canada, the correctional scene was distinctly different from U.S. corrections. Rehabilitation had not been abandoned, and behavioral psychologists played an important role in shaping correctional programs aimed at lowering recidivism. The nearly universal belief within U.S. corrections—that offenders could not be changed in meaningful ways—amounted to a slap in the face to behavioral psychologists; if this were true, their profession held very little value, as understanding and changing human behavior was at the heart of their practice. The almost wholesale dismissal of correctional treatment as useful policy provoked Canadian researchers to stand up and address what they viewed to be a foolhardy decision by their neighbors to the south. Essentially, the contrasting social contexts between Canada and the United States provided the impetus for Canadian scholars to mount a serious challenge to the status quo of U.S. corrections. Even so, this challenge was unlikely to create substantial change all on its own. Instead, other aspects of the broader social context worked in conjunction with this effort made by the Canadian psychologists.

If the prevailing climate in the United States was not signaling a demand for the return of rehabilitation, how is it that Andrews, Zinger, et al.'s (1990) research was able to rekindle interest in correctional treatment? Andrews and his colleagues were certainly not invited to appear on *60 Minutes* to share their knowledge of the issue, as was Robert Martinson, who informed the nation that "nothing works" some 15 years earlier. But even so, there were important elements of social context that undoubtedly convinced policy makers to lend an eventual ear to their research. In large part, this was related to a side effect of the "tough on crime" movement.

The shift from rehabilitation to incarceration resulted in a prison industry that had grown quite unwieldy with regard to at least two related factors. First, prisons began to suffer from severe overcrowding (Franklin, Franklin, & Pratt, 2006). The nature of the problem was straightforward—the growth of the prison industry was not able to keep pace with the rapidly expanding inmate population. In fact, prison conditions had become so troublesome that many institutions were placed under court orders aimed to rectify their inhumane environments. Ultimately, there was only so much that could be done to relieve issues of overcrowding. Some facilities shifted away from reliance on the original *design capacity* of the prison to a more flexible *rated capacity* that could be changed as prisons needed to accommodate more inmates. This strategy created a temporary illusion that the problem was less serious than suspected, but realistically, did little to resolve the overcrowding problem. In the end, many facilities were faced with releasing inmates earlier than planned or constructing new bed space.

The addition of new bed space or the construction of entirely new prisons, however, did not come without setbacks. The second factor faced by prisons was the rising cost of incarceration for states. Reflecting on the years that led up to Andrews, Zinger, et al.'s (1990) article, as well as the years that followed, Spelman (2006) explained that "states doubled their prison populations, then doubled them again, increasing their costs by more than $20 billon per year" (p. 97). Clearly, the expanding prison industry was adding a considerable expense that had to be absorbed by state budgets. Faced with overcrowded prisons that began to consume considerable financial resources, the climate in American corrections eventually became more receptive to alternatives that did not rely solely on lengthy sentences of incarceration. Correctional treatment, particularly community-based treatment, became a potential option—after all, if it could save taxpayers money *and* more effectively reduce recidivism rates, what was there to lose?

The social context of the 1990s was not only shaped by a prison industry that had grown in ways that few would have predicted, but also by a refreshing realization that crime rates were finally on the way down. By the end of the 1990s, the United States was experiencing crime rates that were the lowest in several decades (Spelman, 2006). How might this have influenced the reaffirmation of rehabilitation? A look back to the social context that led to the demise of the rehabilitative ideal indicates that the United States was in a very different position. Crime had been on the rise for some time, and politicians were promising to gain control of the situation. To appease a nation that was becoming increasingly dissatisfied with the crime problem, it made sense to promise a "tough on crime" strategy—and this is precisely what was delivered. Under these circumstances, the "soft on crime" rehabilitative approach was heavily critiqued.

Fast forward two decades or so to the late 1990s and the convergence of several factors appear to once again open the window for a favorable view of rehabilitation: The prison industry had become extremely overcrowded, the cost of sustaining (let alone expanding) the prison system had become a financial burden, and crime had become far less problematic than it had once been. Under these circumstances, it made sense to reintroduce correctional treatment as a means of lowering both recidivism and the financial costs to the criminal justice system. Moreover, this could be accomplished with minimal backlash from those who viewed rehabilitation as "soft on crime," since the state of crime in America was more favorable than it had been in decades.

DISSEMINATING THE PRINCIPLES OF EFFECTIVE REHABILITATION

Andrews, Zinger, et al. (1990) was certainly not the first piece of research to suggest that American corrections had been too hasty in its abandonment of rehabilitation (see Cullen & Gilbert, 1982; Gendreau & Ross, 1979; Martinson, 1979; Palmer 1975). Other scholars were aware that rehabilitation was, quite simply, not as defunct as many would have liked to believe. These researchers were sure to weigh in on the debate, but their responses did not have the same effect of Andrews and colleagues' research. Part of this was, no doubt, related to the timing of the responses, as the previous discussion of social context implies, but there was more to it than that. The nature of Andrews, Zinger, et al.'s research stood out as different in ways that ultimately affected its ability to impact the field. These important nuances are examined here, to help paint a more accurate picture of how their article reached a point of such influence among scholars and even correctional practitioners.

Without doubt, the most important aspect of Andrews, Zinger, et al.'s work was the introduction of a theoretical framework for understanding why some programs failed and why others succeeded at lowering recidivism. Up until this point, researchers who drew conclusions about the empirical status of rehabilitation, whether they were favorable (e.g., Palmer, 1975) or unfavorable (e.g., Bailey, 1966; Martinson, 1974), fell short of clearly explaining why correctional treatment did or did not work (though Palmer did make headway regarding this issue). Martinson suggested that rehabilitation may have failed to work as a result of poor implementation of programming or possibly because even our best efforts were no match against the hardened criminal. In short, Martinson could not really provide, with enough certainty, the reasons for program failure.

The principles of risk, need, and responsivity, on the other hand, were able to add a sense of clarity to a situation that was both complex and confusing. Rather than propagating a message of uncertainty, the introduction of these three straightforward principles offered a clear pathway forward and provided enough specificity for practitioners to implement real change in their treatment strategies. This is precisely why Andrews, Zinger, et al. (1990) referred to their work as "clinically relevant" for those interested in an answer to the *what works* question. Thus, their research did far more than weigh in on the efficacy of rehabilitative treatment—it provided one of the first universal roadmaps for designing effective intervention strategies. The value of this research would eventually prove to be substantial both for practitioners as well as future correctional researchers.

The fact that Andrews, Zinger et al. (1990) relied on a quantitative meta-analysis, rather than a narrative review, to assess the effectiveness of correctional rehabilitation and the principles of risk, need, and responsivity was also crucial to getting their message out. As discussed previously, this technique allowed the researchers to draw direct, quantitative comparisons between the effectiveness of programs that adhered to the risk, need, and responsivity principles and those that did not. Since meta-analysis represented a more advanced and accurate way to summarize large and diverse bodies of literature, their study was able to command substantial attention, even in a field that held a predominantly negative view of rehabilitation. In essence, the use of meta-analysis increased the credibility of the researchers' findings, which was particularly important since they were fighting an uphill battle against an ardent skepticism of correctional treatment. Should the researchers have relied on the traditional narrative review to demonstrate their point, their message might well have been lost among other attempts to accomplish a similar end (Gendreau & Ross, 1979; Palmer, 1975).

Finally, the tone of Andrews and colleagues' research cannot be discounted when examining its eventual impact in the field of corrections. Like Martinson had done some 16 years earlier, Andrews and his colleagues were very much calling out and challenging the status quo of American corrections. Their research findings were not meant as a benign statement offering casual support for correctional treatment. In noting the dismal effects of incarceration and other methods adopted shortly after the demise of rehabilitation, Andrews, Zinger, et al. (1990) asserted that "[c]ritics of rehabilitation are correct when they note that the average correlation between treatment and recidivism is not 1.00. At the same time, critics might be asked to report on the variation that their 'preferred' variable shares with recidivism" (p. 385). The message to the field of criminology was clear: Rehabilitation had been foolishly abandoned in favor of techniques that were no better at reducing offender recidivism, but were actually *worse.*

In the end, Andrews, Zinger, et al. (1990) produced a piece of research that did several things right. By introducing the principles of risk, need, and responsivity, these researchers brought much-needed guidance to a field that had been largely atheoretical. They provided strong empirical evidence to back up their perspective and relied on the advanced technique of meta-analysis to do so. Finally, they structured their article not only to offer real-world guidance for practitioners (via the principles of effective rehabilitation), but also to pose a serious challenge to academic naysayers of rehabilitation by highlighting the failures of alternative responses to criminal behavior. These factors, taken together with a social context that would eventually force policy makers and academics to rethink the staunch emphasis on incarceration, provided the catalyst for Andrews and colleagues' research to become truly impactful in American corrections.

THE IMPACT OF META-ANALYSIS AND THE PRINCIPLES OF EFFECTIVE REHABILITATION

The effect that Andrews, Zinger, et al.'s (1990) research had on the field of corrections was certainly a powerful one, but it did not produce immediate change. As mentioned earlier, the death of rehabilitation had been shockingly quick, particularly in light of the fact that most significant policy reforms take ample time to implement. Breathing life back into rehabilitation proved to be far more challenging and certainly more time consuming. Even so, Andrews and his colleagues made considerable headway with their research, which is evident in at least three changes that took place in the years following their work.

First, the publication of their meta-analysis drew considerable attention from academics and sparked other scholars to join their cause. Though Andrews and colleagues' study was not the first meta-analysis of correctional treatment (for example, see Whitehead & Lab, 1989), it was the first to demonstrate that, when guided by effective principles, rehabilitation could be more than just *somewhat* effective. This led to several additional meta-analyses by other researchers that assessed correctional treatment among different populations (e.g., serious juvenile offenders) and settings (community versus institutional) and further tested the hypotheses related to risk, need, and responsivity. Soon after, a body of evidence emerged that was quite supportive of the rehabilitative ideal as an effective means for crime reduction. For example, 2 years later, in 1992, Mark Lipsey published a meta-analysis that included more than 400 studies of correctional treatment and provided confirmation that rehabilitation was, in fact, able to lower recidivism rates, especially in the case of programs that adhered to the principles of risk, need, and responsivity. As the meta-analytic research began to pile up (Lipsey, 1999; Lipsey & Wilson, 1993, 1998; see also Pratt, 2009), the balance of empirical evidence demonstrated that rehabilitation clearly outperformed alternative methods such as relying on incarceration, deterrence, and fear. As we will see, this eventually altered the reputation of rehabilitation among criminologists.

Second, though it would be inaccurate to suggest that Andrews, Zinger, et al.'s (1990) research single-handedly shifted beliefs away from the "nothing works" doctrine, it certainly played an important role. Leading up to the early 1990s, the professional ideology among criminologists was very much in line with the "nothing works" assessment (see Cullen & Gendreau, 2001). Along with other researchers (e.g., Palmer, 1975; Lipsey, 1992; Lipsey & Wilson, 1998), Andrews and colleagues' research highlighted the weak ground on which these scholars stood. Eventually, a shift took place in which scholars became more interested in discovering "what works" rather than attempting to demonstrate that "nothing works" (e.g., MacKenzie, 1997, 2000; Taxman, 1999). Of course, discovering what works in correctional treatment also entails identifying and understanding failures, but even so, the focus of correctional research has since concerned itself with "knowledge construction" rather than "knowledge destruction" (Cullen & Gendreau, 2001, p. 314). In short, the landscape of correctional treatment is decidedly different from what it was during the post-Martinson years, and part of this change can be attributed to the work of Andrews and his colleagues as well as to others who convincingly demonstrated that rehabilitation could be effective under the proper circumstances.

Finally—and this is of considerable importance—Andrews, Zinger, et al.'s research did more than simply influence criminologists' disposition toward correctional treatment. Since their 1990 work, the principles they put forth regarding effective rehabilitation have been adopted by various agencies across the nation to help enhance the performance of treatment in real-world applications. In describing the dissemination of Andrews, Zinger, et al.'s (1990) principles of effective rehabilitation, Cullen (2005) explains that, "[p]erhaps not surprisingly, advocates of the 'what works' movement were besieged with numerous and continuing requests to address conferences, to give workshops, and to conduct evaluations" (p. 17). Armed with the knowledge that correctional treatment could be quite effective, scholars ventured well beyond the comforts of their academic environments to take up the often difficult task of raising awareness among correctional practitioners (see Latessa 2004; Latessa, Cullen, & Gendreau, 2002). Ultimately, the state of corrections in the United States has not returned to the "medical model" of the 1950s, but the emergence of the risk, need, and responsivity principles have certainly helped to create a more balanced approach to managing offenders in American society.

CONCLUSION

The mid-1970s brought considerable changes to the practice of corrections in the United States. Once predicated on a medical model of offender treatment, corrections had become intensely focused on instilling harsh punishment and incarcerating offenders for lengthy periods of time. The rehabilitative movement had been severely wounded by its critics, and conventional wisdom among academics, practitioners, and the American public indicated that "nothing works" to rehabilitate offenders. Despite the negative image cast upon offender rehabilitation, there were a few notable scholars who vehemently disagreed with this assessment. These researchers offered an immediate response to the abandonment of rehabilitation and attempted to demonstrate the foolhardy nature of such a decision (e.g., Gendreau & Ross, 1979; Palmer, 1975). They argued that the "nothing works" movement had little grounding in reality, but their efforts to communicate this message fell upon deaf ears. It was not until 1990 that supporters of rehabilitation would successfully communicate this point to an audience that eventually became willing to listen.

This message came in the form of a meta-analysis published by Andrews, Zinger, et al. (1990) in which a theory of effective rehabilitation was introduced and tested. Up until this point, researchers had demonstrated that some correctional programs were effective for some offenders. But a clearly stated theory of *which programs* worked best under *which circumstances* had been decidedly absent from the literature. Through the principles of risk, need, and responsivity, Andrews, Zinger, et al. blueprinted a solution to this problem and empirically demonstrated that programs adhering to these principles were able to substantially lower rates of recidivism. The implications of their research were clear: Rehabilitation was not the failed enterprise that many believed it to be.

While previous attempts to dislodge the "nothing works" doctrine as the dominant view of correctional treatment had received little attention (Cullen & Gilbert, 1982; Gendreau & Ross, 1979; Palmer, 1975), Andrews, Zinger, et al.'s work was more difficult to ignore. Several factors related to the work itself, as well as the social context of the era, played an important role in directing attention to their findings. First, the principles of risk, need, and responsivity provided a very clear and practical path for the development of more effective programs; thus, the application of their research had a very real appeal to correctional practitioners. Second, the use of meta-analysis to assess the efficacy of offender treatment represented a significant improvement over prior narrative reviews of the treatment literature. This quantitative and transparent method afforded their research more legitimacy in the eyes of most researchers (for an exception, see Logan & Gaes, 1993). Third, the "get tough" movement that emerged after the demise of rehabilitation had begun to place considerable stress on the correctional system, both in terms of overcrowding and cost. This signaled a need to consider alternatives to lengthy incarceration sentences. Fourth, the crime rate in the United States, though still on the rise when Andrews, Zinger, et al. (1990) published their article, soon began to plummet to levels not seen for decades. Since critics of rehabilitation often argued that treatment was "soft on crime," this created an environment more conducive to the rehabilitative approach. The coalescence of these factors eventually became the catalyst for change, and ultimately, new life was found in the practice of correctional rehabilitation.

DISCUSSION QUESTIONS

1. Describe the three principles of effective rehabilitation discussed by Andrews, Zinger, et al. (1990).
2. What were the major findings of Andrews, Zinger, et al.'s (1990) meta-analysis, and how did they compare to the findings reported by Martinson's (1974) earlier assessment of rehabilitation?
3. What factors in the broader social context of the 1990s eventually led to the reconsideration of rehabilitation as meaningful correctional policy?

REFERENCES

Andrews, D. A., Bonta, J., & Hoge, R. D. (1990). Classification for effective rehabilitation: Rediscovering psychology. *Criminal Justice and Behavior, 17,* 19–52.

Andrews, D. A., Zinger, I., Hoge, R. D., Bonta, J., Gendreau, P., & Cullen, F. T. (1990). Does correctional treatment work? A clinically relevant and psychologically informed meta-analysis. *Criminology, 28,* 369–404.

Bailey, W. (1966). Correctional outcome: An evaluation of 100 reports. *Journal of Criminal Law, Criminology, and Police Science, 57,* 153–160.

Cullen, F. T. (2005). The twelve people who saved rehabilitation: How the science of criminology made a difference. *Criminology, 43*(1), 1–42.

Cullen, F. T., & Gendreau, P. (2000). Assessing correctional rehabilitation: Policy, practice, and prospects. In J. Horney (Ed.), *Criminal justice 2000* (Vol. 3, pp. 109–176). Washington, DC: National Institute of Justice, U.S. Department of Justice.

Cullen, F. T., & Gendreau, P. (2001). From nothing works to what works: Changing professional ideology in the 21st Century. *The Prison Journal, 81*(3), 313–338.

Cullen, F. T., & Gilbert, K. (1982). *Reaffirming rehabilitation.* Cincinnati, OH: Anderson.

Franklin, T. F., Franklin, C. A., & Pratt, T. C. (2006). The effect of prison crowding on prison violence: A meta-analysis of conflicting empirical research results. *Journal of Criminal Justice, 34,* 401–412.

Gendreau, P., & Ross, B. (1979). Effective correctional treatment: Bibliotherapy for cynics. *Crime & Delinquency, 25,* 463–489.

Latessa, E. (2004). The challenge of change: Correctional programs and evidence-based practices. *Criminology and Public Policy, 3*(4), 547–559.

Latessa, E., Cullen, F., & Gendreau, P. (2002). Beyond correctional quackery: Professionalism and the possibility of correctional treatment. *Federal Probation, 66*(2), 43–49.

Lipsey, M. (1992). Juvenile delinquency treatment: A meta-analytic inquiry into the variability of effects. In T. D. Cook, H. Cooper, D. S. Cordray, H. Hartmann, L. V. Hedges, R. J. Light, et al. (Eds.), *Meta-analysis for explanation: A casebook* (pp. 83–127). New York: Russell Sage Foundation.

Lipsey, M. (1999). Can intervention rehabilitate serious delinquents? *Annals of the American Academy of Political and Social Science, 564,* 142–166.

Lipsey, M., & Wilson, D. (1993). The efficacy of psychological, educational, and behavioral treatment. *American Psychologist, 48*(12), 1181–1209.

Lipsey, M., & Wilson, D. (1998). Effective intervention for serious juvenile offenders: A synthesis of the research. In R. Loeber & D. P. Farrington (Eds.), *Serious and violent juvenile offenders: Risk factors and successful interventions* (pp. 313–345). Thousand Oaks, CA: Sage.

Lipsey, M., & Wilson, D. (2001). *Practical meta-analysis.* Thousand Oaks, CA: Sage.

Logan, C., & Gaes, G. (1993). Meta-analysis and the rehabilitation of punishment. *Justice Quarterly, 10,* 245–263.

MacKenzie, D. L. (1997). Criminal justice and crime prevention. In L. Sherman, D. Gottfredson, D. MacKenzie, J. Eck, P. Reuter, & S. Bushway (Eds.), *Preventing crime: What works, what doesn't, what's promising* (pp. 9.1–9.76). Washington, DC: National Institute of Justice.

MacKenzie, D. L. (2000). Evidence-based corrections: Identifying what works. *Crime & Delinquency, 46*(4), 457–471.

Martinson, R. (1974). What works? Questions and answers about prison reform. *The Public Interest, 35,* 22–54.

Martinson, R. (1979). New findings, new views: A note of caution regarding sentencing reform. *Hofstra Law Review, 7,* 243–258.

Palmer, T. (1975). Martinson revisited. *Journal of Research in Crime and Delinquency, 12*(2), 133–152.

Petrosino, A., Turpin-Petrosino, C., & Finckenauer, J. (2000). Well-meaning programs can have harmful effects! Lessons from experiments of programs such as Scared Straight. *Crime & Delinquency, 46*(3), 354–379.

Pratt, T. C. (2009). *Addicted to incarceration: Corrections policy and the politics of misinformation in the United States.* Thousand Oaks, CA: Sage.

Snell, T. (1995). *Correctional populations in the United States, 1993.* Washington, DC: U.S. Department of Justice, Bureau of Justice Statistics.

Spelman, W. (2006). The limited importance of prison expansion. In A. Blumstein & J. Wallman (Eds.), *The crime drop in America* (2nd ed.). Cambridge, UK: Cambridge University Press.

Taxman, F. S. (1999). Unraveling "what works" for offenders in substance abuse treatment services. *National Drug Court Institute Review II*(2), 93–134.

Whitehead, J. T., & Lab, S. P. (1989). A meta-analysis of juvenile correctional treatment. *Journal of Research in Crime and Delinquency, 26*(3), 276–295.

ELEVEN

KEY IDEA: CRIME AND THE LIFE COURSE

KEY WORKS

Moffitt, T. E. (1993). Adolescence-limited and life-course persistent antisocial behavior: A developmental taxonomy. *Psychological Review, 100,* 674–701.

Sampson, R. J., & Laub, J. H. (1993). *Crime in the making: Pathways and turning points through life.* Cambridge, MA: Harvard University Press.

In 1994, Richard Herrnstein and Charles Murray published *The Bell Curve: Intelligence and Class Structure in American Life,* in which they attributed a host of social problems—from unemployment to out-of-wedlock births to structured inequality—to a single, immutable, individual characteristic that they argued was largely established at conception: intelligence (IQ). In relating their argument to the problem of crime, Herrnstein and Murray held that criminal propensity (caused primarily by a substandard IQ) starts early and stays with someone for his or her whole life. This was not a new idea (see, e.g., Dugdale, 1887; Lombroso-Ferrero, 1911), and Herrnstein and Murray did not even present new data to bolster their argument,[1] yet it revived the nature-nurture debate in a new way by bringing quantitative data to bear on the assumption that nothing that happens after the sperm meets the egg is all that important for understanding why people misbehave.

With the possible exception of a few scholars who kept their opinions to themselves, criminologists didn't like this. On the one hand, many journalists and social commentators balked at the research with vague references that "something was wrong"—especially in the way that Herrnstein and Murray (1994) tied differences in IQ to different racial groups in the United States—but they lacked the methodological expertise to know exactly what it was (see, e.g., the discussion by Gould, 1995). Criminologists, on the other hand, responded with reanalyses of the data used by Herrnstein and Murray (the National Longitudinal Survey of Youth [NLSY]) to show that the IQ–crime link was fully mediated when other criminogenic risk factors (like social bonds) were controlled statistically (see Cullen, Gendreau, Jarjoura, & Wright, 1997). Other reanalyses of the same data found that the relationship between IQ and crime only exists cross-sectionally, whereas the relationship essentially disappears when assessed over time (McGloin, Pratt, & Maahs, 2004).[2]

More broadly, criminologists noted that Herrnstein and Murray's contentions were fundamentally inconsistent with the life course tradition in criminology—the subject of this chapter. The life course perspective recognizes that individuals vary in the degree to which they engage in criminal behavior from childhood to adolescence to adulthood; accordingly, life course criminology attempts to provide an explanation for the nature of these changes. To that end, understanding where life course criminology came from—and perhaps why *The Bell Curve* caused such a ruckus among criminologists—requires an understanding of the context of criminology in the early 1990s.

THE CRIMINOLOGICAL CONTEXT OF THE EARLY 1990s

Throughout much of the history of criminological thought, theories of crime have largely been theories of delinquency. Indeed, many of the "key ideas" discussed in this book were ideas about why people misbehave when they're young, including Shaw and McKay's (1942) *Juvenile Delinquency and Urban Areas* (see Chapter 4) and Travis Hirschi's (1969) *Causes of Delinquency* (see Chapter 5). Bolstered by "age-crime curve" data that consistently show that individuals tend to "peak" with regard to their bad behavior around age 17 or so and then decline after that (see Blumstein, Cohen, Roth, & Visher, 1986; Farrington, 1986; Piquero, Farrington, & Blumstein, 2003; Wolfgang, Figlio, & Selin, 1972), most criminologists have assumed—either implicitly or explicitly—that "the crime problem is mainly a teenage problem" (Lilly, Cullen, & Ball, 2002, p. 248).

Thinking about crime in almost exclusively youthful terms was reinforced in recent decades with the growth and sophistication of self-report survey methods. Beginning with Hirschi's (1969) work, scholars discovered that they could devise survey instruments that contained operational definitions of the core propositions made by various theories, which could then be used to test them against one another. Furthermore, they also realized that an entire community's young population can be found in schools, where large samples of subjects could be drawn conveniently and inexpensively because they were, in a sense, "captive"—just sitting at their desks, pencils in hand, waiting to fill out the surveys that criminologists had developed for them. As this approach gained in popularity—which it certainly did (Akers & Sellers, 2009)—criminologists found that they were largely exempt from having to study these kids over time, and instead could get away with gathering all of the data they thought they needed in one shot when their subjects were in their teens.

Not only was this approach enormously convenient, but there was also a growing body of empirical evidence pointing to its theoretical legitimacy. For example, research has consistently shown that there is a considerable amount of stability in offending over time; that is, those who are offenders in adulthood were also quite likely to have been offenders when they were juveniles (Piquero et al., 2003). Thus, it would appear that little "new" insight into criminal behavior could be gained by following deviant youths into their deviant adulthoods if the "causes" of their wayward behavior remained the same. Gottfredson and Hirschi's (1990) self-control theory is a prime example of this way of thinking: that criminal and deviant acts among the young and old alike all stem from the common problem of low self-control—a perspective that has an impressive amount of empirical support (Pratt & Cullen, 2000).

The problem, however, is that the simple interpretation of the age-crime curve—one where the linchpin to understanding crime and deviance will be found merely by examining why young people break the law—may be masking significant within-person changes over time that are important for understanding criminal behavior. For example, on a most basic level, it is plausible that the kinds of factors that may initiate offending (e.g., poor parental supervision, exposure to deviant peer associations; see Lowenkamp, Cullen, & Pratt, 2003; Perrone, Sullivan, Pratt, & Margaryan, 2004; Pratt et al., in press; Unnever, Cullen, & Pratt, 2003) might not be identical to the ones that prompt those same offenders to desist from crime when they get older (e.g., securing stable employment, desisting from excessive use of alcohol; see Laub & Sampson, 2003; Sampson & Laub, 1993). In short, both stability and change in offending over time seem to be present, and criminology needed a theory that could account for both. With that agenda in mind, life course criminology entered the picture.

LIFE COURSE THEORIES IN CRIMINOLOGY

The life course perspective in criminology carries with it two fundamental assumptions, the first of which is that examining lives over time "matters" when it comes to fully understanding the nature of criminal behavior. To be sure, no longer would cross-sectional research and theorizing "cut it" in the criminological arena. Second, given Robins' (1978) famous quote that "adult antisocial behaviour virtually requires childhood antisocial behaviour . . . [yet] most antisocial children do not become antisocial adults" (p. 611), life course theories begin with the assumption that both stability and change in criminal behavior need to be explained theoretically. While variations on the life course theme exist (see, e.g., Leblanc & Loeber, 1998; Loeber & Stouthamer-Loeber, 1996, for discussions of "developmental criminology"), the two most dominant explanations within the life course tradition are those espoused by Moffitt (1993) and by Sampson and Laub (1993).

Stability or Change: Moffitt's Dual Taxonomy

In one of the most noteworthy criminological perspectives to emerge out of developmental psychology, Terrie Moffitt (1993) argued that patterns of criminal offending over time are characterized be *either* stability or change (see also Caspi & Moffitt, 1995). Specifically, she held that the well-known age-crime curve masks the presence of two distinct groups of offending trajectories, each of which requires separate and distinct theoretical explanations. The first group, which involves a relatively small proportion of the population (perhaps as small as 5–10 percent of males) that start offending early on in life and show continuity in antisocial behavior throughout adolescence and adulthood, is referred to as life-course persistent (LCP) offenders.

Life-course persistent offenders, Moffitt argued, exhibit a variety of forms of antisocial behavior even at an extremely early age. These individuals hit and bite others when just out of the toddler stage, they steal from stores and are disruptive in classrooms in early childhood, they drink and do drugs in early adolescence, they steal cars and beat people up in their teens, and they defraud their places of work and engage in child abuse as adults. Accordingly, Moffitt (1993) argued that "if some individuals' antisocial behavior is stable from preschool to adulthood, then investigators are compelled to look for its roots early in life, in factors that are present before or soon after birth" (p. 680). The key variable specified by Moffitt for explaining life-course persistent antisocial behavior is the presence of "neuropsychological deficits" within such offenders. Neuropsychological deficits refer to physiological problems with brain development that can later inhibit an individual's "executive functioning"—that is, one's ability to control his or her impulses and to fully evaluate the consequences of one's actions, both of which have been linked to the problem of low self-control, an extremely strong criminogenic risk factor (Pratt & Cullen, 2000). These problems can emerge during the prenatal period as a result of both voluntary risk factors (e.g., mother's drug and alcohol use; see McGloin, Pratt, & Piquero, 2006; Pratt, McGloin, & Fearn, 2006) and a resource-deprived environment (e.g., restricted access to quality health care services), and can also emerge as the result of postnatal exposure to toxins (e.g., lead) and to child abuse (Wright et al., 2008). As a result of these neuropsychological deficits, at virtually every developmental stage, LCP offenders will engage in nearly all forms of misbehavior at a higher rate than those who are not burdened by such problems.

Standing in stark contrast to the life-course persistent offenders—those whose antisocial behavior tends to occur at a relatively constant rate throughout the life course—is the second group of offenders. This second group, according to Moffitt (1993), describes most youths—those who are fairly well-behaved early on but who "get into trouble" during their teen years, only to desist from such behavior once they reach early adulthood. In noting that delinquent behavior is so common among the general population that it may almost be considered to be a "normal" part of adolescent development, Moffitt referred to this group as "adolescence-limited offenders" (AL). In explaining why most individuals follow this developmental trajectory of offending, Moffitt noted that adolescents are faced with a bit of a dilemma: On the one hand, they are biologically mature, sexually capable, and seemingly ready for "adult" behavioral roles. On the other hand, however, they are also subject to a host of informal social control mechanisms that sanction the display of that very behavior. This results in a "maturity gap" that adolescents attempt to bridge through the "social mimicry" of older youths. In short, delinquent behavior becomes an adaptive strategy that adolescents employ in an effort to demonstrate their autonomy in a way that prosocial behavior—like doing homework—doesn't really convey. As they get older, Moffitt argued, the motivation among ALs to offend diminishes because they themselves transition into legitimate adult roles. To be sure, attempting to bridge the maturity gap may make sense to the 16-year-old who wishes to emulate the 19-year-old, yet by the time the youth is 27, there is little that the 30-year-old is doing that holds the same kind of deviant attraction.

Stability and Change: Sampson and Laub's Theory of Age-Graded Informal Social Control

Robert Sampson and John Laub (1993) took issue with Moffitt's argument for a dual taxonomy of either stability *or* change in criminal behavior over the life course. The problem, according to Sampson and Laub, was that stability *and* change in patterns of criminal offending often seem to occur within individuals over time. Indeed, Sampson and Laub observed that even those individuals who were seemingly on the path to becoming life-course persistent offenders could still be diverted from a life of crime by certain changes that can occur in adulthood. In short, as opposed to being locked into a pattern of either stability or change, life-course trajectories of offending can be dynamic. What, then, are these dynamic factors and how might they affect criminal behavior? For Sampson and Laub, the explanation could be found in an age-graded model of informal social control.

In this perspective, Sampson and Laub drew heavily on Hirschi's (1969) social bond theory. Yet, as opposed to limiting the applicability of social bonds to juveniles only, Sampson and Laub (1993) extended the model to include the formation of adult social bonds (see also Laub & Sampson, 2003). Viewed in this way, the quality of relationships that adults have "matters" with regard to their criminal behavior. In one sense, Sampson and Laub argued that delinquent behavior early on in life—which can be attributed to a host of risk factors, from early temperament problems to cumulative disadvantage—can disrupt the formation of bonds to prosocial institutions like school and family, which may result in continued delinquent behavior. As such, delinquency in youth may, in turn, make the future formation of prosocial bonds to work and marriage less likely because a record of antisocial behavior may make one a less attractive potential employee or marriage partner (Messner & Sampson, 1991; see also Crowder & Tolnay, 2000). Thus, for Sampson and Laub, it is the lack of formation of—or disruption in—social bonds that is responsible for the continuity of antisocial behavior from childhood to adolescence and on to adulthood. Nevertheless, should strong social bonds to employment or marriage be formed by even the most chronic of offenders, these attachments can serve as "turning points" in offenders' lives that can divert them from a life of crime. Put simply, where weak social bonds are responsible for continuity in offending, strong social bonds can be responsible for change (reduction) in offending (see Lilly et al., 2007).

What is more, the kinds of social bonds discussed by Sampson and Laub (1993) are "age-graded"; that is, the types of bonds that are responsible for keeping our behavior in check are different depending upon at what stage we are in the life course. For example, as children, the most important social bonds are likely to be those to parents, who may be a child's primary agents of social control and models for prosocial behavior (Kempf, 1993). Evidence suggests, however, that as kids get older, the direct effect of parenting on their behavior diminishes (Harris, 1998), and peer groups and social institutions like schools become more important (Haynie, 2002; McGloin et al., 2004; McGloin, Sullivan, Piquero, & Bacon, 2008; Pratt, 2009b; Turner, Piquero, & Pratt, 2005; Warr, 2002).

Finally, in adulthood, schools and parents take a backseat to jobs and spouses as the primary mechanisms of social control (Laub & Sampson, 2003; Sampson & Laub, 1990). What is important to recognize, then, is that regardless of the form that informal social control comes in, according to Sampson and Laub (1993), the causal mechanism controlling our behavior—be it good behavior or bad behavior—is still our social bonds.

CONSTRUCTING TESTABLE THEORIES

As stated above, neither Moffitt (1993) nor Sampson and Laub (1993) were the first to suggest that examining lives over time was important to the understanding of criminal behavior. Indeed, other scholars had set forth ideas that resembled the contemporary life course perspective dating all the way back to the Gluecks (Glueck & Glueck, 1950), as well as later perspectives such as labeling theory, which held that certain key events in people's lives—such as contact with the criminal justice system—could significantly influence the direction of one's life, independent of the person's early childhood socialization experiences (see Lemert, 1972). Why, then, did certain "versions" of life course theory catch on and others did not? A portion of that question can be answered in terms of timing, where the ideas contained within the life course tradition may simply have been inconsistent with conventional ways of thinking about criminal behavior at previous times in our criminological history (see Lilly et al., 2007). Yet, while persuasive, timing is only part of the answer; consistent with the broader theme of this book, an often overlooked part of that explanation has to do with the way Moffitt (1993) and Sampson and Laub (1993) went about constructing and presenting their theories.

Specifically, scholars have long complained that, unlike the systematic way in which empirical tests of theories tend to be conducted and presented, the presentation of criminological theories themselves tends to occur in a haphazard way (Gibbs, 1987; see also Cullen, Wright, & Blevins, 2006). To be sure, most theories of criminal behavior were introduced to the field discursively by scholars with little in the way of specific, detailed, causal statements concerning which factors should be related to crime and delinquency under certain conditions (Gibbons, 1994). In addition, rarely were these perspectives summarized fully in one publication; instead, they were spread out among multiple works with theoretical propositions that were often unclear in terms of how they could be measured in empirical tests. This approach to theory construction characterized much of the previous efforts at building life course theories—to the extent that they were theoretical at all.[3] What made Moffitt's (1993) and Sampson and Laub's (1993) work different from the rest of the pack was that they presented their theories in ways that could be easily translated into empirical tests.

For example, Moffitt's (1993) piece, published in *Psychological Review,* contained a number of clearly stated, testable hypotheses regarding her life course perspective. Among the more notable of these is the notion that there are two separate groups of offenders with their own behavioral trajectories (life-course persistent and adolescence-limited offenders), and that what should separate LCP from AL offenders is the presence of neuropsychological deficits. Other "secondary" yet still important propositions included the argument that factors associated with both voluntary and involuntary prenatal risk should predict neuropsychological problems in children, and that neuropsychological deficits, poor parental efficacy, and a resource-deprived social environment should all combine to create a condition of "cumulative disadvantage" for children, which should exacerbate the behavioral tendencies of those prone to life-course persistent antisocial behavior.

Sampson and Laub (1993) were equally clear in the way they presented their theory in terms of its testable hypotheses. In particular, their core theoretical proposition was that, controlling for early childhood behavioral problems or prior criminal/delinquent behavior—either of which should capture the kinds of early risk factors specified by "continuity" theories like those of Gottfredson and Hirschi (1990) and even Moffitt (1993)—the quality of adult social bonds to marriage and work should predict desistance from criminal behavior. Other secondary propositions that are equally important—and were presented equally clearly by Sampson and Laub (1993)—included the statements that stints of incarceration and engaging in criminal or delinquent behavior should weaken ties to prosocial bonds like family, school, and employment. Their book even contained a visual diagram of their fully specified theory (on pp. 244–245) to help scholars understand the logical flow of their ideas and to provide an explicit roadmap that scholars could follow when going about testing the various propositions stated in their theory. In short, it doesn't get much clearer than that!

The bottom line is that, unlike most of the previous iterations of what came to be known as the life course perspective, what constituted testable hypotheses was not a mystery in Moffitt (1993) and Sampson and Laub's (1993) work. Indeed, there was a clear empirical agenda for criminologists to follow, and causal statements that could be translated into operational definitions and tested empirically were presented unambiguously. Thus, it was not merely the ideas themselves that made Moffitt's and Sampson and Laub's work stand out, but rather, it was the way in which these theories were presented that contributed significantly to their status as "key ideas."

LIFE COURSE THEORY CATCHES ON

While theory development and empirical work within the life course tradition sputtered a bit in the 1980s, with much of it mired under the rather broad and vague heading of "criminal career" research (see Blumstein et al., 1986; see also Piquero et al., 2003), there is no doubt that it gathered plenty of steam and the attention of scholars in the 1990s and beyond. In short, it has definitely "caught on" with criminologists. In the process, criminologists discovered that a number of data sets that had long been available to them already contained measures of some of the key concepts specified by the life course perspective. Accordingly, these data sets (e.g., the National Youth Survey; the National Longitudinal Survey of Youth) were used in new ways, new techniques for statistical modeling were developed (e.g., trajectory modeling) to capture dynamic changes in offending over time (see Nagin & Piquero, 2010), and a new literature on "desistance" from crime has been initiated (Bushway, Piquero, Broidy, Cauffman, & Mazerolle, 2001; Laub & Sampson, 2001; Maruna, 2001). So, while scholars have tackled these questions aggressively, the question becomes, what has been the result of these efforts?

With regard to Moffitt's (1993) dual taxonomy, scholars have examined the author's work in detail, repeatedly. Overall, there appears to be general support for certain propositions contained in her version of life course theory—most notably, that neuropsychological deficits appear to be significantly related to life-course persistent offending (McGloin & Pratt, 2003; McGloin et al., 2006; Raine et al., 2005). There is also evidence from a meta-analysis conducted by Pratt et al. (2006) of 18 studies that indicated that factors associated with voluntary prenatal risk—specifically, maternal cigarette smoking during pregnancy—are associated with offending over the life course. Thus, there is ample empirical evidence present that points to the validity of Moffitt's dual taxonomy.

Nevertheless, support for Moffitt's ideas is not unqualified. One of the more damaging sets of findings has emerged from studies using trajectory modeling techniques, which have revealed evidence of more than two categories of offenders (i.e., more than just AL and LCP offenders). Following this line of research, Hirschi and Gottfredson (1995) have argued that the AL-LCP distinction is merely an arbitrary cutoff point that reflects different levels of self-control within the offender population. Bolstering this point is the study by McGloin et al. (2006) that showed that voluntary prenatal risk operated through both parental efficacy (as Gottfredson and Hirschi would contend it would) as well as through neuropsychological deficits when influencing executive functioning. In short, what could also be viewed as self-control (executive functioning) may contain causal pathways that are, at best, only partially consistent with Moffitt's theory of it having largely physiological roots, yet a growing roster of studies seem to be showing just that (e.g., compare Brannigan, Gemmel, Pevalin, & Wade, 2002; Pratt, Cullen, Blevins, Daigle, & Unnever, 2002; Pratt, Turner, & Piquero, 2004; Turner et al., 2005; Unnever et al., 2003; Wright & Beaver, 2005). Either way, future work will need to continue disentangling empirically the relative effects of neuropsychological deficit and parental efficacy precursors to executive functioning and low self-control.

Conversely, empirical support for Sampson and Laub's (1993) theory of age-graded informal social control is a bit more universal. Support has emerged in the form of Sampson and Laub's own examinations of the Gluecks' data set, showing that even after controlling for lifelong patterns of antisocial behavior (even beginning in early childhood), quality attachments to employment and marriage still predict desistance from criminal behavior in adulthood (see also Sampson & Laub, 1992). It is important to note that critiques have been raised concerning *why* employment and marriage should "matter"—in particular, Warr (1998) has argued that the effects Sampson and Laub are attributing to informal social control may really reflect changes in the peer group composition and routine activities of those who become entrenched in family and work roles. Even so, this potentially competing explanation was taken into account with Laub and Sampson's (2003) follow-up study of the Gluecks' offenders up to age 70. In general, then, Sampson and Laub's (1993) theory is extremely well supported by the existing evidence, in no small part because of their willingness to revisit their perspective when new findings and challenges emerge.

CONCLUSION

Can the problem of crime be traced back to conception, the way Herrnstein and Murray (1994) say it can? And if not at that point, then are Gottfredson and Hirschi (1990) correct in that it can be pinpointed shortly thereafter, once early childhood socialization has taken place? Or does the kid who is born to a mother who placed her own needs for nicotine and alcohol ahead of the health of her baby, and who resides in an abusive household in an economically deprived community, already have his ticket punched in the way that Moffitt (1993) hints that he might? Can even the most hardened life-course persistent criminal end up leading a law-abiding life if he can form meaningful ties to a job or a spouse in the way that Sampson and Laub (1993) say he should? According to the life course perspective in criminology, the answer to each of these questions can range from a "yes" to a "no" to a "maybe" to a "perhaps but not necessarily."

The problem, as life course theorists see it, is that simple explanations of criminal behavior are at best incomplete. Indeed, the working assumption within the life course tradition is that the full nature and distribution of crime cannot be blamed solely on faulty genetics, parenting when one was a child, or even a disadvantaged community. Instead, understanding why some people offend and others do not, why some people commit crimes at a high rate while others do so at a low rate, and why some people stop behaving badly while others continue to offend even as senior citizens, requires the detailed examination of lives over time.

Accordingly, the policy implications that can be drawn from the life course theory tradition run a wide spectrum, from developing assistance programs for high-risk youth and their families to lifting the barriers to offender reintegration with regard to certain employment restrictions upon release from prison (see Manza & Uggen, 2004). However, while it is clear that such policies "matter," it is also clear that serious discussions of life course theory have yet to make much of a dent in public policy discussions, where discourse concerning crime control policy is often still couched in the language of rational choice/deterrence and economic efficiency (Pratt, 2009a). Nevertheless, momentum for the creation and expansion of early intervention programs for at-risk youth is growing, and public support for such programs is high (Cullen, Fisher, & Applegate, 2000). Thus, apparently, even in the policy arena, where thinking about crime in simplistic terms is protected with a form of near religious observance, they are ready to start thinking about crime in life course terms. It remains to be seen, however, whether life course theory's influence on the field of criminology will be matched in the realm of crime control policy.

DISCUSSION QUESTIONS

1. What was unique about the criminological context of the 1990s that allowed life course theories to "make sense" during this time period more than at other times?
2. How do Gottfredson and Hirschi (1990), Moffitt (1993), and Sampson and Laub (1993) each view the concepts of stability and change in criminal behavior over time?
3. What made the work of Moffitt (1993) and of Sampson and Laub (1993) "stand out" among the various life course ideas of the time?

REFERENCES

Akers, R. L., & Sellers, C. S. (2009). *Criminological theories: Introduction, evaluation, and application.* New York: Oxford University Press.

Blumstein, A., Cohen, J., Roth, J. A., & Visher, C. (Eds.). (1986). *Criminal careers and "career criminals."* Washington, DC: National Academy Press.

Brannigan, A., Gemmel, W., Pevalin, D. J., & Wade, T. J. (2002). Self-control and social control in childhood misconduct and aggression: The role of family structure, hyperactivity, and hostile parenting. *Canadian Journal of Criminology, 44,* 119–143.

Burt, C. (1912). The inheritance of mental characters. *Eugenics Review, 4,* 168–200.

Burt, C. (1914). The measurement of intelligence by the Binet tests. *Eugenics Review, 6,* 36–50, 140–152.

Burt, C. (1972). The inheritance of general intelligence. *American Psychology, 27,* 175–190.

Bushway, S. D., Piquero, A. R., Broidy, L. M., Cauffman, E., & Mazerolle, P. (2001). An empirical framework for studying desistance as a process. *Criminology, 39,* 491–515.

Caspi, A., & Moffitt, T. E. (1995). The continuity of maladaptive behavior: From description to understanding in the study of antisocial behavior. In D. Cicchetti & D. Cohen (Eds.), *Developmental psychology* (Vol. 2, pp. 472–511). New York: Wiley.

Crowder, K. D., & Tolnay, S. E. (2000). A new marriage squeeze for black women: The role of racial intermarriage by black men. *Journal of Marriage and the Family, 62,* 792–807.

Cullen, F. T., Fisher, B. S., & Applegate, B. K. (2000). Public opinion about crime and punishment. In M. Tonry (Ed.), *Crime and justice: A review of research* (Vol. 27, pp. 1–79). Chicago: University of Chicago Press.

Cullen, F. T., Gendreau, P., Jarjoura, G. R., & Wright, J. P. (1997). Crime and the bell curve: Lessons from intelligent criminology. *Crime & Delinquency, 43*(4), 387–411.

Cullen, F. T., Wright, J. P., & Blevins, K. R. (2006). Introduction: Taking stock in criminological theory. In F. T. Cullen, J. P. Wright, & K. R. Blevins (Eds.), *Taking stock: The status of criminological theory—Advances in criminological theory* (Vol. 15, pp. 1–34). New Brunswick, NJ: Transaction.

Dugdale, R. (1877). *The Jukes: A study in crime, pauperism, and heredity.* New York: Putman.

Farrington, D. P. (1986). Age and crime. In M. Tonry & N. Morris (Eds.), *Crime and justice: A review of research* (Vol. 7, pp. 189–250). Chicago: University of Chicago Press.

Gibbons, D. C. (1994). *Talking about crime and criminals: Problems and issues in theory development in criminology.* Englewood Cliffs, NJ: Prentice Hall.

Gibbs, J. P. (1987). The state of criminological theory. *Criminology, 25,* 821–840.

Glueck, S., & Glueck, E. (1950). *Unraveling juvenile delinquency.* New York: Commonwealth Fund.

Gottfredson, M. R., & Hirschi, T. (1990). *A general theory of crime.* Palo Alto, CA: Stanford University Press.

Gould, S. J. (1995). Curveball. In S. Fraser (Ed.), *The bell curve wars: Race, intelligence, and the future of America* (pp. 11–22). New York: Basic Books.

Gould, S. J. (1996). *The mismeasure of man* (Rev. ed.). New York: Norton.

Harris, J. R. (1998). *The nurture assumption: Why children turn out the way they do.* New York: The Free Press.

Haynie, D. L. (2002). Friendship networks and delinquency: The relative nature of peer delinquency. *Journal of Quantitative Criminology, 18*(2), 99–134.

Herrnstein, R. J., & Murray, C. (1994). *The bell curve: Intelligence and class structure in American life.* New York: The Free Press.

Hirschi, T. (1969). *Causes of delinquency.* Berkeley: University of California Press.

Hirschi, T., & Gottfredson, M. R. (1995). Control theory and the life-course perspective. *Studies on Crime and Crime Prevention, 4,* 131–142.

Kempf, K. L. (1993). The empirical status of Hirschi's control theory. In F. Adler & W. S. Laufer (Eds.), *New directions in criminological theory—Advances in criminological theory* (Vol. 4, pp. 143–185). New Brunswick, NJ: Transaction.

Laub, J. H., & Sampson, R. J. (2001). Understanding desistance from crime. In M. Tonry (Ed.), *Crime and justice: A review of research* (Vol. 28, pp 1–69). Chicago: University of Chicago Press.

Laub, J. H. & Sampson, R. J. (2003). *Shared beginnings, divergent lives: Delinquent boys to age 70.* Cambridge, MA: Harvard University Press.

Leblanc, M., & Loeber, R. (1998). Developmental criminology updated. In M. Tonry (Ed.), *Crime and justice: A review of research* (Vol. 23, pp. 115–198). Chicago: University of Chicago Press.

Lemert, E. M. (1972). *Human deviance, social problems, and social control* (2nd ed.). Englewood Cliffs, NJ: Prentice Hall.

Lilly, J. R., Cullen, F. T., & Ball, R. A. (2007). *Criminological theory: Context and consequences* (4th ed.). Thousand Oaks, CA: Sage.

Loeber, R., & Stouthamer-Loeber, M. (1996). The development of offending. *Criminal Justice and Behavior, 23*(1), 12–24.

Lombroso-Ferrero, G. (1911). *Criminal man, according to the classification of Cesare Lombroso.* New York: Putnam.

Lowenkamp, C. T., Cullen, F. T., & Pratt, T. C. (2003). Replicating Sampson and Groves's test of social disorganization theory: Revisiting a criminological classic. *Journal of Research in Crime and Delinquency, 40*(4), 351–373.

Manza, J., & Uggen, C. (2004). Punishment and democracy: Disenfranchisement of nonincarcerated felons in the United States. *Perspectives on Politics, 2,* 491–505.

Maruna, S. (2001). *Making good: How ex-convicts reform and rebuild their lives.* Washington, DC: American Psychological Association.

McGloin, J. M., & Pratt, T. C. (2003). Cognitive ability and delinquent behavior among inner-city youth: A life-course analysis of main, mediating, and interaction effects. *International Journal of Offender Therapy and Comparative Criminology, 47*(3), 253–271.

McGloin, J. M., Pratt, T. C., & Maahs, J. (2004). Rethinking the IQ-delinquency relationship: A longitudinal analysis of multiple theoretical models. *Justice Quarterly, 21*(3), 601–631.

McGloin, J. M., Pratt, T. C., & Piquero, A. (2006). A life-course analysis of the criminogenic effects of maternal cigarette smoking during pregnancy: A research note on the mediating impact of neuropsychological deficit. *Journal of Research in Crime and Delinquency, 43*(4), 412–426.

McGloin, J. M., Sullivan, C. J., Piquero, A. R., & Bacon, S. (2008). Investigating the stability of co-offending and co-offenders among a sample of youthful offenders. *Criminology, 46*(1), 155–188.

Messner, S. F., & Sampson, R. J. (1991). The sex ratio, family disruption, and rates of violent crime: The paradox of demographic structure. *Social Forces, 69*(3), 693–713.

Moffitt, T. E. (1993). Adolescence-limited and life-course persistent antisocial behavior: A developmental taxonomy. *Psychological Review, 100,* 674–701.

Nagin, D. S., & Piquero, A. R. (2010). Using group based trajectory modeling to study crime over the life course. *Journal of Criminal Justice Education, 21*(2), 105–116.

Nagin, D. S., & Tremblay, R. E. (2005). Developmental trajectory groups: Fact or a useful statistical fiction? *Criminology, 43*(4), 873–904.

Perrone, D. M., Sullivan, C., Pratt, T. C., & Margaryan, S. (2004). Parental efficacy, self-control, and delinquent behavior: A test of a general theory of crime on a nationally representative sample. *International Journal of Offender Therapy and Comparative Criminology, 48*(3), 298–312.

Piquero, A. R., Farrington, D. P., & Blumstein, A. (2003). The criminal career paradigm. In M. Tonry (Ed.), *Crime and justice: A review of research* (Vol. 30, pp. 359–506). Chicago: University of Chicago Press.

Pratt, T. C. (2009a). *Addicted to incarceration: Corrections policy and the politics of misinformation in the United States.* Thousand Oaks, CA: Sage.

Pratt, T. C. (2009b). Reconsidering Gottfredson and Hirschi's general theory of crime: Linking the micro- and macro-level sources of self-control and criminal behavior over the life course. In J. Savage (Ed.), *The development of persistent criminality.* New York: Oxford University Press.

Pratt, T. C., & Cullen, F. T. (2000). The empirical status of Gottfredson and Hirschi's general theory of crime: A meta-analysis. *Criminology, 38,* 961–934.

Pratt, T. C., Cullen, F. T., Blevins, K. R., Daigle, L., & Unnever, J. D. (2002). The relationship of attention deficit hyperactivity disorder to crime and delinquency: A meta-analysis. *International Journal of Policy Science and Management, 4,* 433–360.

Pratt, T. C., Cullen, F. T., Sellers, C. S., Winfree, L. T., Madensen, T., Daigle, L., et al. (in press). The empirical status of social learning theory: A meta-analysis. *Justice Quarterly.*

Pratt, T. C., McGloin, J. M., & Fearn, N. E. (2006). Maternal cigarette smoking during pregnancy and criminal/deviant behavior: A meta-analysis. *International Journal of Offender Therapy and Comparative Criminology, 50*(6), 672–690.

Pratt, T. C., Turner, M. G., & Piquero, A. R. (2004). Parental socialization and community context: A longitudinal analysis of the structural sources of low self-control. *Journal of Research in Crime and Delinquency, 41*(3), 219–243.

Raine, A., Moffitt, T. E., Caspi, A., Loeber, R., Stouthamer-Loeber, M., & Lynam, D. (2005). Neurocognitive impairments in boys on the life-course persistent antisocial path. *Journal of Abnormal Psychology, 114,* 38–49.

Robins, L. N. (1978). Sturdy childhood predictors of adult antisocial behaviour: Replications from longitudinal studies. *Psychological Medicine, 8,* 611–622.

Sampson, R. J., & Laub, J. H. (1990). Crime and deviance over the life course: The salience of adult social bonds. *American Sociological Review, 55*(5), 609–627.

Sampson, R. J., & Laub, J. H. (1992). Crime and deviance in the life course. *Annual Review of Sociology, 18,* 63–84.

Sampson, R. J., & Laub, J. H. (1993). *Crime in the making: Pathways and turning points through life.* Cambridge, MA: Harvard University Press.

Sampson, R. J., & Laub, J. H. (2005). Seductions of method: Rejoinder to Nagin and Tremblay's "Developmental trajectory groups: Fact or fiction?" *Criminology, 43*(4), 905–914.

Shaw, C. R., & McKay, H. D. (1942). *Juvenile delinquency and urban areas.* Chicago: University of Chicago Press.

Turner, M. G., Piquero, A. R., & Pratt, T. C. (2005). The school context as a source of self-control. *Journal of Criminal Justice, 33*(4), 327–339.

Unnever, J. D., Cullen, F. T., & Pratt, T. C. (2003). Parental management, ADHD, and delinquent involvement: Reassessing Gottfredson and Hirschi's general theory. *Justice Quarterly, 20*(3), 471–500.

Warr, M. (1998). Life-course transitions and desistance from crime. *Criminology, 36*(2), 183–216.

Warr, M. (2002). *Companions in crime: The social aspects of criminal conduct.* Cambridge, MA: Cambridge University Press.

Wolfgang, M., Figlio, R., & Selin, T. (1972). *Delinquency in a birth cohort.* Chicago: University of Chicago Press.

Wright, J. P., & Beaver, K. M. (2005). Do parents matter in creating self-control in their children? A genetically informed test of Gottfredson and Hirschi's theory of low self-control. *Criminology, 43,* 1169–1202.

Wright, J. P., Dietrich, K., Tis, M. D., Hornung, R. W., Wessel, S. D., Lamphear, B. P., et al. (2008). Association of prenatal and childhood lead concentrations with criminal arrests in early adulthood. *PLoS Medicine, 5*(5), 732–740.

NOTES

1. For example, they cited the work of Cyril Burt, whose "twin studies" assessing the degree to which IQ is genetically heritable (see Burt, 1912, 1914, 1972) were found long ago to have been based on data that Burt had faked for decades (see Gould, 1996).

2. It is also worth noting that Herrnstein and Murray (1994) limited their crime analyses to the males in the NLSY sample. They did so for "simplicity," yet it was unclear why the inclusion of females in their analyses would have complicated things in any substantive sense. Either way, their measure of IQ—the factor that they assumed to be the primary "cause" of criminal behavior—explained, at most, 5% of the variation in offending in their own statistical models.

3. The charge that much of the work in the life course tradition is atheoretical remains in play today, where debates among scholars still take place concerning whether "methods-driven" work, like plotting various life-course trajectory groups over time, is theoretically meaningful or merely amounts to mindless empiricism that fails to move our understanding of criminal behavior forward in any substantive way (e.g., compare Nagin & Tremblay, 2005; Sampson & Laub, 2005).

TWELVE

LOOKING BACK, LOOKING FORWARD

CONCLUSIONS

By their very nature, lists are political documents. Whenever a list gets made, decisions that can never be fully bias-free will inevitably be reached concerning what does or does not get on the list. Even if the criteria one uses to construct the list are "objective," it is still a subjective choice on the part of the list maker to adopt such criteria instead of others. Lists can even reflect value judgments—either implicitly or explicitly—concerning best and worst, depending upon how close to the "top of the list" something can be found. Yet perhaps most importantly, lists contain the tacit property that the quality of the list itself is inversely related to the number of items it contains, with short lists claiming an air of greater exclusivity.

We have, of course, created a list with this book, and a rather short one at that—after all, what good is any list if it contains everything? In compiling it, we had to make some sort of determination about what would constitute a "key idea" in criminology and criminal justice—a task that could never be completely divorced from our own biases, experiences, and substantive interests as scholars doing work in this field. But what kinds of indicators should be used to judge which ideas deserve to make such a list? We considered multiple sources: the body of empirical tests that have been devoted to an idea, the roster of citations attributed to it in the scholarly literature, substantive coverage in undergraduate textbooks, even the impact it may have had on crime control policy development—all of which have been used as barometers for the impact an idea has had in criminology and criminal justice (Cohn & Farrington, 1999; Wright, 2002). In short, since there can be no "one best way" to determine what is, or is not, a "key idea," we recognize that the entire enterprise of doing so is on its face inherently subjective.

Subjectivity, however, breeds disagreement. Accordingly, reasonable people may agree that some ideas—even some that many scholars would consider to be among the more influential in the field—were snubbed here. Yet, rather than treat this as a game with winners and losers, we would instead encourage both instructors and students to engage in a frank discussion of what does, and does not, constitute a "big" idea. It is certainly possible that we simply got some things wrong. Maybe we gave too much credit to certain ideas and downplayed the contributions of others. If so, hopefully this chapter will at least set the record straight that we realize there is room for honest and open debate here.

As such, this chapter is organized into three sections. The first section involves "looking back" and assessing what might be termed the "glaring omissions" from our roster of key ideas—that is, those ideas that might lead a reader to question our sanity or our criminological expertise as a result of having excluded them from discussion. In the second section, we discuss what we term "the legitimate contenders"—those ideas that could arguably have also made our list of key ideas in criminology and criminal justice. The final section involves "looking forward" to the future of criminology and criminal justice, to those ideas that have the potential to exert the kind of significant influence to warrant their own chapter in a book like this. And with that in mind, let the debates begin!

LOOKING BACK: THE GLARING OMISSIONS?

While opinions will vary concerning which ideas at least deserved an honorable mention in our book, there are two ideas whose exclusion from our discussion thus far is most likely to engender near-universal calls for "what were they thinking?" These ideas include the notions that criminal behavior is learned (social learning theory) and that criminal victimization can be best understood in terms of opportunity structures that surround criminal events (routine activity theory). Both of these "key ideas" are reviewed in this section.

Social Learning Theory

Social learning theory—at least as specified by its most notable advocate within criminology, Ronald Akers—represents an effort to extend Sutherland's "differential association" perspective. As Akers (2001) has observed, "social learning theory retains all of the differential association processes in Sutherland's theory" (p. 194), but then adds additional considerations. In particular, Akers embraced Sutherland's (1939) central proposition that crime is learned through social interaction. Within any society, people vary in their exposure to behavioral and normative patterns through their associations with others (thus the notion of *differential association*). Differential association with others shapes the individual's definitions, described by Akers as "one's own attitudes or meanings that one attaches to given behavior" (p. 195). Moving beyond Sutherland, Akers further argued that definitions may be general (broadly approving or disapproving of crime) or specific to a particular act or situation. Definitions may also be negative (oppositional to crime), positive (defining a criminal behavior as desirable), or neutralizing (defining crime as permissible) (Akers, Krohn, Lanza-Kaduce, & Radosevich, 1979).

Nevertheless, in contrast to Sutherland, who downplayed the role of modeling, Akers (2001) held that criminal behavior—especially when first initiated—can be influenced by *imitation,* which he defined as "the engagement in behavior after the observation of similar behavior in others" (p. 196; see also Warr & Stafford, 1991). Even so, the key, novel explanatory concept added by Akers was *differential reinforcement,* which he defined as "the balance of anticipated or actual rewards and punishments that follow or are consequences of behavior" (p. 195). Acts that are reinforced—either by the reward or the avoidance of discomfort—are likely to be repeated, whereas acts that elicit punishment are less likely to be repeated (Akers & Sellers, 2009). Although reinforcement can be physical (e.g., bodily changes from taking drugs), Akers contended that the most important reinforcers are *social* (e.g., those coming from members of one's intimate social group). The stability of criminal behavior is therefore more likely when an individual is embedded in a social environment where misconduct is reinforced and where differential association with pro-criminal definitions and behavioral patterns is readily available (Akers & Jensen, 2003; Akers & Sellers, 2009).

Thus, the core constructs of Akers' social learning theory are differential association, definitions, imitation, and differential reinforcement. In a sequence that unfolds over time, individuals first initiate criminal acts (mainly through differential association and imitation) and then learn either to cease or to persist in their offending (mainly through differential reinforcement). Nevertheless, existing studies generally do not explore the full "social learning process" outlined by Akers (2001, pp. 196–198). Instead, depending on the measures in the data set under inspection, studies typically explore how one or more of these four constructs are independently related to delinquent or criminal involvement. Even so, to the extent that positive associations between the social learning constructs and misconduct are revealed, support for the theory is generally inferred.

For example, a recent meta-analysis conducted by Pratt et al. (in press) of 133 empirical tests of social learning theory revealed a strong amount of support for the theory's key propositions. Specifically, the mean "effect sizes" (or predictive capacity; see Wolf, 1986) of variables measuring differential association and definitions (or antisocial attitudes) are comparable in magnitude to those of self-control (one of the most consistently robust predictors of criminal behavior)—a finding that is consistent with Pratt and Cullen's (2000) meta-analysis of the self-control criminological literature. Furthermore, the mean effect sizes for the social learning variables presented by Pratt et al. are generally larger than those revealed in Pratt, Cullen, Blevins, Daigle, and Madensen's (2006) meta-analysis of the variables specified by rational choice/deterrence theory (e.g., the relationship between indicators of the perceived certainty and severity of punishment and criminal/deviant behavior).

Despite these impressive results, it is important to note that empirical support for social learning theory is not unqualified. For example, Pratt et al. (in press) also found that some components of social learning theory have received more empirical support than others. For example, their study showed that the mean effect sizes of the differential association and definitions measures were consistently the strongest of the predictors specified by social learning theory, yet the mean effect sizes for the differential reinforcement and modeling/imitation predictors did not fare so well. These latter effect sizes were generally weak and, at times, statistically insignificant across the sample of 133 studies. The weak effects for differential reinforcement are particularly problematic since that is the key causal mechanism by which deviant peer associations are assumed to cause deviant behavior (Akers, 1998).

The combination of large mean effect sizes for the differential association measures with the relatively weak effect sizes for the indicators of differential reinforcement highlights two important issues for social learning theory. First, association with deviant others may increase one's own level of criminal/deviant behavior for reasons that have little to do with the "normative influence" of deviant peers that Akers discussed (see Haynie & Osgood, 2005, p. 1109). Instead, scholars have argued that exposure to deviant peers may alter the opportunity structures for particular offenses, including increasing access to drugs and alcohol and greater levels of exposure/proximity to "targets" for personal and property crime (see Felson, 2002; McGloin, Sullivan, Piquero, & Pratt, 2007; Osgood, Wilson, O'Malley, Bachman, & Johnston, 1996). Accordingly, it is possible that, theoretically, *reinforcement* simply may not be as important to the explanation of the peers–deviance link as Akers has consistently held that it is (see also Krohn, 1999).

These potential limitations aside, the results of Pratt et al.'s (in press) meta-analysis clearly show that social learning theory deserves its status as one of the core perspectives in criminology. So why, then, is it not on the list of "key ideas" reviewed in this book? There are three reasons that it appears in summary form here instead of getting its own chapter. First, unlike the majority of the key ideas discussed in this book, social learning theory unfolded and evolved over multiple works and over multiple decades (see, e.g., from Burgess & Akers, 1966, all the way up to Akers, 2001). In essence, the theory has always seemed to be, at least to a certain extent, an idea in process. This is not necessarily a bad thing—indeed, in letting the theory develop in this way, Akers has been able to respond to criticisms and to make changes and revisions so that it has arguably become a stronger theory over the years (Akers & Jensen, 2003). Nevertheless, in having done so, it makes the impact of any single version of social learning theory more difficult to assess.

Second, social learning theory has never fully differentiated itself from other criminological perspectives that focus on the group-based nature of criminal and deviant behavior. To be sure, theoretical traditions as diverse as strain theory (see Cloward & Ohlin, 1960), differential association (Matsueda, 1988), self-control (Gottfredson & Hirschi, 1990), and opportunity models (McGloin et al., 2007) all provide explanations for why influences such as "deviant peers" matter. It is therefore questionable whether the "key idea" raised by social learning theory—that the reason delinquent peers are important is because they provide models and reinforcement contingencies for one's own criminal/deviant behavior—is any more logically convincing or empirically supported than these alternative explanations.

Finally, and relatedly, social learning theory often does not stand on its own when used in a criminological context. For example, elements of social learning theory have been merged into multiple integrated theoretical frameworks, including social disorganization (Lowenkamp, Cullen, & Pratt, 2003; Sampson & Groves, 1989), rational choice (Paternoster & Piquero, 1995; Pratt et al., 2006; Stafford & Warr, 1993), neuropsychological (Beaver, Wright, & DeLisi, 2008; McGloin, Pratt, & Maahs, 2004), and life course explanations of criminal behavior (Wiesner, Capaldi, & Patterson, 2003). Thus, unlike the other ideas covered in this book, an argument could be made that social learning theory suffers from a bit of an "independence problem" in criminology.

Routine Activity Theory

Virtually all perspectives on crime causation discussed thus far in this book, while differing in their central theoretical propositions, have shared a common purpose: Each attempts, in some way, to outline a theory of why individuals (or collectives of individuals) may be *motivated* to commit crimes. In a major departure from this way of thinking, Cohen and Felson (1979) conceptualized the prediction of crime and victimization differently (see also Felson & Cohen, 1980). In particular, they largely assumed the existence of motivated offenders and thus did not focus much attention on why the propensity to commit crime fluctuated across ecological units. Instead, they argued that criminal events occurred when motivated offenders had the *opportunity* to victimize property or people. In their view, opportunities consisted of attractive or suitable targets (e.g., a stereo, a person with money) and a lack of capable guardianship (e.g., presence of a family member or neighbor). For crimes to occur, there must be a "convergence in space and time of the three minimal elements of direct-contact predatory violations": offenders, targets, and an absence of guardianship (Cohen & Felson, 1979, p. 589). In turn, the likelihood of this convergence taking place was largely shaped by the social organization of daily life, or the "routine activity" in which people engaged (e.g., when and where they were at home, shopped, attended school, worked, or traveled about; see Felson, 1987). Rates of crime and victimization would be highest in those places where motivated offenders were most likely to encounter attractive and unguarded targets.

Again, a central feature of the routine activity model is that opportunities for crime are increased by attenuated guardianship, which in practice typically involves the absence of informal social control (Bryant & Miller, 1997; see also Carroll & Jackson, 1983; Cohen & Felson, 1979; Cohen & Land, 1987; Felson, 1987). Empirical tests of routine activity theory (e.g., Cohen, Felson, & Land, 1980; Cohen & Land, 1987; Copes, 1999; Jackson, 1984), therefore, typically derive proxy measures of criminal opportunity. At the macro level, for example, these measures generally come in the form of either the *household activity ratio* (the sum of the number of married female workers and the number of non–husband-and-wife—or primary individual—households divided by the total number of households) or some measure of aggregate-level *unemployment.* Felson (1993) noted that these measures can serve as indicators of the exposure to motivated offenders (e.g., women moving out of their houses and into the labor force will therefore have a higher likelihood of interacting with potential motivated offenders). Furthermore, measures such as unemployment may be used as indicators of guardianship—particularly against property offenses such as theft and residential burglary—since unemployed persons are more likely to spend a greater portion of their time at home (see, e.g., Felson, 1993; Land, Cantor, & Russell, 1995).

For the most part, the empirical evidence in favor of routine activity theory is rather impressive. For example, Pratt and Cullen's (2005) meta-analysis of the macro-level criminological literature revealed that the variables specified by routine activity theory are fairly consistent—although somewhat modest—predictors of crime rates. Perhaps more impressive is the more recent work that has integrated concepts derived from routine activity theory with the low self-control framework to explain criminal victimization (see, e.g., Holtfreter, Reisig, & Pratt, 2008). By showing how individuals' impulses and predispositions can influence the way they go about their daily routines—and in the process can place them into situations where victimization is more likely—these studies arguably show more promise for the routine activity perspective than has ever been revealed in the past.

Why, then, is routine activity theory not on our list of key ideas in criminology and criminal justice? While this may strike some as theoretical blasphemy, we contend here that the primary reason it did not get its own chapter in our book was because the concept of routine activity is not fully separate from the broader opportunity/rational choice frameworks, nor the theory and research regarding situational crime prevention strategies (Cornish & Clarke, 1986). To be sure, criminologists cannot even agree on what this idea should be called—routine activity theory (Cohen & Felson, 1979), opportunity theory (Miethe & Meier, 1990), or lifestyle theory (Forde & Kennedy, 1997). In short, the line between routine activity theory and other ideas within that same general theoretical family is still rather fuzzy. Put differently, routine activity theory has failed to fully separate itself from the pack of ideas it has been running with in the way that the other "key ideas" featured in this book have done.

THE LEGITIMATE CONTENDERS

While it would be a stretch to say that, to our knowledge, there are any additional "glaring omissions" to our list of key ideas beyond social learning and routine activity theory, there are a couple of other ideas that should at least be considered as "legitimate contenders." These ideas include the notions that criminal behavior can actually be exacerbated as a consequence of punishment (labeling theory), and the idea that punishment strategies have shifted the focus away from harming the body of the offender to instead focus on inflicting pain onto the soul of the offender (see Michel Foucault's *Discipline and Punish,* 1977). Both of these "legitimate contenders" are reviewed in this section.

Labeling Theory

In the late 1960s, a growing distrust of the state to treat offenders fairly fueled the rise of a new way of thinking about the effects of formal sanctions for criminal behavior. Where the deterrence perspective would hold that punishment is a good thing, since it would teach the offender a lesson and make them "think twice" about misbehaving again, a new idea was formed that held just the opposite: that sanctions themselves can be harmful (Lemert, 1967). Under the assumption that individuals—especially juveniles—will take it upon themselves as a "master status" if they are branded an offender or "delinquent," and will continue to offend into the future as a result of seeing themselves through the eyes of that master status, labeling theory was born. This idea made sense in that particular social and political context, and its impact was felt in widespread policy changes within the criminal justice system, from the creation and expansion of diversion programs designed to keep youths out of the juvenile justice system altogether, to Jerome Miller closing all of the juvenile detention centers in Massachusetts (Pratt, Maahs, & Stehr, 1998).

The reason labeling theory did not make our list of key ideas is that, from its very inception, its core concepts have always suffered from a lack of empirical attention and confirmation among criminologists. Indeed, while a handful of studies have emerged demonstrating that youths who receive formal punishments early are likely to continue to behave badly into adulthood, the explanation of this phenomenon appears to have less to do with the social-psychological process of "labeling" than it does with how such punishments tend to disrupt the formation of prosocial bonds (Laub & Sampson, 2003; Sampson & Laub, 1993). In the end, the tail was wagging the dog, the cart was placed before the horse, and the unhatched chickens were counted (or choose your own metaphor), as the public popularity of labeling theory has always outpaced its empirical legitimacy.

Discipline and Punish: Michel Foucault

Michel Foucault's *Discipline and Punish* has endured as a staple of thinking about crime and punishment—particularly in Western European circles—since its publication in 1977. Foucault noted that early forms of criminal punishments were both public and physically brutal, where offenders were routinely gutted, disemboweled, or their limbs torn off by horses moving in opposite directions, while other offenders were subject to public whippings, hangings, or beheadings. Yet, as we moved to the more "enlightened" form of modern punishment—imprisonment—we have shifted away from harming the physical body of the offender to harming his or her soul. This pain inflicted on the soul, argued Foucault, is every bit as damaging as the very forms of public physical punishment that imprisonment was intended to replace.

Part of Foucault's appeal is that his work transcends the form of intellectual ethnocentrism associated with "American criminology" (see, e.g., the discussion by Cohn & Farrington, 1994). As a result, his impact can be seen in his influence on the works developed by contemporary punishment philosophy scholars. While Foucault's influence is certainly substantial within this particular intellectual tradition, the central challenge facing his work is that it has yet to reach a broader audience outside of the rather limited sphere of punishment philosophy. In essence, *Discipline and Punish* represents a big idea within a very narrowly defined territory of scholarship and has, at least to date, failed to generate "general" appeal within criminology and criminal justice.

LOOKING FORWARD: THE FUTURE OF CRIMINOLOGY AND CRIMINAL JUSTICE

Assessing what should or should not be considered a "key idea" in criminology and criminal justice is inherently an exercise in looking backward, yet looking forward can be just as useful, if not more so, for this exercise. To that end, we argue here that there are two intellectual developments in criminology and criminal justice that appear to hold significant potential for influencing the way we think about criminal behavior and its effective public control. These ideas include the integration of the deterrence and labeling perspectives into a comprehensive theory of the effects of sanctions on criminal behavior (Braithwaite's reintegrative shaming theory) and the revival of the biological tradition within criminology. Both of these perspectives are reviewed in this section.

Reintegrative Shaming

Braithwaite's (1989) theory of reintegrative shaming represented an explicit attempt to integrate the way we think about the causes of criminal behavior (criminology) with the various strategies used to control criminal behavior (criminal justice). He noted that formal sanctions can have either a deterrent or a stigmatizing effect on an individual's likelihood of engaging in future criminal behavior, depending on how the shame associated with the sanctions is delivered. In particular, a sanction can be "disintegrative" if the shame is mean-spirited and meant to inflict pain simply for its own sake, and may actually increase the likelihood that the offender will continue to misbehave in the future. Sanctions can be "reintegrative," however, when the shaming is intended to call attention to the harm caused by the offense, and an attempt is made to rebuild trust between the offender and the victim. This form of shaming, according to Braithwaite, should have a deterrent effect on future criminal behavior.

On the one hand, Braithwaite's work has had considerable impact: It has been heavily cited by scholars (Cohn & Farrington, 1999), and the author's ideas have been translated into the policy domain in the form of drug courts and restorative justice programs that are intended to reduce the stigmatization associated with involvement in the criminal justice system (Levrant, Cullen, Fulton, & Wozniak, 1999). On the other hand, the central challenge facing the theory of reintegrative shaming is that, much like its theoretical cousin, labeling theory, Braithwaite's work is long on influence yet somewhat short on empirical validation. Few studies assessing the theory exist, and those that have been conducted have revealed somewhat mixed results (Pratt & Cullen, 2005). Just as important, Braithwaite's (1989) ideas are not terribly dissimilar conceptually from labeling (or even social disorganization) theory or from other works that specify the potentially differential effects of sanctions (see, e.g., Sherman, 1993), at least not enough in our estimation to warrant "key idea" status at this time.

Biology Redux

As the field of criminology has become more interdisciplinary in recent years, new data sets have been compiled and released to scholars that allow for questions to be asked that couldn't have been before—in particular, those related to the biosocial perspective in criminology. As Beaver (2009) has recently noted, biological discussions of criminal behavior have largely been relegated to the dustbin of criminological thought. Such thinking was marginalized initially for legitimate reasons, because of a lack of scientific rigor and an explicitly racist motive among certain theorists, yet a certain disdain has remained toward a biologically informed version of criminological thought, primarily as the result of the intellectual constraints associated with sociological criminology (see Pratt, 2009).

Just as important, however, is the role that data limitations have traditionally placed on the biosocial paradigm: the absence of data on genetic and biological indicators that can be examined directly. Much of the recent work within this revived tradition is rooted in data sets from the biological and health sciences, and others like the National Longitudinal Study of Adolescent Health (also known as Add Health). These data sets contain a rich amount of information on health and biological indicators that have traditionally been absent from the kinds of surveys that sociological criminologists like to dispense to their college classrooms. Put simply, it was easy for criminologists to dismiss the effects of biological and genetic factors on criminal behavior when they were simply ignoring them in their research designs. Now, with the availability of this new data, scholars can integrate these concepts into existing criminological models, such as Moffitt's (1993) life course perspective and self-control theory (see Gottfredson & Hirschi, 1990), and challenge other models that may explicitly deny biosocial influences. The primary challenge facing the new biosocial perspective is a professional culture that is still quite politically charged and resistant to the notion that crime can have biological roots, particularly in the face of evidence that crime is also strongly connected to inequalities in racially bound resource distributions (see Pratt & Cullen, 2005). This is a fine line to walk for those working within the biosocial criminological tradition, and it remains to be seen which idea or ideas emerge out of the pack to lead this intellectual charge.

CONCLUSION

While it might be tempting to treat theories—or what we conceive of as intellectual frameworks intended to explain how the world works—as "mere ideas," it is important to note that ideas have consequences. These consequences are easy to see when we think of how the idea that women's bodies couldn't handle intense physical exercise led to them only being able to play half-court basketball in high school through the 1950s, how the idea that the Earth was at the center of the solar system led the Catholic Church to condemn Galileo up until just a few decades ago, and how the idea that television viewers only wanted to watch cheesy reality shows led the Fox network to cancel the space Western series *Firefly* after just one season.

Criminology is certainly no different, where as we discussed in the introductory chapter, ideas about crime causation will inevitably shape in important ways our thoughts about how best to combat crime. To be sure, ideas concerning how the nature of the "problem" of crime is conceptualized will influence heavily the kinds of "solutions" that will make sense in the context of that problem conceptualization. Stated in the reverse, every proposed "solution" to the crime problem contains at least some implicit set of assumptions about what causes crime in the first place. This relationship can be clearly observed when looking at "solutions" to crime such as the nature-based Outward Bound programs for juvenile offenders (the problem? Crime is apparently caused by the inability to climb a really big rock), acupuncture treatment for drug offenders with a heroin addiction (the problem? Crime is apparently caused by a misalignment of the chakras in one's chi), and military-style boot camp prisons (the problem? Crime is apparently caused by the absence of fear of push-ups and proper bed making).

It is this problem-solution nexus that is too often missed when discussions of "criminology" and "criminal justice" are divorced from one another. That is why we chose not to do so in this book. We instead wanted students to have an appreciation for the various ways in which these two prongs of our discipline are interrelated. Moreover, as important as that is, we encourage students to also take note of one of the central points we have tried to hammer home in each of these chapters: It isn't just the idea itself that matters, but also how it was delivered, that truly sets it apart from its peers and makes it a "key idea" in criminology and criminal justice.

DISCUSSION QUESTIONS

1. What makes a "key idea" in criminology or criminal justice?
2. Why does criminology/criminal justice seem to be moving in the direction that it is?
3. What potentially "key ideas" were missed altogether in this book?

REFERENCES

Akers, R. L. (1998). *Social learning and social structure: A general theory of crime and deviance.* Boston: Northeastern University Press.

Akers, R. L. (2001). Social learning theory. In R. Paternoster & R. Bachman (Eds.), *Explaining criminals and crime: Essays in contemporary criminological theory* (pp. 192–210). Los Angeles: Roxbury.

Akers, R. L., & Jensen, G. F. (2003). Editors' introduction. In R. L. Akers & G. F. Jensen (Eds.), *Social learning theory and the explanation of crime—Advances in Criminological* Theory (Vol. 11, pp. 1–8). New Brunswick, NJ: Transaction.

Akers, R. L., Krohn, M. D., Lanza-Kaduce, L., & Radosevich, M. (1979). Social learning and deviant behavior: A specific test of a general theory. *American Sociological Review, 44,* 636–655.

Akers, R. L., & Sellers, C. S. (2009). *Criminological theories: Introduction, evaluation, and application* (5th ed.). New York: Oxford University Press.

Beaver, K. M. (2009). *Biosocial criminology: A primer.* Dubuque, IA: Kendall/Hunt.

Beaver, K. M., Wright, J. P., & DeLisi, M. (2008). Delinquent peer group formation: Evidence of a gene X environment correlation. *Journal of Genetic Psychology, 169*(3), 227–244.

Braithwaite, J. (1989). *Crime, shame and reintegration.* New York: Cambridge University Press.

Bryant, K. M., & Miller, J. M. (1997). Routine activity and labor market segmentation: An empirical test of a revised approach. *American Journal of Criminal Justice, 22*(1), 71–100.

Burgess, R. L., & Akers, R. L. (1966). A differential association-reinforcement theory of criminal behavior. *Social Problems, 14,* 128–147.

Carroll, L., & Jackson, P. I. (1983). Inequality, opportunity, and crime rates in central cities. *Criminology, 21,* 178–194.

Cloward, R. A., & Ohlin, L. E. (1960). *Delinquency and opportunity: A theory of delinquent gangs.* New York: The Free Press.

Cohen, L. E., & Felson, M. (1979). Social change and crime rate trends: A routine activities approach. *American Sociological Review, 44,* 588–608.

Cohen, L. E., Felson, M., & Land, K. C. (1980). Property crime rates in the United States: A macrodynamic analysis, 1947–1977; with ex ante forecasts for the mid-1980s. *American Journal of Sociology, 86*(1), 90–117.

Cohen, L. E., & Land, K. C. (1987). Age structure and crime: Symmetry versus asymmetry and the projection of crime rates through the 1990s. *American Sociological Review, 52,* 170–183.

Cohn, E. G., & Farrington, D. P. (1994). Who are the most influential criminologists in the English-speaking world? *British Journal of Criminology, 34,* 204–225.

Cohn, E. G., & Farrington, D. P. (1999). Changes in the most-cited scholars in twenty criminology and criminal justice journals between 1990 and 1995. *Journal of Criminal Justice, 27*(4), 345–359.

Copes, H. (1999). Routine activities and motor vehicle theft: A crime specific approach. *Journal of Crime and Justice, 22*(2), 125–146.

Cornish, D. B., & Clarke, R. V. (1986). *The reasoning criminal.* New York: Springer-Verlag.

Felson, M. (1987). Routine activities and crime prevention in the developing metropolis. *Criminology, 25,* 911–931.

Felson, M. (1993). Social indicators for criminology. *Journal of Research in Crime and Delinquency, 30*(4), 400–411.

Felson, M. (2002). *Crime and everyday life* (3rd ed.). Thousand Oaks, CA: Sage.

Felson, M., & Cohen, L. E. (1980). Human ecology and crime: A routine activities approach. *Human Ecology, 8*(4), 389–406.

Forde, D. R., & Kennedy, L. W. (1997). Risky lifestyles, routine activities, and the general theory of crime. *Justice Quarterly, 14*(2), 265–294.

Foucault, M. (1977). *Discipline and punish: The birth of the prison.* New York: Vintage.

Gottfredson, M. R., & Hirschi, T. (1990). *A general theory of crime.* Palo Alto, CA: Stanford University Press.

Haynie, D. L., & Osgood, D. W. (2005). Reconsidering peers and delinquency: How do peers matter? *Social Forces, 84,* 1109–1130.

Holtfreter, K., Reisig, M. D., & Pratt, T. C. (2008). Low self-control, routine activities, and fraud victimization. *Criminology, 46,* 189–220.

Jackson, P. I. (1984). Opportunities and crime: A function of city size. *Sociology and Social Research, 68*(2), 173–193.

Krohn, M. D. (1999). Social learning theory: The continuing development of a perspective. *Theoretical Criminology, 3*(4), 462–476.

Land, K. C., Cantor, D., & Russell, S. T. (1995). Unemployment and crime rate fluctuations in the post–World War II United States. In J. Hagan & R. D. Peterson (Eds.), *Crime and inequality* (pp. 55–79). Palo Alto, CA: Stanford University Press.

Laub, J. H., & Sampson, R. J. (2003). *Shared beginnings, divergent lives: Delinquent boys to age 70.* Cambridge, MA: Harvard University Press.

Lemert, E. M. (1967). *Social problems and social control.* Englewood Cliffs, NJ: Prentice Hall.

Levrant, S., Cullen, F. T., Fulton, B., & Wozniak, J. F. (1999). Reconsidering restorative justice: The corruption of benevolence revisited? *Crime & Delinquency, 45*(1), 3–27.

Lowenkamp, C. T., Cullen, F. T., & Pratt, T. C. (2003). Replicating Sampson and Groves's test of social disorganization theory: Revisiting a criminological classic. *Journal of Research in Crime and Delinquency, 40*(4), 351–373.

Matsueda, R. (1988). The current state of differential association theory. *Crime and Delinquency, 34*(3), 277–306.

McGloin, J. M., Pratt, T. C., & Maahs, J. (2004). Rethinking the IQ–delinquency relationship: A longitudinal analysis of multiple theoretical frameworks. *Justice Quarterly, 21*(3), 601–631.

McGloin, J. M., Sullivan, C., Piquero, A. R., & Pratt, T. C. (2007). Local life circumstances and offending specialization/diversity: Comparing opportunity and propensity models. *Journal of Research in Crime and Delinquency, 44*(3), 321–346.

Miethe, T. D., & Meier, R. F. (1990). Opportunity, choice, and criminal victimization. *Journal of Research in Crime and Delinquency, 27*(3), 243–266.

Moffitt, T. E. (1993). Adolescence-limited and life-course persistent antisocial behavior: A developmental taxonomy. *Psychological Review, 100,* 674–701.

Osgood, D. W., Wilson, J. K., O'Malley, P. M., Bachman, J. G., & Johnston, L. D. (1996). Routine activities and individual deviant behavior. *American Sociological Review, 61,* 635–655.

Paternoster, R., & Piquero, A. R. (1995). Reconceptualizing deterrence: An empirical test of personal and vicarious experiences. *Journal of Research in Crime and Delinquency, 32*(3), 251–286.

Pratt, T. C. (2009). Foreword. In K. M. Beaver, *Biosocial criminology: A primer.* Dubuque, IA: Kendall/Hunt.

Pratt, T. C., & Cullen, F. T. (2000). The empirical status of Gottfredson and Hirschi's general theory of crime: A meta-analysis. *Criminology, 38*(3), 931–964.

Pratt, T. C., & Cullen, F. T. (2005). Assessing macro-level predictors and theories of crime: A meta-analysis. In M. Tonry (Ed.), *Crime and justice: A review of research* (Vol. 32, pp. 373–450). Chicago: University of Chicago Press.

Pratt, T. C., Cullen, F. T., Blevins, K. R., Daigle, L. E., & Madensen, T. D. (2006). The empirical status of deterrence theory: A meta-analysis. In F. T. Cullen, J. P. Wright, & K. R. Blevins (Eds.), *Taking stock: The status of criminological theory—Advances in criminological theory* (Vol. 15, pp. 367–396). New Brunswick, NJ: Transaction.

Pratt, T. C., Cullen, F. T., Sellers, C. S., Winfree, L. T., Madensen, T., Daigle, L., et al. (in press). The empirical status of social learning theory: A meta-analysis. *Justice Quarterly.*

Pratt, T. C., Maahs, J., & Stehr, S. D. (1998). The symbolic ownership of the corrections "problem": A framework for understanding the development of corrections policy in the United States. *The Prison Journal, 78*(4), 451–464.

Sampson, R. J., & Groves, W. B. (1989). Community structure and crime: Testing social-disorganization theory. *American Journal of Sociology, 94*(4), 774–802.

Sampson, R. J., & Laub, J. H. (1993). *Crime in the making: Pathways and turning points through life.* Cambridge, MA: Harvard University Press.

Sherman, L. W. (1993). Deterrence, defiance, and irrelevance: A theory of the criminal sanction. *Journal of Research in Crime and Delinquency, 30*(4), 445–473.

Stafford, M. C., & Warr, M. (1993). A reconceptualization of general and specific deterrence. *Journal of Research in Crime and Delinquency, 30*(2), 123–135.

Sutherland, E. H. (1939). *Principles of criminology* (3rd ed.). Philadelphia: Lippincott.

Warr, M., & Stafford, M. (1991). The influence of delinquent peers: What they think or what they do? *Criminology, 29*(4), 851–866.

Wiesner, M., Capaldi, D. M., & Patterson, G. (2003). Development of antisocial behavior and crime across the life-span from a social interaction perspective: The coercion model. In R. L. Akers & G. F. Jensen (Eds.), *Social learning theory and the explanation of crime—Advances in criminological theory* (Vol. 11, pp. 317–338). New Brunswick, NJ: Transaction.

Wolf, F. M. (1986). *Meta-analysis: Quantitative methods for research synthesis.* Thousand Oaks, CA: Sage.

Wright, R. A. (2002). Recent changes in the most-cited scholars in criminal justice textbooks. *Journal of Criminal Justice, 30*(3), 183–195.

NAME INDEX

SUBJECT INDEX

ABOUT THE AUTHORS

Travis W. Franklin earned his PhD in criminal justice from Washington State University in 2008 and is currently an assistant professor in the College of Criminal Justice at Sam Houston State University. His research interests focus on the effects of race and ethnicity on the processing of offenders through criminal courts, violence in correctional institutions, the causes and correlates of fear of crime, and biological predictors of crime and delinquency. His recent work has appeared in *Criminal Justice and Behavior, Journal of Criminal Justice, Feminist Criminology,* and *Social Justice Research.*

Jacinta M. Gau has a PhD in criminal justice and is an assistant professor in the Department of Criminal Justice at California State University, San Bernardino. Her research focuses on policing, including procedural justice, order maintenance and broken windows, and issues concerning race and policing. Her work has appeared in journals such as *Justice Quarterly, Criminology & Public Policy, Police Quarterly,* and *Policing: An International Journal of Police Strategies and Management.*

Travis C. Pratt, received his PhD in criminal justice from the University of Cincinnati. He is currently a professor in the School of Criminology and Criminal Justice at Arizona State University. (He was previously on the faculty at Rutgers University–Newark and Washington State University.) Pratt's research focuses on structural theories of crime/delinquency and correctional policy. His recent work on correctional policy in particular has appeared in the *Corrections Management Quarterly, Crime & Delinquency, Criminal Justice Policy Review, Journal of Criminal Justice,* the *Journal of Offender Rehabilitation,* the *Prison Journal,* and *Justice Quarterly.*

Supporting researchers for more than 40 years

Research methods have always been at the core of SAGE's publishing program. Founder Sara Miller McCune published SAGE's first methods book, *Public Policy Evaluation*, in 1970. Soon after, she launched the *Quantitative Applications in the Social Sciences* series—affectionately known as the "little green books."

Always at the forefront of developing and supporting new approaches in methods, SAGE published early groundbreaking texts and journals in the fields of qualitative methods and evaluation.

Today, more than 40 years and two million little green books later, SAGE continues to push the boundaries with a growing list of more than 1,200 research methods books, journals, and reference works across the social, behavioral, and health sciences. Its imprints—Pine Forge Press, home of innovative textbooks in sociology, and Corwin, publisher of PreK–12 resources for teachers and administrators—broaden SAGE's range of offerings in methods. SAGE further extended its impact in 2008 when it acquired CQ Press and its best-selling and highly respected political science research methods list.

From qualitative, quantitative, and mixed methods to evaluation, SAGE is the essential resource for academics and practitioners looking for the latest methods by leading scholars.

For more information, visit **www.sagepub.com**.